A History of the United States

United States

Volume One: A New World 1607-1677

By Jamie Redfern M.A.

To Julene.

Contents

Prologue

It would be the bold historian to say that since its declaration of independence in 1776, any country has had a greater influence on the world than the United States of America: a country founded on the simple idea that all men were created equal, and that all had the right to life, liberty, and the pursuit of happiness. Over the following two hundred years this squabbling strip of states along the Atlantic seaboard grew to become a global superpower. It is a rather impressive rags to riches tale, but there is a dark side to the American dream. Slavery. The treatment of Native Americans. It's certainly a complicated story, which is exactly why I'd like to tell it.

This book is going to tell the whole story. We will start with early voyages to North America, trace the development of the colonies, watch them mature into states, chart the Revolution and the creation of the federal government. We will go through the era of good feelings, the civil war, the reconstruction and examine how America became a superpower. We will go through two world wars, the great depression, and right up to the end of the Cold War. "Mr Gorbachev, tear down this wall!"

But that isn't all. We're going to tell the whole story. We will be covering politics, warfare, social history and economics. There will be no political slant. No edge. Just the facts. If something is just my opinion, believe me, I will make you well aware of it. I mention this as I don't you to think that I'm going to be doing any America bashing, but likewise

I'm not going to be chanting *'USA! USA!'* I'm hoping that the fact that I'm British should give me adequate distance to tell the story fairly.

This is volume one of a series which will chart the history of the United States. It is a long story, and there is a lot of ground to cover. Therefore, it's worth making sure that it is clear immediately exactly what we are going to cover in this volume. We shall look at the initial European exploration of the European continent, before moving on to the history of the first English colony: Virginia. We will cover the story of Virginia from its foundation up until the resolution of Bacon's Rebellion in the 1670s. We shall then cover the creation of the New England Colonies before finally looking at the colonisation efforts of the Dutch and Swedes, up to the English capture of New York. We will introduce various themes which will play a greater role later on in the story. If I don't fully explore an idea, assume that it will come up later rather than that the theme has been omitted. There is a lot of material to cover, and it cannot all be covered at the same time.

Part 1

The Planting of Virginia to 1677

Chapter 1 – The New World

In fourteen-hundred and ninety-two, Columbus sailed the ocean blue. Despite thinking that he had actually made his way to India, Columbus accidentally discovered America. Except by 'discovered', of course I mean that he found something millions of people knew about already. There were the indigenous peoples who had been living in the Americas for thousands of years, in addition to Norse Vikings having landed in Newfoundland five centuries beforehand. Columbus would really be an odd place to start telling the American story. The Spanish conquest of Mesoamerica is highly interesting, and it shall be covered elsewhere in this narrative.

The Spanish and Portuguese were the first to begin exploring (well, invading) this new land in earnest. They went so far as to divide the world between them. The Spanish began creating New Spain following on from the voyages of Columbus, and Portugal claimed the land of Brazil in 1500. They were driven by greed for the vast amounts of gold to be found in the New World by the Inca and the Aztecs. That isn't moralising. The sheer volume of gold taken back to Spain and Portugal would cause rampant inflation throughout the 16th century. There were obviously other reasons, such as a desire to explore, to find a new route to the east, to see the mysterious civilisations of the Americas, and to spread Christianity to the heathens. This was a mission to save souls, the gold was just a bonus. At least that was the official version of events. I will reiterate the amount of gold taken, and mention that 90% of natives had died of disease by 1600.[1]

You can draw your own conclusion about why the Europeans were there.

Very little was done regarding North America for some time. There were early voyages, such as Giovanni Caboto, more commonly known as John Cabot. Cabot landed in Newfoundland in 1497 and claimed it for England, but he was in no position to actually claim the land. He discovered the ample supply of fish the region held. This may seem trivial, but fish was a precious resource in the middle ages. The diet of the average European lacked protein, and Catholics needed fish to eat on Fridays and in Lent. The pace of events began to pick up in the 1520s with the French. King Francois I encouraged French activity in the region, in 1524 funding Giovanni da Verrazano to explore the Atlantic coast. He found Manhattan Island and the Hudson River.

Jaques Cartier of St. Malo would be the next great explorer. Fascinated by the voyages of Verrazano, Cartier was determined to launch an expedition. He sent a letter in 1533 to Philippe de Chabot, Sieur de Brion, High Admiral of France. He passed the letter

---

[1] I've tried to be politically correct throughout this book, although that is quite difficult. Basically, there is no real consensus on what the best words are. Native American is a term the United States Federal Government introduced in the late 20th century and caught on as the PC word outsiders use, but it isn't how they describe themselves. Indian isn't a particularly useful word either, it has a lot of negative connotations, but it is about as good as we've got. American Indians often refer to themselves as such. A 1995 survey by the Census Bureau saw that 49% preferred the term Indian, while only 37% preferred Native American. Plus, Indian is a standard word in academic books on the matter.

on to Francis I who loved the idea. The next year, the expedition set sail with the intention of finding the north west passage to the Indies. It landed in Newfoundland and then explored the Saint Lawrence Gulf. A second expedition was launched in 1535 in which the Saint Lawrence River was explored. Cartier constructed a fort during this expedition, it would only survive a year before being abandoned (something very common with these early settlements), but is noteworthy for its location. It was the site of the city of Quebec. It was Cartier who named the area New France, and also gave it another name which has stuck. Canada. This was the first interior exploration of North America by a European.

The logical next step would be further investment and ensuring the establishment of a permanent colony, but this would not happen for over half a century following Cartier. France was about to become entangled in the 16th century religious wars, dreams of an empire in the new world were placed on the back burner. For the second half of the 16th century it would be England trying to challenge Spanish hegemony.

The conflict between Spain and England is long, and complicated, and I don't want to get into the whole thing here. I want to, but we need to make it to Jamestown. As Inigo Montoya of the Princess Bride would say, "Let me explain, no, there is too much, let me sum up".

Medieval Europe was a world of warfare. It was a constant struggle to get ahead, but the game changed when Columbus landed in America. Her empire made Spain a global superpower, and so the states of Europe became hostile to Spain. England was particularly hostile due to the whole 'Mary I marrying Philip II of Spain' thing, so when Elizabeth I came to the throne Spain would be no friend. Attempts were made to disrupt the Spanish empire. Francis Drake caused trouble for the Spanish in the Caribbean, so the Spanish retaliated by causing trouble in Ireland. Walter Raleigh, the greatest of the English privateers, decided that he would cause trouble in return by founding a colony on the Atlantic coast. He named the area Virginia, after the Virgin queen Elizabeth. It must be noted that this Virginia bares very little resemblance to the modern state of Virginia. Defining American geography was very fast and loose at this stage in history, and place names don't have exact definitions.

Florida was pretty established by this point. While it would not join the Union until 1845 to become the 27th State, Florida's has a very long history. It was discovered in 1513 by Juan Ponce de Leon and was named after the Spanish Easter festival, Pascua Florida, the Feast of Flowers. Ponce de Leon would make another expedition in 1521 in which he tried to establish a colony, but it was attacked by natives and failed. Hernando de Soto would go treasure hunting in 1539, but Florida did not have the riches of other areas of the New World, and nothing was really done with Florida by Spain. The French became interested, Jean Ribault explored the region in 1562 and in 1564 René Goulaine de Laudonnière founded Fort Caroline at the mouth of the St. John River, not too far away from Jacksonville. Once the French were involved the Spanish accelerated their plans. In 1565 Pedro Menéndez de Avilés founded San Augustin, which has the honour of being the first permanent European settlement in the United

States. Fort Caroline was quickly captured and renamed San Mateo. A French assault was launched to take it back, but it was unsuccessful. The Spanish were permanently entrenched in Florida.

So, Florida was pretty defined at this point. Then to the north was the area of Norumbega. There was a pretty big difference between the two. Florida, unlike Norumbega, actually existed. People tell tall tales, and rumours existed of a powerful civilisation somewhere in what is known today as New England called Norumbega, and for a while the name stuck. So, when Raleigh named the region Virginia, he was naming everything between Norumbega and Florida.

This was a prime location to prey on Spanish ships, so in 1585 Raleigh placed a colony on Roanoke Island, in modern North Carolina. It didn't last very long, the settlers wanted to return and Francis Drake brought them back in 1586. The following year Raleigh moved more colonists back, but then the English became a bit distracted dealing with the Spanish armada. Understandably. When Raleigh returned to Roanoke the settlement had disappeared. This brought to an end English attempts to settle Virginia for moment, though the name would stick.

Spain began to take a calmer approach to her empire. As the 16th century closed she began to expand from Florida. Spain advanced north, moving into Georgia and then the Carolinas. But Spain was no longer as powerful as she once was. New Spain was more secure. Defences had been improved in the Caribbean and Drake's attempted attack of Panama in 1595 was unsuccessful. It was a larger state, but less powerful. In the 17th century other states would not be kept out of North America as they had been in the 16th. New France would develop along the Saint Lawrence, New England in Massachusetts, New Netherland along the Hudson River centred on New Amsterdam, which would eventually be renamed New York, and New Sweden along the Delaware River, not to mention Jamestown. Of all of these it would be England who would have the most success, and it's worth spending a moment asking why.

You see, there was an important realisation with Jamestown and New England which would change the nature of the new world. The previous colonies had been set up for profit. Either taking gold, or for launching raids. This was why Raleigh wanted to set up the colony at Roanoke. It was realised that land would be what kept a colony going. The land would need to be worked, they would need to farm. There would need to be plenty of colonists in order to do this, those colonists would need to be kept well supplied and the sea routes open, and the culture would need to adapt to the new situation. England was best suited to these things.

As the dominant power on an island, as long as the navy was kept powerful it was impossible for England to be invaded, and the distance from the continent meant that England was not lured into a continental empire. While there was an English Civil War, it was small scale compared to the conflicts on the continent, and the lasting result was the strengthening of the English political institutions. The English had done little during the 16th century. It was one of the weakest states in Europe. It was still divided between the Houses of Lancaster and

York. Henry VIII had numerous costly foreign wars. There was no real trade to speak of. England produced wool and cloth, both of which declined after 1550. Yet, all this toughened up the English. It produced the great privateers, Drake and Raleigh. Numerous trading companies were set up, the most famous of these being the East India Company, but it was one of many. Wealth steadily grew, as did the desire to get back at Spain for the armada. Richard Hakluyt published Principal Navigations, Voyages, and Discoveries of the English Nation in 1600 which excited the mind about the possibilities in America. It was believed that Virginia would be a rich land. There were concerns about the restless population caused by the wars, and sending them to America seemed like a great way to avert social troubles. and they could spread Christianity to the heathens. It was believed that if the Irish could be civilised, then so could the Native Americans. Sigh. It's really not hard to work out where the British self-loathing comes from. We have Shakespeare, and then find out that they thought things like that. Sigh.

The Virginia Company of London

The fortunes of the English had greatly improved since 1580. The English desperately wanted to get on with the process of founding a colony, but they couldn't because of problems with the Spanish. Things would change though in 1603. In 1603 the Elizabeth I, the last member of the House of Tudor, would die, and she would be replaced as monarch by her last living relative, James VI of Scotland of the House of Stuart. He became James I of England, and had little interest in continuing the war with Spain. It was not his war, and peace was made in August 1604. Things did not take long to get going.

While powerful men, such as Sir Thomas Smythe, head of the East India Company, had been pushing for some time to establish a colony along the Atlantic Seaboard, it is not sure exactly how the Jamestown settlement came about. The idea has been credited to one Bartholomew Gosnold, a man well connected with the early explorers. He had made a voyage to New England to trade in 1602, and had been trying to gather support for the colony for some time, but had little success. Gosnold was able to recruit his cousin, Edward Wingfield, who had serve on the continent and was connected with the governor of the fort at Portsmouth, the heart of the English Navy. The other figure of importance brought on to the expedition was John Smith.

John Smith was born in a small village in Lincolnshire, by the East coast of England, in 1580, but was not cut out for the farmer's life. At the age of 19 he travelled to the continent to fight with the Austrian armies against the Turks, and he returned in 1604 weary of war, but still eager for adventure. Gosnold's plan sounded perfect to Smith, and the three of them set about gathering support. Other gentlemen of their position in society were interested, but this wasn't enough to fund such an enterprise. Though, they had a stroke of luck in 1605. They received support from several very prominent figures. Sir John Popham, Lord Chief Justice of the King's Bench, Robert Cecil, the Earl of Salisbury, as well as the merchants of London, Plymouth and Bristol. On 10th April, 1606, The Virginia Company of London was given a charter by King James to go and found a colony.

The Charter did slightly more though than this. A second colony was to be set up too, the Plymouth Company, which would represent the wishes of the West Country merchants, while the Virginia Company would represent those of London. The Plymouth Company was allowed to settle between latitudes 38 degrees and 45 degree (from Chesapeake Bay to Bangor, Maine). The Virginia Company was to found their colony between latitudes 34 degrees and 41 degrees (from Cape Fear in North Carolina to New York). I should make it clear that this was not all the territories between these latitudes being given away, but each colony was to have dominion over 50 miles to the north and south, as well as a hundred miles inland and out to sea. For equality, a Virginia Council was founded which would oversee both companies to ensure that the colonies did not compete with each other. The choice of location was a very pragmatic decision. To the South there could be no competing with Spain, which held power from South Carolina southwards, while in the North the French were establishing themselves along the St. Lawrence. There were only two feasible locations for English colonies, New England and the Chesapeake.

At the time, these would be known as the North Virginia and South Virginia colonies, and until the Pilgrims settled New England, the region would be known as the Northern Colony. Chronologically speaking I should begin with the story of South Virginia, but the settlement there, Jamestown, would have a longer history than that of North Virginia, so I'll tell that tale first.

North Virginia

St. George's Fort, North Virginia, was founded on August 20th 1607, 3 months after its southern sister. It was at the mouth of the Kennebec River in the modern State of Maine. It was an excellent location for a settlement, but would be severely unlucky. The settlement was supposed to have been founded earlier but had run into problems, and so the late summer arrival meant that there was no time to farm food. The winter of 1607-08 was bitterly cold, and the President of the Colony, George Popham, nephew of the aforementioned sir John Popham, died. This was a huge blow, as was the storehouse burning down along with all of the colony's provisions. Popham was replaced as leader by Ralegh Gilbert, nephew of Walter Raleigh. The next year they received word from England that Sir John Popham had died, as had Ralegh Gilbert's brother, Sir John Gilbert. These were huge blows for the colony. Ralegh Gilbert decided to return home, and the rest of the colonists decided to go home too. It hadn't even lasted a year. It should be remembered when telling the story of Jamestown just how quickly its twin had died, and the resulting effect of this on the early colonists. Before we leave St. George's fort behind though I wish to quote a bit of a letter George Popham wrote to King James before he died. He said:

"The Indians positively assure me that there is a certain sea in the opposite or western part of this province, distant not more than seven days journey from our fort of St. George in Sagadahoc: a sea... which cannot be any other than the Southern Ocean, reaching to the regions of China, which unquestionably cannot be far from these parts." I find it incredibly amusing that these early colonists in Maine seemed to think that they were just a few days walk from the Pacific Ocean. These rumours would talk some time to die, and the governor of Virginia would launch an expedition to find something called the East India Sea in 1670. But, that's enough of St. George's Fort and North Virginia, we have to return to the South.

The Jamestown colony was originally intended to be a fort which could then be expanded into a settlement, this initial voyage wasn't going to see a town built. That should be quite clear from who signed up to go. Most strikingly, there were no women. For obvious reasons the settlement wouldn't last very long without them. The expedition was to consist of 3 ships. The flagship, the Susan Constant was 100 tons and was under the command of Captain Christopher Newport. There were also two smaller shops, the Godspeed, 40 tons, and the Discovery, 20 tons, captained by Bartholomew Gosnold and John Ratcliffe respectably.

In addition to the crew of 39 there were 105 colonists. These included 59 gentlemen, in it for the adventure and to get rich quick. These were, well, completely useless to the expedition. Of far more value were the soldiers, 4 carpenters 2 bricklayers, 2 barbers, a mason, a blacksmith, a tailor, a surgeon and a clergymen. There were also some unskilled labourers and small boys.

Under the auspices of Hallie's Comet, considered unlucky by some, these three ships set of down the river Thames in the closing days of 1606. When I first saw that this voyage across the Atlantic was taking place in December I was a bit sceptical. I'm no expert on sailing, but even to a landlubber like me that seems like a bad idea. Winter storms and whatnot. I was therefore not surprised at all to find out that once the ships left the Thames they sailed into the English Channel where they were held for 6 weeks by storms coming in from the Atlantic. They hugged the English coast beset by seasickness and were ready to abandon the whole enterprise, were it not for Reverend Robert Hunt, the one clergyman who had sailed with them. He convinced them to hold firm while "making wild vomits into the black night". I'm not entirely sure where that quote comes from originally, but I found it in Virginia: The New Dominion by Virginius Dabney, and I couldn't resist throwing it in. While Hunt was using his Godly exhortations to raise the men's spirits, it must be noted that it really wound up some of the gentlemen. The infighting would continue for the whole voyage. On February 13th John Smith would even be arrested for mutiny, apparently he was trying to make himself the king of the colony, and wouldn't be released until over a month after Jamestown was founded. It's probably more likely that he was merely insubordinate than actively trying to found a monarchy.

The wild winds abated and they could begin the voyage proper in in Mid-February. The time lost was bad, but worse was the loss of 6 weeks rations. They took the southern route, as was the style at the time, following in the footsteps of Columbus. The colonists made their way to the Fortunate Isles, known today as the Canaries, where they collected fresh water. They made their way over the open ocean to the West Indies in late March and enjoyed the local food. But still, the colonists were deeply divided.

Newport, who commanded the flagship, did not like Smith at all and ordered that gallows be built. This was a double insult to Smith. Not only was he to be executed, but he was to be hanged in the gallows like some commoner, rather than being shot as befits a gentleman! I'm not joking. From the way my material reads it seems he was more upset about the way he was to be killed than the fact that Newport wanted him dead. But as Smith was needed to go on to star in a Disney movie he wasn't killed. Reverend Hunt and Gosnold managed to calm down the situation, but by this point Newport and Wingfield loathed Smith. After their cruise around the West Indies they set sail north on April 10th and were hit by storms, but somehow the ships did not stink. On April 26th they caught sight of Virginia.

Virginia

"And cheerfully at sea
Success you still entice
To get the pearl and gold,
And ours to hold
Virginia,
Earths only paradise.

Where nature hath in store
Fowl, venison and fish,
And the fruitfull'st soil
Without your toil
Three harvests more,
All greater than your wish.

And the ambitious vine
Crowns with his purple mass
The cedar reaching high

To kiss the sky,
The cypress, pine,
And useful Sassafras."
Michael Drayton

The place they landed, at the mouth of the James River, was particularly agreeable. England is a famously mild country. The winter isn't too cold, the summer isn't too hot. This had caused problems for St. George's Fort when they had been broken by the Maine winter. Virginia was much more reasonable. John Smith would write that it had the summer of Spain and the winter of England. Plus, more famous than England's mildness is its rain. I can personally attest to this.[2]

The land was also fertile, there was plenty of timber and game. Captain George Percy, one of our sources for the expedition, raved about sea food which could be easily found on the coast and strawberries four times the size of those back in England. The James River was great for trading, and the Natives weren't as hostile as they might have been. This wasn't because they were particularly weak individuals, more that European diseases were already causing plenty of damage. There were signs then that this little colony might just thrive. As Jamestown is where the American story begins, it should be reasonably clear how all this turns out.

---

[2] Thomas - Jefferson would remark that it was fairly common to see a clear blue sky in Virginia, the kind which didn't exist in Europe. Haha, very funny, Jefferson, but yeah he's got point.

Chapter 2 – The Founding of Jamestown

On April 26th, 1607, three ships sailed into Chesapeake Bay in Virginia. These were the Susan Constant, the Godspeed and the Discovery, and they had just travelled across the ocean to found a colony. The Captain of the flagship the Susan Constant, one Christopher Newport, decided that they would disembark and get the lay of the land. He went with Wingfield, Gosnold, and a few dozen others including George Percy, one of our sources for the expedition. They explored the coast and country and liked what they saw, before returning to the ships as night fell. Percy wrote:

> "At night, when we were going aboard, there came the Savages creeping upon all foure, from the Hills like Beares, with their Bowes in their mouthes, charged us very desperately in the faces, hurt Captaine Gabrill Archer in both his hands, and a sayler in two places of the body very dangerous. After they had spent their Arrowes, and felt the sharpnesse of our shot, they retired into the Woods with a great noise, and so left us."

The story of the United States starts with Jamestown, but that doesn't mean there wasn't anything going on before the colonists arrived. We'll discuss the Native Americans in more detail in another volume. But, for the moment, I want to introduce the Powhatan Confederacy.

The Powhatan Confederacy

A common criticism levelled at the Native Americans is their failure to effectively unite against the European threat, but this isn't completely true. In the 1560s the Spanish ventured as north as the modern state of Virginia and came into contact with the Powhatan. One of the Native Americans was taken to New Spain where he was given the name Don Luis, but he returned home and forced the Spanish back. This sparked rapid political development as the tribes along the Chesapeake united to force back a possible Spanish threat which ultimately never materialised. But it did mean that when the English arrived the natives were prepared to meet them.

The Powhatan Confederacy was led principally by two brothers, Wahunsonacock and Opechancanough.[3] Towards the south of the Chesapeake Bay are two rivers, the James River and the York River. This was the heartland of the Powhatan Confederacy, but under the leadership of the warlike Wahunsonacock their influence expanded as far north as the Potomac. His leadership was totalitarian in the core of his empire which is why our sources describe him as a despot, but beyond this relatively small area he was more of a chief of chiefs. He certainly never attempted to go seriously against the more established tribal groupings of the interior, such as the Iroquois and the Siouans, but there were raids.

---

[3] Some, most notably Carl Bridenbaugh, theorise that Opechancanough is the very same Don Luis, but I'm not entirely sure how convinced I am by these suggestions. They are interesting to say the least.

Wahunsonacock collected tribute in food, peals, beads, skins and tobacco, in addition he had a monopoly on the trade of luxury goods such as copper and iron. Wahunsonacock placed family members in positions of power and used this to control his wider empire, the most powerful of these was Opechancanough.

The Powhatan Confederacy had a population of around 15,000. Most people avoided the exposed areas of the coast, they instead lived in villages of usually less than a hundred people on high ground next to the rivers. Though you shouldn't think of them as anything like European villages, of groups of houses gathered together. These tended to be rather spread out. 20 houses could easily be spread out over ten acres. The rivers provided transport and communication while the high ground meant that they wouldn't be affected by flooding. This was just part of a wider network which connected the entire Eastern Seaboard from Canada to Florida. These people really weren't ignorant savages. That said, they certainly weren't peaceful. The Powhatan Confederacy was built for war and Wahunsonacock was able to pull together a force of 1,200-1,500 warriors which was easily enough to assert his will upon the region.

Custom demanded that when making important decisions the chiefs consult with the cawcawwasoughs, a word which I can probably translate as counsellors. They were a group of village elders, warriors and priests. The elders had experience, the warriors would have to deal with the fighting if going to war, and the priests had the ability to see the future and more broadly act as an intermediary between the tribe and spiritual force.

They would read omens and then give the appropriate advice.

Powhatan religion worshiped a god called 'Ahone' who was perfect, and who created the world and all the lesser gods. He was however a distant god, and so the most important god was Okeus, this was with whom the priests communicated. He was a vengeful god who needed to be appeased. That should serve as a reasonable introduction to the Powhatans, and allows us to get back to our narrative. April 26th, 1607.

The First Days

Our sources have very little to say about the Indian attack, aside from the fact that it happened. The English made their way back to the ship and then there was the small matter of choosing a leader. That isn't quite the right way to put it. Perhaps I should say, there was the small matter of finding out who was to lead them. You see the choice of leadership was made by the Virginia Council, the body which had been created to oversee both the south Virginia Company's colony at Jamestown and the Plymouth Company's colony at St. George's Fort. The Council was worried that if they announced the leadership before the expedition took place that some of the gentlemen simply wouldn't be interested. What they decided to do instead was to put the name of the leaders inside of a box which could then be opened when they had arrived safely in Virginia. By that point, it would be too late for any grumpy gentlemen to go home.

So, Newport opened the box to reveal the names of the ruling 7. You'll already know several of these names. There was Newport, Captain of the Susan Constant; Gosnold, founder of the enterprise and Captain of the Godspeed; Wingfield, Gosnold's cousin and key early mover in getting funding for the expedition; and Ratcliffe, Captain of the Discovery. There was also Sir Richard Martin, Master of the Royal Mint and three times Lord Mayor of London, he had sailed with Drake to bring home the colonists at Roanoke. Member number six was Captain George Kendall, he was connected both with parliamentarian Sir Edwin Sandys and Lord Salisbury. The seventh of the leaders was John Smith, currently under arrest. These 7 would then choose a President who would serve for a year, unless he was removed. This could be done by a vote of the majority of the council. It was expected that the 7 would make decisions together, but it could come down to a vote with the President carrying 2 votes. It was a good system. But it had a couple of problems.

One of the council, Smith, was in custody and was hated by Newport and Wingfield. They wouldn't let him take his seat. In addition, George Percy and Gabriel Archer had both expected to be named on the council. There was now the question of just what their role in the expedition would be.

Well, the council voted. Wingfield was elected President of the Colony, but he shared command with Newport who was tasked with exploring the country for a couple of months before returning to England with the ships. Archer was made secretary, which answered the particular problem about what to do with him.

They spent a couple of weeks exploring the James River, even moving a couple of miles inland. They then had a great stroke of luck when they discovered a channel of deep water in the James. This was significant as it allowed the ships to safely move upriver, this would save weeks of finding a suitable harbour. The natives also appeared to be friendly for the most part. They had been attacked on their first night, so I'm not sure you could call them completely friendly. It was now time to found the settlement.

The Site

Gosnold favoured a point called Archers Hope, but Wingfield wouldn't allow this because the ships couldn't get close enough. Instead a locale was chosen 2 miles upstream. A peninsula which they named Jamestown Island. Jamestown Island was about 3 miles long in the yellowish James River. The island was dominated by reedy marshes which cut into the woods and meadows. It was 50 miles from the coast which should protect it from the Spanish, and the fact that it was only connected to the mainland by a narrow causeway offered it protection from the natives. The boats could easily dock their due to a deep channel of water and there was plenty of nearby timber. It seemed like a great location. But the marshes would cause problems. The Virginia council had instructed the settlers to not choose a low or moist site due as this would cause disease. This instruction was ignored. We'll see the effects of this later.

On 14th of May they disembarked and set up camp. They broke into small groups. One team began building fortifications in a half moon shape, others cleared away the undergrowth, others cut trees, and the rest made fishing nets and prepared the ground to grow crops. The beachhead was established.

A week later Newport set off on his mission. He was to find a mountain which might have gold, and find a river which went to the East India Sea. This is the same sea I mentioned last week, and seems to be referring to the Pacific Ocean. He sailed with 23 men, these included Percy, Archer and Smith. Smith appears to have still been technically under some sort of arrest, but he would be properly released sometime in mid-June. While Newport didn't find the Pacific, Newport did find natives who wanted to trade and gave him information. It was here that the English learned of Wahunsonacock. He explored up the James as far as he could go, and to mark the occasion on the 24th of May he planted a cross with the Latin inscription "Jacobus Rex". In English, King James. This act claimed the territory for England. Not that the natives realised this.

Newport very happily misled the natives about the true significance of planting the cross. He kept up the pretence that this was only a trading mission. But he was not the only one putting up a show. The Powhatans misled Newport over the identity of Wahunsonacock. They told him that it was Chesapeake tribes who had attacked him on the 26th April, not the upriver Powhatans. Newport was quite happy to believe them. It was very good to know that they had friends upriver. What he didn't realise was that the reasons the Powhatans were putting no such a show of hospitality was to keep them upriver while a force of 200 warriors launched an assault on the Jamestown colonists. The fighting was hard but the English held out and used the ships' cannon to force back the Powhatans. In the fighting two were killed, a boy and one of the gentlemen named Eustace Clovell. In addition, 11 were injured including Gosnold, Ratcliffe, Martin and Kendall, while an arrow was actually shot through Wingfield's beard.

While we do not know who launched the attack, it seems likely that Wahunsonacock wanted to test the Europeans. If this is what happened, he was very likely troubled at how easily they had held off 200 of his finest warriors. He would need to rethink his approach. It also convinced the English that they would need to rethink their approach. The Virginia council had recommended that a square fortification be built around a market square which would hold the church and storehouse. This would allow a more gradual expansion as more settlers arrived. While this was all well and good, it wouldn't be remotely practical if the colonists had been killed by the time new settlers arrived. They needed to increase their fortifications. It was decided that the settlement would become a triangle with three defensive walls, with the main south wall along the coast of the island about one hundred and forty yards in length, while the other two walls were a hundred yards. At every corner a half moon fortification was be built with a watchtower which could house a canon. The walls were a palisade about 8 feet high to protect them from arrows, but there were holes in the timber allowing the English to fire back. The canons would also be located so that if a Spanish ship wanted to get close the island, because of the water channels they would have to get within the firing line. The houses of the fort were around 10 yards inside of the walls. The colony was established. Jamestown was founded. Newport had completed his exploration mission and on Monday June 22nd 1607 he set sail back to London to report to the council how things had gone so far.

Newport had with him a letter from the governors addressed to the Virginia Council back in London to spread word on how the expedition was going. The colonists were spectacularly excited about Jamestown. The seas were plentiful, as was the land. There was plenty of game and timber, and it would be able to supply all the tobacco the English could need. All they needed was more labourers. When Newport arrived back in London on August 12th and got off the boat, it wasn't so much these resources that caused excitement back home, but instead the gold. There was talk of mountains in the interior which had plentiful gold, and this was the really exciting stuff. They'd all be rich! However, a sample was taken back to England for testing, and it was found out that the colonists hadn't discovered gold at all, it was instead Iron Pyrite. Fool's gold. This put the future of the colony in jeopardy. Sure there were good resources. But there was no gold. Was it really worth in the investment. The Spanish ambassador in London, Don Pedro de Zuniga, wrote to King Philip III to inform him that the English colony was sterile, and it was likely it would be used as a base for piracy instead. While there may have been no gold, there was enough good news that the company decided to send a second expedition to the colony with more supplies.

The First Summer

Meanwhile, in Jamestown, things were not going well. There had been some notable successes so far. They had built their fortifications, they had built houses, they had fought back the Powhatans, they had planted their first crop and they had seemingly overcome their internal struggles. Before Newport sailed back to England John Smith was restored to the council. This left Wingfield as President with Gosnold, Ratcliffe, Smith, Martin and Kendall also on the governing council of seven. Newport was absent.

Wahunsonacock had realised that a frontal assault of the colony wasn't a good idea, so he waited. If any Englishman strayed outside of the colony with their guard down, they would not last very long. The shelters were also flimsy, boiling in the summer, and offered little to no protection from either the wind or rain. And then there was the choice of location. Jamestown Island was marshy. The choice of settlement was low lying. It was exactly where the Virginia Council told the colonists not to settle, in an unhealthy place.

Problems began almost as soon as Newport left when the colony entered the sickly season, which lasted from July to September. It began on 6th of August when John Asbie died of bloody flux. Three days later George Flowre died of swelling, the next day William Bruster died of a wound received from the Powhatans, and from then the men just kept dropping.

Percy attributed it to famine, but famine really doesn't make sense. During these months the colonists would have been able to fish for sturgeon from the river. Rather, they were suffering from typhoid. If you have a sensitive stomach you may want to skip past this bit. Typhoid Fever is a disease caused by the bacteria *Salmonella Typhi*, closely related to the salmonella more commonly associated with food poisoning. It is highly contagious. The bacteria can be passed out of the body through waste. Mostly faeces, but sometimes urine too. If a person come into contact with infected waste, they too will catch the disease. This is why typhoid is such a problem in areas with low sanitation. While it is less of a problem than it was even a hundred years ago, Typhoid Fever affects about 21 million people annually, killing 200,000. That is with modern medicine. It had a much higher mortality rate before antibiotics of around one in five. Once the *Salmonella Typhi* enters the body, usually through infected food or water, it will work its way through the digestive system until it reaches the small intestines. The bacteria then moves into the bloodstream where it can gain access to the other organs by attaching itself to the white blood cells. It gets into the liver, the spleen and bone marrow where it can grow before moving back into the bloodstream. From there it attacks the biliary system, the part of the body which creates bile for digesting food. This is the gallbladder as well as bits of the liver. It also begins to attack tissue in the gut. This is when symptoms develop include a fever of around 40C (104F) headaches, stomach pain, loss of appetite, lethargy, constipation and diarrhoea. The disease takes about a month to run its course, but the infected may take longer to die.

It is suspected that the original carrier was Reverend Hunt, who you'll remember was ill during the initial 6 week delay off the coast of England. He lectured the gentlemen not to abandon the expedition in between bouts of vomiting. This would fit. You see, while the boats were there the men could drink beer, but once Newport sailed away the men were forced to have something called the common kettell. It was a drink of wheat and barley boiled in water, and it was Hunt who tended the common kettell. It is suspected by a leading authority on the subject, Dr. Wyndham Blanton, that Typhoid killed more of the Jamestown colonists than all the other diseases combined.

So, the men started dropping like flies. This was bad, but things got worse on August 22nd. Bartholomew Gosnold, the founder of the Jamestown movement, died, aged 36. Gosnold was a great calming influence amongst the senior figures, you should remember how he had stopped Wingfield and Newport from killing Smith in the Caribbean. With him dead, things really began to go to hell in a handbasket.

On 10th September Ratcliffe, Smith, and Martin removed Wingfield from office as President. They accused him of hording food and drink while the rest of the colony staved, while he accused Smith of planning to abandon the colony and fleeing to Newfoundland. Wingfield was also accused of plotting with the Spanish. It does seem that there was someone communicating with the Spanish, but it is now thought that it was Kendall rather than Wingfield. Anyway, Wingfield was exiled back to the England and Ratcliffe was made the colony's second president. According to Wingfield, the triumvirate of Ratcliffe, Smith, and Martin usurped power and the rule of law disappeared from the colony. He related one account that James Reed, a blacksmith, was sentenced to executed for hitting Ratcliffe, but he saved himself by revealing a plot by Kendall. How much of this was true? To be blunt, we don't know. The Company chose to not follow up either the council's allegations against Wingfield, or Wingfield's allegations against the council. We don't know if this was because they didn't believe them, or because it would have been terrible publicity for the venture if word of what was going on got out. Whether these complaints were real or imagined, the 6 were plainly no longer friends.

Could things BE any worse for the colony? 104 colonists had landed at Jamestown in May. By the time winter was setting in there were fewer than 40 of them left. And those few settlers were in fighting. As a historian I much prefer a sarcastic comment to advice, but even to me such constant arguing doesn't seem like a good idea. The colony should not have survived. They desperately needed the supplies that Newport would bring back with him, and some labour too. When Newport did return, I wonder just how brutal the welcoming committee for the new settlers was. "Welcome to the New World. It sucks. You're going to love it!" Not that this really matters in the grand scheme of things, it's a moot point. It is almost certain that the colony wouldn't have survived were it not for the Native Americans. They had become a lot friendlier since the big ships, the Susan Constant and the Godspeed, had left with Newport. The English seemed much less imposing without their ability to patrol the coast, and so they supplied the English with desperately needed goods.

Things were still not going well for the English. Ratcliffe and Martin were not loved, and so Smith took charge of day to day operations. This cannot have been easy for Smith. He had few men, most of those were ill, and those that weren't wished they were dead. But Smith kept things going, such as constructing cabins to replace their falling apart tents.

When the food supply began to run low he sailed downstream to trade with a tribe known as the Kecoughtans. They laughed in Smith's face and gave him a few beans in exchange. Smith was not amused. He launched an attack, not to kill, but to demonstrate that he could kill if he wanted. He could just take their things, but he wanted to trade. The Kecoughtans were suitably frightened and then traded as Smith wished. Even these didn't last long and they were in trouble again by November. The leaders drew lots and it fell to Smith to sail upriver. Once he reached the shallow water Smith decided against risking the barge and so found two some Native Americans who were willing to sail him in a canoe, and so Smith carried on up river with Jehu Robinson and Thomas Emry. They disembarked and Smith decided to explore with one of the Native Americans as a guide, while Robinson and Emry and stayed with the canoe and other Native American.

Within 15 minutes Smith heard a shout, and he was very quickly surrounded by 200 Powhatan warriors. While Smith had a pistol and managed to fend them off for a while, he was literally outnumbered 200 to one. He was captured. Robinson and Emry were both killed. He was then led to Opechancanough, the brother of Wahunsonacock. In an effort to try and buy him some time he took out a compass from his pocket and gave it to the chief as a gift, the Powhatan who had acted as a guide spoke some

English, and so Smith was able to explain just about what it could do. To quote Smith himself:

> "Much they marvailed at the playing of the fly and Needle, which they could see so plainely, and yet not touch it, because of the glasse that covered them. But when he demonstrated by that Globe-like Jewell, the roundnesse of the earth, and skies, the sphere of the Sunne, Moone, and Starres, and how the Sunne did chase the night round about the world continually; the greatnesse of the Land and Sea, the diversitie of Nations, varietie of complextions, and how we were to them the Antipodes, and many other such like matters, they all stood amazed with admiration."

The more we deal with the Powhatans you'll see that these interactions are far more complicated than they seem at first. Every meeting has the flavour of they don't know that we know that they know. There is a lot of both sides acting like friends when they really don't like each other, and sudden changes of mood. For instance, as impressed as they were by his compass, this was not enough to stop them tying Smith up to a tree and preparing to shoot him. All seemed lost, but then Opechancanough held up the compass, and the warriors put down their bows. Smith was then marched to Orapaks, a town about six miles away.

Assumed Simplicity

The villagers gawked at him, and performed a celebratory dance. Smith was then taken to a house where he was given so much food that he thought they were fattening him up so that they could eat him. He was given back his things, including his compass, and he was even allowed to speak with Opechancanough. They took great interest in each other, and Smith very soon realised why he had been spared. Opechancanough was planning an attack on Jamestown and wanted Smith to provide him with the information on how best to take it. In return, he wouldn't be killed.

Smith pretended to accept the deal, because, well, he didn't want to die. He would instead live and try and warn Jamestown of the trouble that was coming. What follows next is... a bit strange. Smith warned the Powhatans of the dangers of assaulting Jamestown, and of the power of English weaponry. Smith wanted to send a letter to Jamestown to let them know he was alive, and so 3 Powhatans travelled there, and returned with goods Smith had requested. The Powhatans never launched the attack, and Smith was kept alive. That's what we know happened. But, how did that happen. What were the reasons?

Smith seemed to think that the Powhatans had no knowledge or understanding of writing, and therefore assumed that the Powhatans assumed that either Smith could communicate through long distances or had made the paper talk. Either way, he was magic. This was what kept him alive. Meanwhile his request for weaponry to give to the Powhatans was enough to convince them that attacking Jamestown was a bad idea. This was how

Smith understood the situation, but it has several problems with it.

If you'll allow me to become a grumpy historian for a moment, well, a grumpier historian anyway, one of my biggest pet peeves is the assumption of simplicity. So often written accounts assume that they are far smarter than the people they are writing about. Not in an arrogant way, although sometimes that. More that they don't allow the possibility of sophisticated thought by what they deem lesser civilisations. One of my huge criticisms with most scholarship on the fall of the Roman Empire is that they are dominated by assumed simplicity. They look for chaos in the fall of the Roman Empire, and so find it. They don't look for patterns or higher levels of thought, such as counter-logic. Now, I'm sure you're saying this is all well and good Jamie, but what does it have to do with John Smith?

He is working under the assumption of assumed simplicity. Smith didn't realise that the Powhatans had already had plenty of experience with Europeans, and that it was very possible that Opechancanough was Don Luis who had spent time in Mexico City. At the very least, we can be reasonably confident that if he wasn't Don Luis Opechancanough knew of Don Luis, and probably spoke with him. He would have known all about writing. So, just like when they tricked Newport into staying upriver for the first attack on Jamestown, the Powhatans were playing a game just like Smith. The only question is what where they doing, and why were they doing it. That is a question we simply don't know the answer to, but we can make some pretty good guesses.

It could be they were using Smith to get some sort of ransom. This would explain why they sent men to Jamestown, they were seeing just how important Smith was. From what they brought back from Jamestown apparently he was valuable, worth keeping alive, and worth presenting to Wahunsonacock himself, which they did a few weeks later.

Werowocomoco

He went to Werowocomoco on the north side of the York River, 15 miles from Jamestown. The meeting was very ritualistic and ceremonial, no doubt intended to impress Smith. Indeed, he was. Wahunsonacock welcomed Smith, and let him know that he would be freed in four days. He was interested by what Opechancanough had told him, and wanted to know more. For instance, just why were the English there?

Smith replied that they had been in a fight with the Spaniards and fled into Chesapeake Bay. They then went up river in order to find fresh water. They had encamped at Jamestown to make repairs while waiting for the return of Newport, who Smith described as his father. Not the most convincing explanation, but Wahunsonacock didn't ask too many questions about it. What he did do was ask Smith and the English to abandon Jamestown and resettle on the York River where they would become part of his chiefdom. Smith describes what happened in a scene which has since become legendary, describing himself in the third person.

"two great stones were brought before Powhatan: then as many as could lay hands on him dragged him to them, and thereon aid his head, and being ready with their clubs to beate out his braines, Pocahontas the Kings dearest daughter, when no intreaty could prevaile, got his head in her armes, and laid her owne upon his to save him from death."

Did this happen? No. Probably not. James Horn notes that Smith is our only source for the event and that he was writing years after the fact.[4] Not even considering the fact that Smith probably had a poor grasp of understanding Powhatan rituals, he either accidentally or purposefully got it wrong. I mean, just think about it. Pocahontas (yes, that Pocahontas) was the daughter of Wahunsonacock and was only 11 years old. While it makes for a happy story about the power of love over violence, was she really going to risk her life and publicly humiliate her father for the sake of some stranger? No. Of course she wasn't.

Horn finds far more likely the possibility that this was some sort of adoption ceremony involving a ritualistic dying and rebirth as an Anglo-Powhatan. Pocahontas was playing a role within the ceremony, and it would fit with Wahunsonacock asking Smith and the other English to join his tribe. It seems likely that this approach was due to the rapidly declining numbers of the English. They weren't much of a

---

[4] Horn (2005) A Land as God Made It: Jamestown and the Birth of America.

41

threat anymore, and having them as part of his empire would give him trading access to English goods.

Two days later there was another ceremony in which Smith was made a son of Wahunsonacock, he was given the name Nantaquoud. Smith would be freed, and to confirm their friendship he was to give Wahunsonacock two guns and a grindstone. It is assumed that he accepted the terms. Smith never seriously considered Wahunsonacock's offer. He was an Englishman and a gentleman, not some barbarian chief. With all his knowledge gained on this misadventure, Smith's position of pre-eminence in the colony would be confirmed.

He returned to the fort and presented his guides with the canons that Wahunsonacock wanted. However, these weighed one and a half tonnes each. The Powhatans had no way of dragging them back. Smith showed off what they could do by firing some rocks at trees, which terrified the guides. Smith mollified them by giving them other gifts to take back to Wahunsonacock.

The reaction to Smith's return was mixed. The men were happy to see him, but the council wasn't. Archer was particularly upset. He had been promoted to the council in Smith's absence. Even before he was captured, Ratcliffe and Martin weren't Smith's greatest admirers. Archer blamed Smith for the deaths of Robinson and Emry. Ratcliffe, as president, condemned Smith to death by hanging. You'll recall the double insult of this. As a gentleman Smith should have been shot, not hung. It was January 2nd that Smith returned, and things had been getting ever worse. Ratcliffe,

Archer, and the other gentlemen were planning to abandon the colony. They would flee on the one ship they had left, the Discovery, which was only a small 20 ton pinnace. On it, they would travel either to Newfoundland or England, leaving Reverend Hunt and the surgeon, Thomas Wotton, in charge. But, as had happened for the third time now in our short narrative, this was not Smith's time to die. By pure chance this day, January 2nd 1608, was the day that Newport returned to Jamestown.

The First Supply

The charges against Smith were dropped in the celebrations. There is a brilliant passage by Horn which I'm just going to quote since I don't think I could put it better myself.

> "We do not know what Newport's reactions were upon his return to Jamestown. When he left in the summer, only a couple of men had been lost and the settlement appeared to be in relatively good shape. Six months later, nearly two-thirds of the men were dead, the deposed president of the council was under close arrest, one member of the council had been shot, and another was about to be hanged. The leading gentry had decided to desert the colony, and nothing of value had been discovered or produced."[5]

---

[5] Horn (2005) A Land as God Made It: Jamestown and the Birth of America.

Newport wasn't going to wallow in self-pity though, he wouldn't despair about what had happened to the colony. He was going to fix things. He had with him a hundred or so men, of which we have 73 listed individuals. Including 33 gentlemen, 21 labourers, 6 tailors, 2 apothecaries, 2 refiners, 2 goldsmiths, a gunsmith, a perfumer, a blacksmith and tobacco-pipe maker. For all his new optimism, there would be another setback for Jamestown a few days later. There was a fire. Fires are never nice, but in a settlement made entirely of timber they could do an awful lot of damage. All but 3 buildings were destroyed. The church was burnt, the library, the storehouse, and the fortifications. All most men had left were the clothes on their backs. Fires are not uncommon in structures made of wood when there were open flames, but I will mention that there was, and indeed still is, some suspicion about whether the Spanish had anything to do with it. It was a particularly harmful blow to Reverend Hunt who would die in the following Great Frost. As we saw when dealing with St. George's Fort, 1607-08 was a cold winter.

The English were desperate, and all of a sudden they were reliant on the Powhatan again. Wahunsonacock sent food to Jamestown a couple of times a week. Well, more accurately, they sent food to Smith and Newport. These were the only two they considered leaders, and Newport only because of what Smith had told them about him.

What happened next was Jamestown was left in the hands of Martin and Ratcliffe while Smith and Newport travelled to Werowocomoco with a guard 30 or 40 strong. The reception was warm and friendly. There was another ceremony which confirmed the English as Powhatans and Smith was confirmed as a weroance, which translates as something like leader. It was used to describe the level below the chief.

Once negotiations between Newport and Wahunsonacock began, the chieftain demanded to see the English goods before deciding how much corn to give. Smith advised Newport against this, recognising it as a trick to lower the amount of food they would give. Newport agreed to Wahunsonacock's request and, as Smith expected, less corn was given. Smith was furious. While I've criticised Smith for not understanding the Powhatans, he did understand them far better than his contemporaries. This act greatly weakened the diplomatic stock of the colonists since they had been tricked. Newport was concerned primarily with the immediate problems, but Smith was concerned about long term trade, so maybe Newport was taking a risk to secure the colony's future. They returned in early March with enough food to see the colony into Spring. This was a bad time for the colonists. There was little food, and the men were being put to use to find gold. While Smith was just as interested in gold as the others, he wanted men to be put to a more productive use than finding gold.

Newport set sail back to England on April 10th with Archer, Wingfield, and a Powhatan who had been sent to England by Wahunsonacock named Namontack. Since the council was now getting pretty small, it was down to just Smith, Ratcliffe and Martin, one of the new arrivals, Matthew Scivener, was added, and Smith began doing to real work of repairing the fort. While he was doing this he had a problem with Native Americans sneaking into the fort and stealing things. Eventually some were captured, and they revealed information that Wahunsonacock really hated the English, and his show of friendship was just that, a show. He planned to lure Newport into a trap when he returned and launch a general attack on Jamestown. Smith was troubled by this information, and set above improving the fortifications.

Another ship soon arrived. Newport had set out with Captain Francis Nelson in the Phoenix, but Nelson had gotten lost in bad weather and so made it to Jamestown late. They shared resources, and the colony's strength was raised to around 150. At the beginning of June he set off back to London with Martin, who was rather ill. It would be a while before Newport returned so Smith set off to explore the country.

I won't include a list of all the rivers he went down, but there was one incident of note when Smith's party was attacked by a group of Powhatans. The English easily forced them back with their muskets, but from them Smith learned that they had been ordered to attack by Wahunsonacock, and that he had been egged on by Ratcliffe.

Smith returned on July 21st with knowledge of the local area, as well as furs, fish and fruits. He returned to find Jamestown on the verge of Mutiny. Ratcliffe had become deeply unpopular while Smith was away, apparently he forced the men to work building him a palace in the woods, which is really odd on just about every level. As second in command they asked Smith to depose Ratcliffe,

which he seems to have done, making himself the
third president of Jamestown.

Chapter 3 – The Starving Time

When Jamestown was originally founded there were 7 leading councillors. Within 15 months Gosnold died from illness, Kendall had been shot, Martin had left, Newport was commuting between Jamestown and London, and both Wingfield and Ratcliffe had been deposed. There was only Smith left. So, when he became President of the colony in July 1608 what was his first action? He... erm... left. He didn't abandon the colony, he just decided to continue his exploring and left Scrivener, who you'll recall was added to council last week, in charge for the moment.

I won't bore you with the details since Smith was just looking for a river which would take him to the southern ocean (which didn't exist) and making a lot of deals with local tribes. Various attacks, trading missions, and diplomatic dealings took place which, you can find yourself if you wish. But I really don't think you'd appreciate me throwing name after name at you without any real context. But, basically, this was a 6 week expedition around Chesapeake Bay and they returned to Jamestown on September 7th. He had gained much information, but no gold.

The fort had been worse, but Jamestown couldn't be called in good condition. These had been the sickly months and many had died, while the fort was not at all ready for Newport's expected arrival. First things first, they had to sort out the constitutional mess. On September 10th Smith was formally elected President and he began to set about improving things. The eastern wall was taken down so that the colony could expand, and it doubled in size. The church and storehouse were rebuilt, and a military field was created called Smithfield.

The Second Supply

Newport arrived with the Second Supply in Mid-October, and Smith was not happy about it. A map Smith had drawn had excited people back in England about the possibility of the Roanoke settlers surviving somewhere along the coast, this would be a huge boost to the Company. But Smith, with his practical long term mind-set, thought that the Company back in London was clearly deluded. Newport had been told to return only if he could find gold, a route to the South Sea and the lost survivors of Roanoke. Smith knew that these were all unrealistic, and he wasn't fond of Newport either. However, the historian must be careful when narrating events. Hindsight has 20-20 vision, as they say. We now know there was no gold to be found, that there was no chance of finding the Roanoke survivors, and that Virginia is nowhere near the Pacific. This was not known at the time, and can we really fault Newport and the Virginia Company for not being aware of this?

There was every chance that there was Gold in those mountains, or that a river would be found which would take them through to the Pacific. The Company was worried about how to best secure the future of the colony. Rumours were coming in from Madrid that the Spanish were constructing an Armada to attack and destroy Jamestown. If the Company could report to the king that they had found gold, or a passage to the Pacific, that would greatly increase the chances that the Royal Navy would consider the colony worth protecting.

Newport brought 70 more colonists with him, but not food for those 70. He did, however, have resources for an exploration of the interior which Smith opposed. Most people thought this was Smith being petty since he had been unable to find gold, a route to the south sea, or the Roanoke colonists, and that he didn't want Newport to upstage him. Newport also was to coronate Wahunsonacock as it was hoped this would tie the English and the Powhatans closer together. Smith objected, and it came to a vote. Which gives us a good opportunity to address the changing nature of the council.

Newport Takes Control

Of the original 7, only 2 were still on the council, Smith and Newport. We also mentioned last time out that Scrivener had been added, but with Newport's return the council was expanded. New members were Captain Richard Waldo, Master Andrew Buckler, Edward Brinton, Samuel Collier and Namontact, the Powhatan whom Wahunsonacock had sent to England. This brought their numbers up to 8. The council sided with Newport over Smith, so Smith went with the council's decision. He and Waldo travelled to Werowocomoco to discuss the coronation idea with Wahunsonacock. He agreed, on one condition. He would not travel to Jamestown. If the English wanted to do this, they would come to him. They had little choice but to agree. The negotiation was a farce. As was the whole coronation.

Wahunsonacock accepted the gifts, but refused to bow to be crowned. They eventually forced him to drop his head enough for Newport to put the crown on his head. He in return gave the English a sign of his royal favour, one of his cloaks and some shoes. Smith found the whole experience very strange, and thought that what had happened was that Wahunsonacock hadn't understood what the crown meant. This is true, but perhaps a better way of saying it would be that Wahunsonacock didn't understand what the crown meant to the English, just as the English didn't really understand how the Powhatan chief had twisted the meaning of the ceremony. To the Powhatans, it had become the English giving them tribute, rather than what it was supposed to be, them recognising the supreme power of King James. As part of this, Wahunsonacock also refused to help with English expeditions against the Monacans, an interior tribe to the west of the Powhatans. He wouldn't give them any guides, aside from allowing them to use Namontact.

The English returned to Jamestown, and Newport was annoyed. Smith had been right, the coronation was a terrible idea. But Newport wasn't one to be discouraged, and so he set about his exploration mission. He would take 120 men, including all the councillors apart from Smith, who would stay behind in Jamestown with 80 men to produce something to send back to England.

Smith was annoyed at this deliberate snub, he was the most qualified explorer, but I completely sympathise with Newport. The two had had a rocky relationship ever since they set out for Virginia two years ago, Smith had failed in his explorations, it was now Newport's turn. Smith had also been telling them that they needed to do something practical, this was his chance.

Newport set off into the heartland of Virginia, and may have made it as far as to see the Blue Ridge Mountains, but they found no gold, no Roanoke survivors, no route to the Pacific, and the locals wouldn't trade. It was a complete disaster. I bet Smith was unbearably smug when Newport returned.

Since Newport's get rich quick scheme hadn't worked, the English set about far more mundane matters. Making practical products. These included a glass works for which 8 Germans and Poles had been hired to work on. He also took a group of men into the forest to work on their survival skills. When he returned he found Jamestown short on food, so he went to trade with the natives, they were unwilling, so Smith terrified them into handing over their food. While a few of the gentry hated Smith his ability to feed the men was making him practically untouchable.

Newport set off back to London in December 1608, and had with him letters sent from Smith. He told them point blank that what they planned was deluded. They were not going to find gold, a route to the Pacific, or the Roanoke survivors. There would be quicker ways of getting rich. It would take time to build up industry, but that was the only way to advance with the colony. They needed to think in the long term. They needed to send men with practical skills, not the gentry who were worse than useless as far as Smith was concerned.

It was a brilliant work of propaganda. He described things which could be found in Europe, and so were familiar to the masses, but stressed their abundance. He also stressed the small numbers of the natives. This was a golden opportunity for the English, they shouldn't let it slip.

December was spent with the English trying to secure food, but there was one particular event of note. I mentioned earlier that it was interesting that the colonists were all men, and the limitations this meant for the colony. Well, as part of Newport's Second Supply two women made the voyage. Unfortunately we don't know the name of one of them, the wife of a settler. We only know of her as Mistress Forrest. But we do know the name of the other, Ann Burras. She was a maid to Mistress Forrest. In December she married a carpenter, John Laydon, in the first Anglo-American marriage. In 1609 they would have a daughter named Virginia. The first child born in Jamestown. I think that's a pretty big moment.

The Relationship with the Powhatans Collapses

But, back to the quest for food. By January things were getting pretty bad in Jamestown, and Smith travelled to Werowocomoco, arriving there on January 12th 1609. What followed was a pretty blunt exchange. The English wanted food. Wahunsonacock wanted their weapons. Neither was prepared to budge. They both posed as the wronged parties, and Smith began to fear for his life. He agreed to Wahunsonacock's terms, but only to buy himself some time. He planned to kidnap Wahunsonacock and steal as much food as his men could carry. After a few days negotiations ended and Wahunsonacock left. Then the hall was surrounded by warriors, and Smith was in trouble. He managed to force his way through with his pistol, but he was just too outnumbered. The Powhatans lied to him to keep him in place, while Wahunsonacock had ordered Smith to be killed later that day.

During the evening, he was warned by Pocahontas of what was coming. Smith thanked her, and with this knowledge was able to make his escape later that night. He fled to Opechancanough, hoping to get food. It was risky, but Smith was desperate. Opechancanough seemed open to the deal, but when Smith went to meet him the next day he found Opechancanough with food. They went and spoke, but were soon surrounded by 500 warriors. Smith challenged Opechancanough to single combat, which Opechancanough obviously ignored. Smith was desperate. He grabbed Opechancanough and put his pistol in his face. This was enough to force Opechancanough to 'trade'. Smith departed on friendly terms, but this was just an act. The Powhatans and the English were no longer friends. Smith returned to Jamestown in early February with food, but the winter had been a complete disaster.

Why? Just how had all this happened? Despite the show of friendship, the English and Powhatans had been trying to trick each other and get one up over each other since they met, but the hostility had never been quite this open. The answer to why this was going on was in Werowocomoco. For while Smith was negotiating with Wahunsonacock, the English were not the only Europeans there. There was also a group of German colonists.

Wahunsonacock made them the same offer he had made to Smith a year before, except without making any of them weroances. They could settle in his land, be part of his chiefdom, and he would supply them with food and other necessities. They accepted. All of a sudden the Powhatans had no need of Smith or the English, which explains why Smith's negotiating position fell apart so rapidly. Indeed, while Smith was out trying to secure food several of these Germans travelled to Jamestown and managed to deceive their way into getting some supplies and took them to Werowocomoco. In addition to a few defectors, they secured three hundred hatchets, 50 swords, 8 pikes and 8 cannons. It was a huge blow to the English, and a huge gain for the Powhatans. Things were looking bad, but next week they will only get worse. The years 1609-1610 are known in the historical record as 'The Starving Time' to give you a sense of what's coming.

The Starving Time

When Smith returned to Jamestown, he was met with more bad news. There had been an accident when some of the men were sailing to Hog Island. 11 were killed, including two councillors, Scrivener and Waldo. Word then came of the Germans with Wahunsonacock encouraging further defection. When Smith went out to investigate he was attacked by a group of Paspaheghs commanded by their chief Wowinchopunck, in which Smith was almost killed.

This would prove beneficial in the long term though. The Paspaheghs were not as powerful as the Powhatans and Smith was able to outman then.

When Smith launched a counter attack the two sides reached an agreement whereby Smith would leave the Paspaheghs alone, and in return they would supply him with food.

As winter turned into spring Smith continued improving the colony. They were producing pitch, tar, soap asses and glass, a second fort was built on the other side of the river in case they should ever need to abandon Jamestown, Hog Island had hogs, and they planted corn over 30 to 40 acres. The problem was food.

Their supplies had either rotted or been eaten by rats. Smith had no choice but spread out his force or risk starvation. He sent a group of 70 about 20 miles downriver to live on oyster. This worked at providing them food, but there are problems with an all oyster diet. Their skin started to peel off. 70 more were went upriver to live on food they could find by the waterfalls. This left 70 at Jamestown. And these didn't want to work. They wanted to be soldiers, not farmers. They had no interest in forming careers, and just traded privately with the natives.

Smith was forced into desperate action to try and keep the peace. He threatened to hang anyone who talked of abandoning the colony for Newfoundland, and to expel anyone from Jamestown who didn't produce as much food as he did. I don't really want to repeat myself, but this was the Starving Time. Smith was just preoccupied with food which is why he eagerly awaited Newport and the Third Supply which was due in the spring of 1609. But Newport didn't come. Smith dealt with problems caused by the Germans, and the colony stumbled along, but still Newport didn't come. Wahunsonacock didn't attack, despite encouragement from the Germans. He was happy to wait, and watch. And things got worse. Still Newport didn't come. Then, finally, in mid-July, two ships were spotted. But it wasn't Newport.

Was Smith's doom to come from either the angry Powhatans, his own men on the verge of mutiny, or perhaps a Spanish raid? No. It was to come from London.

Back in England

We must see what was happening with Newport after he arrived back in England following the Second Supply in January 1609. It had been realised for some time that Jamestown wasn't going well. The colony had done anything the company had intended. They had spent a lot of money, and earned very little back. Henry Clinton, the Earl of Lincoln, had been saying that a different approach was needed for a year by this point. This need was made abundantly clear by Smith's letters back to London, and by speaking with Ratcliffe who had returned to England with Newport. Sir Thomas Smythe knew that something needed to be done.

It's been a long time since we've talked about Sir Thomas Smythe, so I'll reintroduce him. He was, quite simply, the leading merchant of the day. He was the governor of the East India Company, he had also set up the Turkey Company and the Russia Company, not to mention others he was merely involved with. He was an MP, was a high ranking official in the Royal Navy and had been appointed Ambassador to Russia in 1604. Thomas Smythe was one of the major backers of the Jamestown expedition, and he called a meeting in late January 1609 to work out just what was wrong. They found two problems.

The system of government wasn't working. They would need to create a new charter for the colony to fix it, and the second issue was the route. It was taking far too long for ships to travel back and forth, this was causing supply problems. You only really need to look at a map to realise how big this particular problem was. The English were sailing along the southern route. They were getting to the Chesapeake from England via the Canary Islands and the Caribbean. There had to be a more effective route than this. To fix the problems the company turned to Captain Samuel Argall to find a shorter route, which would get the ships to Virginia directly from the canaries without sailing to the Caribbean. This would see them avoid Spanish patrols and most of the pirates. Sir Edwin Sandys, a well-connected figure in the aristocracy and merchant circles, was tasked with writing a new charter, which he did.

What was created was a new corporation, The Tresorer and Companie of Adventurers and Planters of the Citty of London for the Firste Collonie in Virginia. It would have a treasurer and governing council to form a permanent administrative body which would report how things were going by both weekly and quarterly meetings. In addition to this change, a new council was made up of adventurers which the company would nominate, rather than the King. This new company would have the power to change the government of the colony. It had total legal power as long as it was not contrary to

English law. A new position was created, the governor. The governor would be the principal officer of the Company in Virginia and would have extensive powers, such as to introduce martial law. There would be an advisory council, but the governor could overrule the council and could not be removed by the council. It was hoped that this would introduce some sort of stability, the type which Jamestown desperately needed. The first lord-governor would be Sir Thomas West, the twelfth Baron De Le Warr. Sir Thomas Gates, a prominent figure within the company, would be appointed his deputy, the lieutenant governor.

It also expanded the territory of the colony because of the collapse of the North Virginia Company. There wasn't really a need to stop the colonies competing with each other if one of them had collapsed. Jamestown's domain was expanded from 50 to 200 miles north and south, and its domain the west was expanded from 100 miles to the Pacific Ocean. Although, to those making the decision in London, it wasn't known just how far it was to the Pacific.

Thomas Smythe then worked on funding what was to be a large scale expedition. It would be done through stock. Bills of Adventure could be purchased for the cost of £12 10s. per share, or a person could join the expedition for a share equivalent to the rank and skills of the colonist. A lowly labourer would be worth a single share, while an artisan or officer would be worth more. Attempts were made to recruit craftsmen from abroad too. Requests for investments were made to the Lord Mayor of London and the other governing bodies and merchants.

The Charter received royal approval on May 23rd 1609, by which point 619 people and 55 London companies had invested with hundreds signing up for the voyage. Don Pedro de Zuniga, the Spanish ambassador in London, was particularly alarmed by this in the messages he sent to King Philip III. He wrote that Lord De La Warr was to set sail with six or seven hundred, and was to be closely followed by Gates with four or five hundred men and a hundred women. This was ambitious, but Sir Thomas Smythe was working on far more ambitious things. Jamestown was considered too small to be a primary base and would be reduced to a garrison and another site selected for the capital.

Much of the new policy was a reaction to what had been done by Wahunsonacock. He was not to be trusted. The other Native Americans were to be converted to Christianity, and they were not longer to give tribe to Wahunsonacock, but to the English. Wahunsonacock and the priests would be captured as part of this. While all this had been going on London, we must return to Jamestown.

We left Smith in mid-July seeing two ships arriving, these were the Mary and the John, commanded by Samuel Argill who had been tasked with finding an alternative to the southern route. He sailed from Portsmouth in May where he travelled southwest until reaching 30 degrees north. Then he headed west until he was a few hundred miles away from Bermuda, and then he turned North, making landfall on July 13th. A 9 week voyage. He was to let Smith know of all that had gone on in London over the past few months, and what he found was Jamestown in chaos.

The leadership was divided and the colony was beset by idleness. Men were starving, but wouldn't do anything to feed themselves. They instead sold their goods on the black market, causing inflation making their goods relatively valueless. Smith was annoyed by the company's harsh criticism of him. They thought he had been too hard on the Powhatans, which Smith felt sort of ignored the fact that they had repeatedly tried to kill him. But, Smith was delighted by the food they brought, and by news of the funds the colony would receive.

Meanwhile in Spain

You wait ages for a ship, then two turn up at once. In addition to Argill, the next day, July 14th, another ship arrived. This time it was the Spanish. We now need to go to Madrid. Philip III of Spain came to the throne at the age 20 in 1598, and he would rule over the Spanish Empire at its height. He had been told continually by his ambassador in London, Don Pedro de Zuniga, of the potential dangers of the colony at Virginia. It was going to become a pirate's den, and none of the wealth of the New World would make it back to Spain. The English would steal it all. The only solution to this issue would be to destroy Jamestown, and to destroy it now. But Philip wasn't going to just blindly charge into such an adventure, he wanted to properly scope out the situation. He sent instructions to General Pedro de Ibarra, the governor of Florida, to investigate. De Ibarra chose Captain Francisco Fernandez de Ecija to conduct the mission, and he set out from San Augustin on June 11th on the La Asunsion de Cristo. Ecija sailed at a very leisurely pace, meaning that a voyage which I think should have taken a week or so took over a month. He arrived the day after Argill while his ship was still in the mouth of the river, which spooked Ecija who didn't go upstream. He was instead chased off. Had Ecija taken a few less days travelling north from Florida he would have found a Jamestown in chaos, perhaps he could have destroyed it; or, at the very least, caused significant damage. It is a very interesting "What if?"

The Third Supply

Two and a half years previously three ships at set sail for Virginia, the 100 ton Susan Constant, the 40 ton Godspeed and the twenty ton Discovery. In early June 1609, 8 ships were setting sail, commanded by the 250 ton Sea Venture. Lord De La Warr had been made the first Lord Governor of Virginia, but he was to set sail later in the year. For the moment the interim governor was to be his Lieutenant Governor, Sir Thomas Gates. He was aboard the Sea Venture, but the ship was captained by Newport. Also travelling were the Diamond, which was second in command, it was captained by Radcliffe; the Blessing, commanded by Archer, the Unity, the Lion, the Swallow, the Virginia and the Falcon which was commanded by Martin and Nelson. Other names of importance are Sir George Somers who was to be the Admiral of Virginia, William Strachey, a writer, Reverend Richard Buck, the minister for Jamestown, and John Rolfe, who will have a very important role in our story. This was a big expedition. I can't stress this enough. 500 settlers were on board.

They set out from Plymouth and sailed along the English coast before turning southwest until they reached 26 degrees latitude and then sailed west. It was a very hot voyage and there was disease, but things went pretty well until July 24th when the ships were hit by a great storm, which may have been a hurricane. It's thought that Strachey's descriptions were inspiration for Shakespeare's Tempest. This was a disaster. Hurricanes cause significant damage to modern vessels, so just think how a seventeenth century wooden boat would hold up. The flagship, the Sea Venture, was damaged, and began to take in water. People panicked, Strachey thought they were going to die, but Gates kept his cool. He put men to work around the clock clearing out the water and threw their belongings overboard, but still the Sea Venture continued to sink. When all looked lost, the miraculous happened. The sky began to lighten, and they saw land. The storm had blown them widely off course and into the Bermudas: an archipelago of small islands about 600 miles off North American coast which were uninhabited.

The men of the Sea Venture were pretty depressed, it was widely known that Bermuda was an evil place. But it was land, so 150 or so of them disembarked and set themselves up on an island they named St. George's. Very soon they realised just what a paradise Bermuda was, and that it had bountiful food. They constructed cabins, and Gates sent a small ship to Jamestown in September asking for help. There were a couple of conspiracies by those who didn't want to leave Bermuda, but Gates was a seasoned commander. He was able to swiftly end the mutiny. When no news came from Jamestown they assumed that their ship had gotten lost, and so they started work building 2 more over the winter. They soon began to suffer the same problems of factionalism as Jamestown had suffered, Gates and Somers not getting on in particular. We shall leave these men here, but for the moment, we shall return to Jamestown.

Smith's Finale

Once Argill arrived at Jamestown in mid-July 1609 he had informed Smith of what was coming, but all this was based on the Sea Venture arriving as part of the Third Supply. But it didn't. It was stuck in Bermuda. Instead the Unity, the Lion, the Blessing and the Falcon arrived at Jamestown on August 11th, shortly followed by the Diamond and the Swallow. Straight away the infighting started. Smith was convinced that the leaders of the new arrivals, namely his old adversaries, Ratcliffe, Martin, and Archer, had poisoned the minds of their crews against him to usurp his presidency, while the new arrivals believed that Smith was consorting with the mariners to secure his support without acting appropriately to the other gentry.

While they waited for the Sea Venture to arrive with Gates, or for Lord De La Warr, the gentry proposed that De La Warr's brother, Francis West, lead the expedition once Smith's presidency expired. Smith was able to go along with this since it would leave him in charge for the moment. He then removed the possibility of further arguments by, well, removing the people who may cause those arguments from Jamestown. The new arrivals had quadrupled the size of the colony to 400, Jamestown couldn't supply that many. They needed to disperse, so West would set up base with about 120 men at the falls and Percy and Martin would go downriver to Nansemond with 60, dropping the number of men at Jamestown to a much more manageable 250.

Nansemond was an island downstream of Jamestown. They tried buying the island of the locals, but the chief had no interest in this and instead killed the messengers. This prompted the English to just take the island. The operation quickly turned very violent. As for West, he set up next to the river with 6 months of food. Smith visited the next week and thought it was too low lying. The place could very easily flood. He recommended they move to higher ground at a village he had secured possession of, and Smith says that this was greeted with open hostility by West's men. Smith was forced to leave, but when the garrison was soon attacked by the Powhatans and it was realised just what a bad location he had chosen, the men then listened to Smith's advance. But West appears to have visited Jamestown while this was going on, and he was furious to learn of the relocation when he returned. He then moved them back to his original fort and Smith left the village.

So, what was going on here? Smith must have known how much local resistance these new forts would create. What was he thinking? Perhaps he was trying to discredit his rivals by sending them on expeditions he knew would fail? Perhaps he was trying to set himself up to save the colony? It was likely some sort of gamble to save his influence in Jamestown before he was removed from power. This would fit with his treatment of Newport. Smith had been vital to the colony's survival, and his ideas of practically were crucial, but he had made too many enemies. When he was on his way back from visiting West's fort, a match fell into his lap. His powder bag exploded, he was terribly burnt and he dived into the river to try and extinguish the flames. When they pulled him out of the water he was more dead than alive. Martin, Ratcliffe and Archer were almost certainly behind the attempt on his life. But he lived. They wrote up a list of charges against him and put him on the ships returning to England. Somehow Smith survived. While the Company would not follow up on the accusations against him and was going to keep the Virginia Company going, John Smith would not be allowed to return to Jamestown. He has been the first real centrepiece of our narrative, but he now exits our stage. He had no further role to play in the story of the United States.

President Percy

We are now around the end of 1609. Things were not going well. Anywhere. Gates was lost in Bermuda. In London there was panic among investors over what was going on in Virginia and about where Gates was. Meanwhile, 1609 had been a year of drought in Virginia. There were more food shortages, both amongst the English and the Powhatans. Martin's settlement at Nansemond was a disaster. Martin fled back to Jamestown, his second in command was killed and the fort was abandoned. Only 30 of the original 60 made it back to Jamestown. West's Fort had also suffered heavy attacks and he had fled back to Jamestown. The only outer settlement left was Fort Algernon, which had been set up at the mouth of James River to see ships which may sail into Chesapeake Bay. The 400 colonists in August had now dropped to 300.

Since Smith had gone, Gates was presumed dead and there was no idea when De La Warr would arrive. Therefore George Percy was elected president. His biggest problem was lack of food. They would soon run out completely, so he sent out two parties to negotiate. One was commanded by Ratcliffe, the other by West. Both ended in disaster. Ratcliffe was ambushed and almost his entire party was killed. Ratcliffe had a particularly horrible end. While he was still alive the Powhatan women scraped the flesh off his bones and burnt it in front of him. Not a good way to go. As for West, he managed to turn a friendly tribe into enemies by killing some of them, and then his men mutinied and fled back to England in the Swallow, their best ship. In a few months, through death and desertion, Jamestown lost another 130 colonists. Jamestown was blockaded by the Powhatans and Nansemonds. Famine hit the colony hard, and there are even stories of cannibalism. Then, thrown into the mix was plague brought over from England in the Diamond. I can't imagine how awful this must have been.

In May 1610 the Powhatans and Nansemonds lifted their siege to plant crops, allowing Percy to check up on Fort Algernon. What he found appalled him. Fort Algernon had plenty of food, they were actually saving up enough food to keep them going on a voyage back to England and were fattening their pigs with the excess. Percy was furious about how many lives could be saved. He told them that he was going to move half the people to Fort Algernon immediately, and when they improved he would take them back and send the other half. If there were still deaths, they would just abandon Jamestown and all move to Fort Algernon. But, before Percy could do anything, two ships sailed into the Chesapeake, it was two the ships Gates had sent from Bermuda. After another rebellion in March, in which Gates had to execute those involved, he and Somers gathered up the settlers and they sailed in the two ships they had been constructing, the Deliverance and the Patience, and set sail for Virginia.

The news was mixed for them, part delight that the rest of the convoy had made it, part dread when they heard of the conditions. Gates sailed up river, and landed at Jamestown. The settlement was a mess. Of the 400 colonists there in August 1609, only 60 were left alive only 9 months later. I hope it is abundantly clear why 1609-1610 is called the Starving time. It had destroyed the colonists. They had lost every trace of civilisation over that winter and had turned into savages. Gates realised he had only one option. Jamestown had to be abandoned. They would sail for Newfoundland, and then back to England. Gates buried the cannons, meaning that this would only be temporary, not that the colonists saw things that way. He had to have his guard make sure that no one threw a match as they left. They fired a round of shots to mark their fairwell, and at midday on June 7th, 1610, they set off home.

Chapter 4 – Birth of Virginia

When Gates set sail down the James, he almost immediately met a longboat. It was the advance party for Lord De La Warr. He had been delayed for half a year ago raising funds, something which had proved more difficult than expected following the loss of the Sea Venture. He finally set off with 3 ships and 150 settlers from Portsmouth on April 11 1610, and arrived in Virginia in early June . Gates was told to go back to Jamestown and prepare the colony for the arrival of De La Warr (much to the unhappiness of the colonists who thought they had finally escaped).

Considering that, before Gates arrived, Jamestown was in anarchy with only 60 inhabitants, these events were a startling turnaround. Jamestown had competent leaders and their numbers were up to 375. Plus, perhaps most importantly, De La Warr brought with him a year's supply of food. The Starving Time was over.

De La Warr's primary concern was breaking the men out of the idleness which had destroyed the colony during Smith's tenure. You'll recall how men were starving, but refused to do anything to solve the problem. De La Warr would solve the problem by installing military values.

He established a more serious government. Gates would be his second in command, the lieutenant general; Sir Ferdinando Wainman would be his master of ordnance; Strachey would be the secretary; and Percy the captain of Jamestown. Together with Admiral Somers and Newport, this would form his governing council. In addition,

Percy, Samuel Argall, Thomas Holcroft, Thomas Lawson and George Yeardley would each command 50 man militias. The laws brought by Gates, known as 'Lawes Devine, Morall and Martiall', were maintained. They were harsh and strict, but this was necessary (or so the commanders felt, given their experiences in Europe).

The infrastructure was rebuilt and De La Warr set to work making the colony sustainable. He had supplies for the moment, but that didn't mean the supplies would last. The sturgeon didn't appear in the James River as normally happened. This compounded the problems of the Powhatans refusing to trade and the loss of all English livestock during the previous winter. De La Warr sent Somers and Argall back to Bermuda to collect 6 months of supplies, including some hogs to re-establish the livestock. However, they wouldn't make it to Bermuda and instead went fishing off the coast of New England. As Jamestown emerged from the ashes, it was a vast improvement compared to the one it replaced. The buildings were suited to the climate. While not quite 'comfortable', it was becoming liveable. It felt as though there is a plan at work. Under Wingfield, Ratcliffe and Smith the colony had been lurching from one disaster to the next, but this was a lot more organised. Though, as we shall soon see, it was just a false dawn.

False Dawn

De La Warr set about repairing the relationship between the English and the Powhatans. Relations had deteriorated, but he didn't want to plunge the colony into war just yet. If there was a chance he could fix things, he would take it. He sent messengers to Wahunsonacock asking for friendship, reminding him of the crowning, and wanting vengeance for the attack on Jamestown.

Wahunsonacock was not in the mood for this. As far as he was concerned, the land was his, not theirs. The English could stay at Jamestown, but they could not be allowed to expand, and they could not explore. If they did, they would be attacked. Wahunsonacock would excuse De La Warr this time, but made it clear that De La Warr should not send Englishmen to Werowocomoco without being invited. Also, he should at least bring gifts. De La Warr held this same attitude of annoyance with the Powhatans. This was war.

The move towards open warfare was probably influenced by an event of the summer of 1610. On an expedition into the Chesapeake, Gates witnessed one of his own men be killed by the Native Americans. Gates had previously advocated a peaceful approach, but this forced him to change his perspective. He wanted revenge. Very shortly after, he attacked a group of Kecoughtans. It would be the first of many such attacks by both sides.

Gates returned to England on July 20th 1610, but the attacks would not stop now that they had begun. The Powhatans were offended that De La Warr was constructing two new forts at the mouth of the Southampton River, Charles and Henry. This may seem odd considering his initial commitment to peace, but just as Smith's attitudes changed as he spent time in the country, so too did those of De La Warr. He realised that his moderate position wouldn't work. If Jamestown was to survive, it needed to be more aggressive. This was war, and it was now treated as such. These forts did not survive long. De La Warr ordered them to be abandoned so the men could relocate at West's fort upriver (which could be a base for finding gold). This went wrong quickly. Men were lost, and the position was soon abandoned without a proper exploration being launched.

This was a return of the colonies old problems. De La Warr had been in Jamestown 6 months, and through a combination of disease and war had lost a third of the settlers. This wore down his legitimacy, and soon the men grew unhappy. De La Warr then made everything worse by falling ill, and in late March 1611 he sailed to Nevis in the Caribbean to recuperate. Percy now had command of the colony. Even this went wrong.

Rather than making it to the Caribbean, winds blew De La Warr off course and he wound up on the other side of the Atlantic in the Azores. From here he returned to England, incredibly embarrassed. De La Warr had to report to the company said that everything was going well. He overplayed the things which went well, and didn't mention the sickness. The usual lies. It wasn't very convincing. This could easily have killed Jamestown, were it not for Gates.

Gates had returned to London in 1610. He had spread the word of how the Sea Venture had been survived, of how Jamestown had been reborn, and enthusiasm for the venture had returned. Gates had been busy preparing a new venture across the Atlantic to be led by himself, and Sir Thomas Dale, who had been in service on the continent. Dale had set sail in March 1611 with a year's supply and 300 settlers and he arrived 8 weeks later, 10 days after

De La Warr had departed. With Somers and De La Warr absent, Dale assumed command of the colony.

His immediate concern was very similar to that of De La Warr: making the colony self-sufficient. His arrival had upped the number of settlers from 170 to almost 500, and Gates would soon be arriving with even more mouths to feed. Dale immediately set about reoccupying Forts Charles and Henry as they were surrounded by good farmland, and land was cleared and crops planted. He also worked on improving colonial administration by promoting Captain James Davis, who had been in command of fort Algernon, to taskmaster of all three forts.

The other big problem facing Dale was discipline. Of the 300 he had brought with him, Dale estimated than only 60 were of any use and he was forced to expand the harshness of the law code. The fort was rebuilt and more buildings were added to Jamestown, such as a stable, a new well, and stores for the weapons and a sturgeon house for dealing with the fish. Private gardens were also established. This was part of a wider specialisation programme. Forts Charles and Henry would grow corn, while Fort Algernon and Jamestown would raise livestock and produce goods for export. He also had plans for moving the major settlement upriver, a process he felt was all the more urgent when a Spanish ship on a reconnaissance mission arrived and managed to capture one of the settlers.

Henricus

In August, Dale heard reports of more ships arriving. He thought that it was the Spanish coming to destroy them and began to panic, but it turned out it was only Gates with 300 colonists and supplies. This was the sickly period, and with now 750 settlers and fear of Spanish attack it was decided that they needed to push upriver and found a new settlement to replace Jamestown as the capital. 350 settlers, mostly artisans, were handpicked for this adventure. They were continually attacked by Wahunsonacock who recognised the danger of this particular venture, and by December they had constructed a town which they named Henricus, in honour of Henry, the Prince of Wales. Unlike earlier attempts at setting up a settlement upriver, Henricus (located only a few miles away from the modern capital of Virginia, Richmond) would survive longer than a few months, and it would see the English begin to really establish themselves along the James River.

Gates was the person in command in Virginia during these years, and the colony was beginning to look after itself. The founding of Henricus was a turning point, and now the English had 5 strongholds. The towns of Jamestown and Henricus, and the Forts of Henry, Charles and Algernon. There was near constant warfare with the Powhatans. Not in the form of open battles, but plenty of raids took place. Argall formed friendly relationships with some of the tribes along the Potomac River to the north, and conducted plenty of trading missions. John Rolfe in 1612 did something of huge importance by planting the first crop of tobacco. Tobacco is very easy to grow, and it would really take off, but we'll have a lot more to say about tobacco as we go on.

Back in England, the company was struggling to find funds. One of its chief backers, Henry, the Prince of

Wales, died in November 1612. The company started a lottery to try and raise funds. Diplomatic dealings continued with the Spanish over prisoners that had been taken during their reconnaissance in 1611 without really going anywhere, and there was always the looming threat of an actual invasion. That was all of note that happened until April 1613 when the English kidnapped Pocahontas.

Knapping of Pocahontas

The English suddenly decided to kidnap Pocahontas, the now 17-or-18-year-old daughter of Wahunsonacock. Argall had been sailing along the Potomac and had become very friendly with the tribes in the area. This is highly significant as it showed Wahunsonacock's disintegrating powerbase. While the English suffered once the Powhatans were able to deal with other Europeans, so the Powhatans would suffer once the English began to form diplomatic links with other tribes. Argall managed to get some of them to support his plan of kidnapping Pocahontas in order to gain some diplomatic advantage with Wahunsonacock. His friends were persuaded, and they lured her onto an English ship for a meal. She wasn't allowed to leave, and was taken back to Jamestown.

The version of events recorded by Ralph Hamor writes that the English demanded food, prisoners and the stolen weapons from Wahunsonacock in exchange for Pocahontas. Wahunsonacock refused to respond for three months, before offering a couple of the deserters and food, in exchange for the stolen weapons which he claimed the Powhatans had since lost. Dale didn't believe this, and refused. Until the weapons were returned,

Pocahontas would be kept prisoner. She would be well treated, but she was still a hostage. In the meantime, there could be war or peace between the English and the Powhatans, but that choice was up to Wahunsonacock. Then nothing really happened. Pocahontas grew frustrated with her father for doing nothing to try and free her and she was sent to Henricus. She learned English, studied Christianity, and became friends with several of the settlers: including John Rolfe.

Dale decided that he was going to force Wahunsonacock to make a decision. He set out with a hundred and fifty men in order to get the deal he originally offered Wahunsonacock one year previously. They were attacked, and their retaliation scared the locals into leaving them alone. Eventually, they met Opechancanough and a force of 400 warriors. It looked as though fighting was going to break out, but then two of Pocahontas' brothers came forward and demanded to see her. They found that she had been well treated, and this allowed negotiations to begin with Opechancanough who was conferring with Wahunsonacock. What was agreed was that the English weapons and tools would be returned within 15 days along with some food, while Pocahontas would be made a 'daughter' of Dale and allowed to stay at Jamestown. The weapons and food were indeed sent, and 5 years of war was brought to a close.

This suited Pocahontas just fine. She enjoyed living with the English and she had freedom within the settlement. All the sources agree that she was tremendously bright, no doubt spending time immersed in another culture was intellectually stimulating. She had also formed friendships, and had grown very close to Rolfe. Rolfe informed Dale that he wished to marry Pocahontas, and that she wanted to marry him too. She was going to take the name Rebecca and embrace Christianity. Dale was delighted and agreed, Wahunsonacock also consented, and on April 5th 1614 the ceremony was conducted in Jamestown church. It was hoped that this was a sign of the age of peace and unity to come. A change you can paint with all the colours of the wind.

The State of the Colony in the 1610s

Another agreement was soon after made with another tribe which saw them submit to the English, and offer the use of several hundred bowman against the Spanish should they attack. This was good, but it would be foolish to overestimate the closeness of the two peoples. This was in the eyes of Wahunsonacock and Opechancanough a temporary deal, useful so that they could catch their breath, but they certainly did not view themselves as conquered. Dale however was delighted. He had won the war, brought peace, and secured the future of the colony. Another event of significance happened in this year. On a ship back to England Rolfe sent 4 barrels of tobacco, which arrived in June 1614. This was the beginning of the tobacco trade which would come to dominate Virginia. A few years later, Rolfe would conduct an overview of the colony. He estimated there were 351 English colonists in Virginia at this point, of whom 65 were women and children. There were 6 horses, 144 cattle, 216 goats, plenty of hogs and poultry. Virginia was becoming established. It wasn't the biggest settlement in the world. Virginia currently has a population of some 8 million people so 351 isn't impressive, but they were seasoned. They were no longer starving. There wasn't a threat of a Spanish invasion and peace had been achieved. When you think back to the colony being down to 38 before Newport's First Supply in January 1608 or down to 60 before the arrival of Gates and De La Warr in 1610, things were looking pretty good.

There were three types of colonists, the first of which were the officers. The second group were the labourers. These either worked directed for the company or were artisans, such as blacksmiths or carpenters. They could supply the settlement with the products which were needed. Together these groups were made up of 205 people. The third group were the 81 farmers. They were compelled to work for the company one month a year and could be called in to defend the colony if necessary. Aside from this they would support themselves through farming and supplied two and a half barrels of corn to the general store each year.

There were 6 settlements, Henricus, Bermuda which was 5 miles downriver of Henricus which was the largest settlement, West and Sherley Hundred another few miles downriver, Jamestown, Kecoughtan near the mouth of the James River, and Dale's Gift on the far side of Chesapeake Bay.

Soon after this Dale was recalled by the company to England. If you'll allow me to quote James Horn's "A Land As God Made It: Jamestown and the Birth of America" for a moment:

"Leaving the James River on the ebb tide in April 1616, Samuel Argall's Treasurer carried one of the strangest assortments of passengers ever to make the Atlantic crossing. On board were Sir Thomas Dale, returning to England now that the colony was enjoying "great prosperytye & pease"; John Rolfe and Pocahontas (the Lady Rebecca) with their infant son Thomas; Pocahontas's sister, Matachanna, and her husband, Uttamatomakkin (also called Tomakin or Tomocomo), a priest and tribal elder instructed by Wahunsonacock to keep a careful account of everything he saw in the land of the Tassantasses; another ten or so Powhatans, mostly young women who were attending Pocahontas and who, the Virginia Company hoped, might be induced to convert to Christianity and marry suitable Englishman; Don Diego de Molina, relieved to be boarding after five years in the Jamestown; Francis Lembry, the 'hispanyolated inglishe man" captured with Molina, who had served as a piolet with the Spanish Armada of 1588, (he would be hanged from the end of Argall's yardarm as the ship approached the coast of England within sight of the land he had betrayed); and, finally, several of Dale's principals during the war, Captains Francis West, John Martin, and James Davis, who (like Dale) had decided to return home."[6]

The ship brought back tradable goods, but none were as important to the Virginia Council as Pocahontas. She was not the first Native American to go to England, but as the daughter of Wahunsonacock she had much prestige, she was proof that Native Americans could convert to Christianity and she excited the people as she made her way across the south from Devon to London.

---

[6] Horn (2005) A Land As God Made It: Jamestown and the Birth of America

She was the toast of high society, even meeting King James and Queen Anne. It is all very interesting, but everyone has their own agendas at these sorts of things. The English wanted to prove that they could civilise her, and show her off. Pocahontas didn't feel that way at all though. While to the English the Powhatans were savages, a term for people who are uncivilized, to Pocahontas, things were not so black and white. She didn't abandon her own culture, she could be both Powhatan and English. Tragically, Pocahontas died young. As she prepared to travel back to Virginia in March 1617 she fell ill, possibly either tuberculosis or pneumonia, and died soon afterwards. While Pocahontas exits our narrative, the same cannot be said for John Rolfe. We need to talk about tobacco.

Tobacco

Since it had been first brought back to England in the late sixteenth century, smoking tobacco had become highly fashionable. This very quickly spread its way into the lower classes and everybody smoked. And of course, once they were hooked, people kept smoking. Tobacco has many of the same addictive qualities as tomacco. By 1614 it was claimed that the tobacco industry was worth £320,000 annually in London alone. To put that figure in context, that is six and a half times greater than the £50,000 it had taken to establish Virginia. This is what inspired John Rolfe into thinking that tobacco would be a useful enterprise.

The natives grew tobacco which they smoked (*Nicotiana Rustica* to give it its Latin name). It was, however, quite sharp and bitter. The English had been smoking the tobacco grown by the Spanish

(*Nicotiana Tabacum*), so Rolfe thought that it would better suit the English market to develop these varieties in Virginia. He imported seeds from Trinidad and Venezuela and began experimenting. After a couple of years he hit success. The beauty of tobacco was that it was very easy to grow. His was in addition to the fact that it was hugely addictive, and there was already a market for it. I mentioned that Rolfe sent his first shipment of tobacco in 1614, but he brought a far greater amount with him in 1616 and spent a lot of the trip dealing with London merchants himself. He needed to do this since James I and the Company both opposed tobacco.

The King simply opposed the practice of smoking, but the company had a different reason. They desperately wanted to avoid the emergence of a staple crop. This would make the economy much more fragile. They wanted diversity and flexibility, thinking that this instead would be how the company thrived, but most importantly they were eager to get a return on their investment. Things had been quite slow since the 1611 voyages and they needed ways of financing the operation. Many leading figures in the company had also funded an expedition to Bermuda, the island Bermuda that is, not the settlement of Bermuda in Virginia. It had gone very well and had been financed by offering land grants in return for investment.

So, in 1617, 150 or so settlers set off from London going back to Virginia, including Argall who was made deputy governor, and Rolfe. Argall decided to make his base Jamestown and began to rebuild the settlement, it had fallen apart in their absence. Only a couple of buildings were left standing. It wasn't too much trouble to repair the damage, and they sent a shipment back to London in 1618 of 20,000 lbs of tobacco, which selling for 5s. 3d. per pound, making in total £5,250.[7] This wasn't a huge amount, but it was far more than the colony had made previously. The economy of the colony was generally doing well.

The 1618-19 Reorganising of Virginia

By this point in history, Virginia had already gone through 2 governing systems. There was the original somewhat-egalitarian-first-among-equals approach of the council with an elected presidency, but this had quickly dissolved because of in fighting between Smith, Newport, Ratcliffe, Wingfield, and the other leaders. This had forced the creation of the second system, implemented in 1610 with the arrival of De La Warr. This was designed to restore discipline, and had been very militant. By 1618 things had calmed down and the colony was at peace with the Powhatans. The militant approach wasn't necessary nor attractive to the settlers. This lead to the creation of the third system.

First of all, the colony was divided into four areas, either known as the cities or the boroughs. These were James City, Charles City, Henricus, and

---

[7] I should explain briefly the English currency system. It was broken up into three tiers: pounds, shillings, and pence. There were 12 pence in a shilling, and twenty shillings in a pound. When writing this down, a system was used based upon Roman currency: LSD. These stand for the Latin words *Librae*, *Solidi*, and *Denarii*. This means that 5s. 3d. means 5 shillings, three pence. When reading primary documents, it isn't uncommon to see 500l. referring to £500, but I shall use the modern pound symbol instead to avoid unnecessary confusion.

Kiccowtan (which would later be renamed Elizabeth City). Each was given 3,000 acres for the use of the company and 1,500 acres for local administration. There were 3,000 acres near Jamestown for the use of the governor, and 10,000 acres near Henricus for the construction of a university. Those who were already there were each given 100 acres, and then a hundred more for each share in the company they bought. Those who arrived after April 1616 were given 50 acres for themselves and an extra 50 for every person they transported. This would be how Virginia grew in size over the next century.

In addition to this, the government was changed following the instalment of George Yeardley as Governor. The laws were to be less strict, and there were to be two councils. There would be a council of state to aid the governor, similar to the councils already discussed. Then, there was something radically new which was introduced: the General Assembly, known commonly as Virginia's House of Burgesses.

The plan was that the General Assembly would be made up of the council of state and of Burgesses. Burgess was an old English word referring to an elected official who represented a borough (a municipality). Each town, hundred and plantation would elect 2 burgesses, and they would discuss local government. This was not an autonomous legislature, and it certainly wasn't a model of Parliament. It was local government, giving the settlers a voice in the colony. It is important to know that it was just this, a voice. There was no independent political power attached to this. A motion was only valid if the company approved, and the governor had a veto.

22 burgesses met in Jamestown on July 30th 1619 for 5 days. They talked about their own rules, how best to convert the Powhatans, about the crops they should be growing, drew up a few suggestions for the company, and then they all went home. It was nothing grand, it was nothing bold, but it was the first democratic meeting in the Anglo-American colony. This meeting is the origins of a democratic tradition which will be waging war on England in a mere 157 years.

Introduction to Social History

The size of the colony was rapidly increasing, so it's worth dealing with the big question of how Virginia jumped from 6 settlements to almost 30 within 4 years. Argall set sale for Jamestown in 1617 with 150 settlers. 6 ships set sail in 1618 carrying 400 colonists. In 1619 that number rose to 10 ships carrying a thousand, and in 1620 13 ships brought over 1,300 colonists to Virginia. The number could have been even higher, were it not for a storm in late 1620. Sandys, in addition to his wider efforts of getting tradesman and the general population to travel to Virginia, worked on convincing religious dissenters to make the journey. These were the puritans and the nonconformists. He worked particularly hard on a group of separatists who had spent the last decade living in the Netherlands, the Pilgrims. These set sail to settle in the northern reaches of Virginia, the mouth of the Hudson, but this never quite happened. Either they were blown of course by a storm, or they simply changed their minds on route, but either way the Pilgrims instead landed at Cape Cod in December 1620 where they would form New England, but we'll cover this in more detail later.

The English were not the only Europeans involved in Virginia. There were a number of foreign artisans from around Europe who found work at the colony. There were German and Dutch glassmakers, French specialists in vineyards and silk, Poles who could produce pitch and tar, as well as Italian glassblowers. The continentals would never properly settle in Virginia. They and the English were unable to get along. I suspect part of this was to do with the German defections to Wahunsonacock, which had caused so much trouble for the early settlement. There is one line in particular I really want to quote. It is a comment by Sandys concerning the Italians, "A more damned crew hell never vomited". This gives you a good idea off the attitudes of the people we're dealing with. We must also mention the introduction of another group to the colony, in addition to the voluntary migrants. I am of course talking about slavery.

Slavery

We will have a lot to say about slavery in the future, so I'm not going to go into any great detail here. There is no need to lecture you about the evils of the institution. I'm pretty sure that everyone reading knows that slavery was a bad thing. There will be a great deal of time to properly discuss this issue in the future. But, since the topic is being introduced, I want to make a quick point or two.

Firstly, I want to go back to what I learnt in school. In primary school, or elementary school as it's called in the States, history was very… Hodge Podge. We darted all over the place, never covering anything in any detail. This is fair. By the age of 10 I had an interest in world history. I knew about the ancient world, British history, and had a decent grasp of most other periods, but I was the only one. But, me ranting about how annoyed 10-year-old me was that we weren't learning about the complexities of European diplomacy in the thirty years war isn't really the point here.

Once we were done with that and went to high school, we then went through a 3 year required history course. The first year starting with the Romans, and then moved on to the Anglo-Saxons and began to cover the Normans. The second year covered the Normans, the Middle Ages, the Tudors, and the English civil war. The third year covered Slavery and the two world wars. When we were learning about slavery (I would have been 13 at this point) we focused exclusively on the British slave trade in North America. It was all very interesting, but, almost 10 years on, I'm realising just how warped a lot of what we were taught was. I'm not saying that we were lied to, more that we weren't given the full story. This is what I'd like to do from the outset, give you a clearer picture of what is going on. That is the understanding I had in school, and I can't speak with great knowledge about the American school system, but when dealing with slavery I imagine that it also focused on American slavery.

According to current theories on the subject, it is estimated that 400,000 Africans were taken from their homes and brought to British North America. This is terrible, obviously. This is what I was taught in school. What I wasn't taught was that this was less than 5% of the total. The vast majority of the total, some 12 million people, were sent either to the mines or the plantations in the Sugar Islands, Spanish America, or Brazil. We'll be focusing on the portion that went to America since this is a history of America, but just know that this formed a tiny percentage of the total. This isn't to negate what happened in British North America. A terrible act isn't made any less terrible because something worse happened somewhere else. I just want you to have the full picture.

With this in mind, it also explains just how the first slaves made their way to Virginia. These men and women were from the Kingdom of Ndongo (modern Angola) in West Central Africa. They had been captured by the Portuguese and were sailing to Brazil when they were captured by Dutch pirates and then taken to Virginia via the Caribbean.

The Social Classes

Another theme which will define our narrative will be wealth inequality. This can also be viewed in the early years of Virginia. Tobacco very quickly became the go-to cash crop for the early settlers, and they were soon producing plenty of it. Rolfe sent back to England 4 barrels of tobacco in 1614, and by 1620 Virginia was producing 60,000 pounds. Yet, this wealth was concentrated. Settlers travelled with servants which gave them more land, and more ability to make a profit. Men who travelled to work for a company were traded to private individuals for a year, and this trade in servants became the form by which most people had their wealth. This is what most of the population was. It's thought that 95% of the colonists making their way over to Virginia were doing so as servants, rather than as freeholders. Understanding the social composition of the colony at this early stage will be hugely important in its implications further down the road.

The elite began to grow rich off tobacco. The stories of men who had travelled to the new world were exciting to those back in England. They had explored new lands, they had created a new industry, they had met wild savages, civilised them, and John Rolfe had even married a princess and brought her back to England. Life was hard and miserable in England, but Virginia was abundant with food. It was an exciting prospect. Indeed, the American dream is almost as old as America herself. But this was only what happened to the few.

Richard Frethorne was something close to a typical case. He sent a letter home shortly after he arrived in Virginia saying that he was in a miserable state with no clothes or meat. He had spent the last 3 months eating nothing but peas and water gruel. Another planter wrote that he couldn't believe that the boy's parents had sent Richard to Virginia, they should have killed him instead. That would have been kinder. He didn't get to go home. He died a few months later. The turnaround in servants was remarkable. They were malnourished, so many were killed by scurvy. There was also dysentery from the bad water, and they were still beset by the bloody flux. There was no shelter. Many people had been sent to the colony, but Virginia wasn't prepared for them. They were forced to live in the woods while their houses were built. Thousands were travelling to the New World, and they were dying. Three quarters of the servants died within a year of landing. Virginia had been sold to these poor souls as a land of milk and honey. They were instead met by something close to hell on earth.

It wasn't all doom and gloom though. Life was brutal, but there was an opportunity for advancement which didn't exist back in England. The leaders in Virginia were not the aristocracy. There were no earls or lords in the New World. This new leadership was made up of the merchant class. While most indentured servants either died or lived in poverty, there was still an opportunity for them. 7 men who were listed as servants in 1624 were representatives in the House of Burgesses only 5 years later.

The colony was still very male dominated. Remember how big a deal it was when the first two women arrived with the second supply? By now the gender ratio was 7:1. A sign of what life was like for these women was an event which took place in 1619 when the company paid for 90 educated maids to be brought to Virginia. They were, to quote Virginia: The New Dominion by Virginius Dabney, "sent over by the company for the benefit of such settlers as felt the need of matrimony." Quite clearly, things weren't great for women either.

Indian Relations

Virginia had been at peace since 1614 and the marriage between John Rolfe and Pocahontas. This had allowed the English to have food supplies, and gave them the opportunity to properly explore the continent. As we've seen, the driving force of tobacco led to thousands of new acres being farmed up the James River. Wahunsonacock was much less of an influence in these years, and he died in 1618. While there was a technical succession system with the Powhatan Confederacy, and supposedly Opitchapam succeeded Wahunsonacock, effective power completely transferred to Opechancanough. This led to an even closer relationship between the Powhatans and the English. While he had made treaties with the English, Wahunsonacock was always distant from them. The English educated native children in their settlements.

The two groups grew increasingly close. When man of note George Thorpe arrived in 1620, he encouraged that more be done to continue to civilise the Powhatans. This was reflected in the company's next choice of governor to replace Yeardley, Sir Francis Wyatt, in 1621. Wyatt pushed for further unity between the Powhatans and the settlers, stressing that no harm should be done to them. However, as I've already hinted at, things were about to deteriorate rapidly in 1622. There were several key reasons for this.

The most important was English arrogance. Assumed simplicity of our sources is a major issue in our understand of events, but this is just one facet of the arrogance the Europeans had. Europeans were condescending to the Powhatans. They spoke of friendship with the Powhatans, all the while plotting conquest. For all the talk of one Powhatan and English nation, that didn't mean anything. Thousands were travelling to Virginia and the plantations were pushing up the James. This was forcing out Powhatans who had been living there for generations. The Powhatans were paying tribute to the Virginians and were generally treated like a subject people, not partners.

This situation was untenable for the Powhatans. Something had to be done. They were being pushed off their land, and slowly worn down by the English who were growing ever stronger. There was the possibility of a frontal assault, but their early conflicts with the English made them realise that this would end in disaster. The Powhatans could not match the English firepower, therefore they instead played the long game. It's not known at what point exactly the Powhatans decided to pursue this policy, but it's quite possible that Opechancanough came to this conclusion as early as 1614.

If the Powhatans couldn't attack the English openly, they would have to attack the English from within. This would involve ingratiating themselves with the English, working their way slowly into the colony, and then waiting for the perfect moment to attack. This was difficult. Opechancanough needed to ignore many insults to his honour. He did not act when one of his best warriors was killed. He allowed the English settle wherever they wanted. He waited. The English were completely convinced by this deception, and Thorpe – who acted as a go between in negotiations – was delighted to discover in 1622 that Opechancanough was planning to convert to Christianity. This would be an even bigger coup than converting Pocahontas. The English were so excited that they began to overlook things. They didn't read the significance of Opechancanough changing his name, and they didn't notice him building an alliance of Native Americans hostile to the English. This brings us to the fateful morning of Friday, March 22, 1622.

Powhatan Uprising

The morning was just like any other. It was a crisp spring day. The settlements along the James began to stir as the people woke. They began to head into the fields and work on their trades. Nothing was out of the ordinary. It seemed that the day would be a busy day for the traders. A group of Powhatans gathered by one of the plantations. This had happened a hundred times before. The English would have recognised almost all of the Powhatans, and probably knew most of them by name. The Powhatans made there way in. They walked into the fields. They walked into houses. They found families at the table eating breakfast. And then they started killing. Men, women, children. None were spared. On that day, 347 colonists were killed. Many plantations or hamlets were wiped out. Henricus was completely destroyed. When he heard the commotion, Thorpe went out to greet the Powhatans. We have an eyewitness account that he went to see them with a certainly that he had misunderstood something. These people were his friends. He was dead before he realised what was happening. Over half of the English settlements were attacked, mostly those upriver. Those further downriver had received warning the night before that something was going to happen, and Wyatt had managed to prepare his defences.

The aims of the operation were to sweep the English into the sea, and this hadn't quite happened. Many settlements remained intact, such as Jamestown. The Powhatans had burned down Henricus, killed a quarter of the settlers and devastated the colony. It was quite possible that the plan was to starve the English out, exactly has had almost happened in the starving time of 1609-1610. We think this since it can be assumed Opechancanough knew that destroying the whole colony in a day was impossible. It was, all in all, a rather brilliant piece of strategy.

When word of the uprising reached London in the summer of 1622, no one could really believe the news. The company blamed the moral failings of the settlers, and then set about practically fixing the problem. They wrote to the government inquiring about old weapons which were stored in the Tower of London. These weapons were hopelessly out of date and would be useless in any European engagement, but against the Powhatans they would be quite useful. The King gave them to the company as a royal gift. There were some bows and arrows, some old muskets and pistols, some halberds and some armour. There was to be no talk of abandoning the expedition or the settlement. To do so would be an insult to the dead. They would send over new colonists. They would restart their production of goods. The only thing to change was that there could now be no peace with the Powhatans. They must be destroyed. Not that the Virginians needed to be told this.

Governor Wyatt wrote "Our first worke is expulsion of the Salvages to gaine free range of the countrey, for it is infinitely better to have no heathen among us, who at best were but as thornes in our sides, then to be at peace and league with them." The English launched raids against all the tribes. The Powhatans, the Pamunkeys, the Weyanocks, the Chcikahominies, the Quiyoughcohannocks, the Warrascoyacks, the Nansemonds and the

Rappahannocks. They destroyed villages, burned fields and took corn. This was a war of attrition, and there were relatively few casualties on both sides. For all the English attacks, the worse damage had been done by Opechancanough. The English lost most of their allies, and the colony entered a second starving time in winter. It is thought that between the spring of 1622 and the spring of 1623 a thousand colonists died.

In April 1623, word came that the Powhatans were ready for peace. A formal offer for a meeting with Opitchapam came in May. This is very interesting. For instance, why the meeting with Opitchapam and not Opechancanough? No one had heard from Opechancanough in a year, so perhaps he had been forced out of power, maybe by the anti-war party. This would explain why Opitchapam was making the meeting. It could also be a trick to lure the English into an ambush.

The English had no intention of making a deal, but they did indeed meet with Opitchapam. They promised friendship, and then they attempted to poisoned him and 200 other Powhatans. We don't know how many died exactly, but the English failed to kill both Opitchapam and Opechancanough, and so the war continued throughout the summer of 1623, then through the winter and into the next year.

A battle was fought in July 1624 when 800 Powhatan bowmen, in addition to allies, met about 60 armoured Englishmen. The Powhatans had been wise to avoid a pitched battle before this point, and engaging was a mistake. The battle continued for 2 days, but the Powhatans were simply unable to overcome English firepower. It would be years before they were finally defeated, but this spelled the end for the Powhatan Confederacy.

Reflections on the Uprising

The English would win the war, but it is fair to say that the early 1620s had been a complete disaster for Virginia. Disease and the climate were still causing many deaths. English frailties had been exposed by the Powhatan uprising. It's worth exploring these weaknesses in a bit more detail.

Edwin Sandys had been placed in charge of the Virginia Company in 1619, taking over from Sir Thomas Smythe. He had a brother named George who was stuck in the restlessness of middle age. He travelled around Europe and the Holy Land, and he even published a translation of Ovid's Metamorphoses. Considering my background in classics, it would be remiss of me to not mention a factoid featuring the anti-epic, which had such an influence on later Latin poets such as Statius.[8] Following this, he travelled to Virginia, and decided to write back to his brother Edwin on what had been going on.

He shared his brother's distaste for tobacco, but George saw the settlement pattern as the biggest issue facing the colony. The settlements were too spread out along the James River, making them impossible to govern. This also made them vulnerable to attack (as Opechancanough had so ably demonstrated). George thought that these issues could be fixed if the company knew what was

---

[8] Abad del Vecchio, J. (2015) 1

going on, so he wrote back to Edwin, but the letters were intercepted by a royal commission which had been set up to investigate the company's management of Virginia.

Since Edwin took command of the Virginia Company, infighting had gotten a lot worse in the company's hierarchy. These divisions led to damning stories coming out. A faction opposing Sandys decided to petition for a royal investigation, and a royal commission was set up in May 1623. The Jones Commission. A second commission was also set up which would investigate conditions in Virginia in person. While Sandys' enemies had exaggerated, the commission found... well... what we've discussed in this chapter. Everything was a total mess. There was no diversity in the economy, only tobacco. The colony was defenceless against the local Powhatans, and thousands of people had died through disease and malnutrition. In February 1625 there were only 1,095 people in Virginia. 7,549 had made the voyage. That is a survival rate of 14.5%. There wasn't a good way to spin this.

In the summer of 1623, the Jones Commission concluded that the colony was in danger of collapse. The King instructed the Attorney General to dissolve the Company. In November the Company was instructed to provide legal reasons for why they should still control the company, but they were unable to do so while a legal battle dragged on. Finally, on May 24th 1624, the Virginia Company was dissolved and control of the expedition was given to the crown. Virginia was entering a new era, something confirmed in March 1625 when James I died and his son, Charles I came to power.

Chapter 5 – A Royal Colony

James I died. So began the reign of Charles I. I don't want to dwell too much on British history, but it is quite import to discuss Charles. Charles was never supposed to be king. He was the second son of King James, 6 years younger than his brilliant older brother Henry. Charles was born in 1600, and would have spent his early years in his brother's shadow. Everyone was excited about Henry who was involved with politics from a young age. He was an early backer of the Virginia Company and support English colonisation efforts. Henry's death in 1612 was a national tragedy, and pushed it Charles into the public eye.

Ascension of King Charles

He would gain his political education as the Thirty Years' War began to develop across Europe. The overly simplified version is that Europe had a war between its Catholic and Protestant countries. As England was a protestant country, this led to some hostile views of Catholics, particularly Charles' wife, who was a Bourbon of France. Charles' reign was dominated by religious animosity, and accusations that he was too Catholic by the reformed churches. He drew particular opposition from the puritans, and forced Anglican theology on the Scots. He alsobelieved in the divine right of kings which enfurirated parliament. It is safe to say that he wasn't England's most popular king. Which – spoiler alert – is probably why the English killed him.

Anyway, James began to grow ill and Charles took an increasingly important role in governance, eventually becoming king at the age of 24 upon the death of his father in March 1625. This was important both for the history of England, and for the history of Virginia since the colony was now in the direct control of the crown.

Things didn't immediately change for Virginia. The council was replaced, but Wyatt remained as governor. The general assembly was not mentioned. Following this change was a decade of legal confusion. In 1625 the Virginians sent a petition to Charles asking to keep their legislature, but, for someone as obsessed with the Divine Right of Kings as Charles, it should come as no surprise that he ignored the appeals. There were attempts by the governors to bring back the assembly. It occasionally met, and from 1629 it was decided that it would meet annually. However, it had no legal position. It had no constitutional authority. This remained the situation until Charles finally relented in 1639. Bearing in mind the conflict Charles was having with parliament, this was a considerable achievement. Charles made clear that the assembly was only allowed to exist because of royal favour, not because of some right of the settlers, but this does not negate the achievement.

The House of Burgesses

It also aristocratic in nature. It was created as an instrument to reflect the views of the plantation owners and to give them a say in how Virginia was governed, not so that your average commoner could share their views. However, it was a sort of democratic institution that constitutionally had to meet annually. That's important.

Very early on the House of Burgesses began to make claims about its sovereignty, such as that it was the only body in the colony that had the right to levy taxes. It continually reinforced this claim. In 1629 for instance it levied a tobacco tax, but it was a poll tax in which the rich paid just as much as the poor.[9] The House of Burgesses wasn't a real democratic institution. Though, a political revolution was happening in Virginia.

The old English aristocracy didn't travel to the New World, this new aristocracy was made up of the self-made merchant class that had gotten into the tobacco industry early by setting up large plantations to be worked by the indentured servants who had travelled to Virginia in their thousands only to die in their thousands. Once the New Aristocracy gained access to political power through the House of Burgesses it began securing it and truly creating an oligarchy.[10]

---

[9] Though it must be noted that there was such popular outcry against this unfair tax that it was repealed in the 1640s.

[10] I'm going to use aristocracy and oligarchy interchangeably as this is how they are used by most people. But, as a trained classicist, I need to mention that these words do have more specific meanings. You see, these words are Greek. I love Greek because when you want to make a word you can just mash other words together. For instance, there is the word *philos*, which means friend or love, and *sophia*, which means wisdom. If you mash them together you get *philosophia*, the love of wisdom, philosophy. Now, let's bring this logic into political jargon. One of the most famous Greek inventions is democracy. This word is just two other words mashed together. *Demos*, people, and *kratos*, a word which is typically translated as power but means something closer to sovereignty. Mash them together

Once it used the powers it gained from the existence of the House of Burgesses, Virginia developed an aristocracy. It is noteworthy how quickly inequality made its way into the colony, but the creation of a political class allowed the colony to reach political maturity with remarkable speed. For the first few hundred years of America, Virginia was its heart. It was the most important state. The preeminent status could be explained because it was the first US colony, but the New England colony was set up only 13 years later in 1620. New York came into existence in 1621, New Hampshire in 1623, Maine in 1624, Maryland in 1634 and Connecticut in 1635. By this point in our narrative there were 7 colonies. Considering independence wouldn't be achieved for another hundred and fifty years, how much difference could a ten-year head start have made? Not much. What made Virginia stand out was its political maturity. We'll have more to say about this later, but when America became independent, it would be led by the Virginian

---

and you get *demokratia*, the rule of the people. The opposite of democracy is oligarchy. This comes from *oligos*, meaning few, and *archaw*, a verb which means 'I rule'. So, oligarchy means the rule of the few. This *archaw* stem also combines with *monos*, one, to get monarchy, the rule of one person. So, oligarchy, the rule of the few, means something different than *aristokratia*. This is the same *kratos* ending as *demokratia*, power, but instead of the power of the *demos*, it is the power of the *aristos*, which means best. Aristocracy means the rule of the best. This is the sense you would use the word when dealing with 7th century BC Greek history, but we're not. We're dealing with 17th century American history, so I'm going to use aristocracy to mean the wealthy and powerful few, even though it would make my Greek history friends shudder. Sorry guys.

aristocrats. I'm not saying that this aristocracy was anything to equal to the European nobility, it would take a hundred years for that to happen, this was on a much smaller scale.

1630s Politics and Tobacco

Virginian history in the 1630s centres on political clashes between the governors and the assembly. Wyatt remained as governor until 1626 when he was replaced by Yeardly for a second term as governor. In 1628 Sir John Harvey took office, and he spent the next 10 years embroiled in such clashes. Things came to a head in 1635 due to popular outrage at a decision to give Kent Island to the recently formed colony of Maryland. The assembly impeached Harvey who was forced to flee to England where he was restored by royal decree.

While the leadership squabbled, for the most part life was peaceful. The Powhatan Confederacy, while not destroyed, was for the moment no longer a serious threat. Harvey had constructed a four mile long palisade between the James and York rivers as a defence to aid the colony. Defences were also made for the livestock. Crops were diversified so that the colony wasn't as reliant on tobacco, although tobacco was still the main industry of the colony.

I previously mentioned the statistical growth of tobacco, that Rolfe sent back 4 barrels of tobacco in 1614, and that by 1619 this had increased to 20,000 pounds. Now, to put that statistic into perspective, in 1639 Virginia produced 1,500,000 pounds of tobacco. It doesn't take an expert in economics to know that this flooded the market. Really. This changed the global tobacco market.

Before the settlement of Jamestown it cost several pounds sterling per imperial pound of tobacco. By 1619 this had dropped to three shillings per pound of tobacco, and by 1639 it was at a mere threepence a pound.[11] In 1639 the price of tobacco was 160 times lower than it was 30 years previously. A rather large change. It a pretty simple economic cycle, higher production drops prices, so manufacturers need to increase production to maintain revenue which drops prices.

The story of Virginia is in a lot of ways the story of tobacco. The wealth created by tobacco was enough to keep the colony going in its early years. These new riches gave the plantation owners a say in the governance of their colony creating the most democratic body to exist in colonial America, which led to the political sophistication which would define Virginia from the other colonies. This much we've covered, but there is more too. The rapid growth of the colony has its heart in tobacco.

You see, while it is very easy to grow, tobacco exhausts the soil. It will wear it out completely in seven years. This lead the plantation owners to constantly need new soil and saw them push up the James and York rivers. In 1634 the colony had to have its administrative map redrawn and 8 shires, later known as counties, were created.[12] The need

---

[11] The old imperial currency system had four farthings in a penny, 12 pence in a shilling, 20 shillings in a pound. Pence is the plural of penny.
[12] Henrico, Charles City, James City, Warwick River,

for larger estates which could be worked cheaply led to the mass movement of the indentured servants. Following the 1622 Powhatan uprising, the colony had several hundreds of settlers, but its growth picked up. In 1635 it was at around 5,000, a figure which was up to 10,000 by 1639.

This still wasn't cheap enough, and while other colonies were placed in New England, the creation of Maryland in 1634 was a threat to Virginia. The desire for cheap work to cut costs for growing tobacco would, in following decades, lead to the growth of slavery in the region. Virginia's eventual doom was also in the tobacco.[13]

Following Sir John Harvey as governor of Virginia in 1639 was Sir Francis Wyatt, serving for a second term. He ruled in an interim nature while a new governor was selected, and he arrived on the scene in 1642. Sir William Berkeley: one of the great figures of the colonial era. He had a Master of the Arts from Oxford, he was a playwright, and had served in the King's Privy Chamber. He was an able statesman. Not to dismiss all the other governors of the colonial era, but here was a great figure, the sort of person Virginians wanted ruling them.

Berkeley continued the aims of diversification. Tobacco had become something of a staple crop at this point, but he would try to reverse it by

---

Charles River, Warrosquoake, Elizabeth City and Accomack.

[13] The desire for new arable land led to Virginia's push westwards, but once new states were created it would run out of land to plant tobacco, leading to it to fade from the national stage in the nineteenth century, but we're a really long way away from that.

introducing silk growing. He was soon able to produce 300 pounds of it. There was also to be another expedition to find gold. In 1643 the General Assembly gave a 14-year monopoly to a group of 4 who wished to try and find a gold mine along one of the more southern rivers.

Tax Problems of Charles I

I don't want to get too far into the reign of Charles I and the English Civil War, but we do need to mention it. So, here is a very simple version of Charles' tax problems.

Under the Tudor's, England's revenue collection system was woefully out of date. It was a system for the fifteenth century, not the seventeenth. This caused problems for the Stuarts when they came to power in 1603, and the country needed to undergo a lot of structural transformations. However, there was no money to do this. James I had this problem, but things got even worse for the Stuarts when Charles came to power.

Taxes could only be raised by parliament. This is a very strong English tradition. We've seen it emerging in the House of Burgesses. No taxation without representation, as the saying goes. This is a very strong tradition in British politics, and is still relevant today.[14] This tradition of parliament,

---

[14] At the time of writing, November 2015, there is something of a constitutional crisis going on in Britain. It has been a long-established tradition that the House of Commons is the only part of the British government which can decide on monetary policy since it is the only elected element of government. The other two pieces of government, the monarch, and the House of Lords, do

specifically the House of Commons, being the only body able to tax, is a long and important one.

Charles had a lot of disagreements with his parliaments, and he could never keep one together long enough to properly tax people. But he was the king, he needed money, so he therefore had several innovations for raising money through unconventional methods. This involved the regular imposition of ship money, and the expanded use of monopolies. So, what was a monopoly? It's sort of what you'd expect. The government would sell a contract to a business, business would be the only one allowed to conduct that particular task. This could be making and selling soap, or it could be mining for gold. The government would take a set percentage of revenue from the monopoly, and so it was a way of raising money without having to work with parliament. This was the sort of deal agreed in 1643 between the crown and four entrepreneurs who wanted to go looking for gold by heading south of the Appomattox River, the monopoly was granted for 14 years and the crown would take the royal fifth of whatever might be produced. This would set a precedent for later agreements, but the venture would never get going due to an event which took place the following year.

---

what the House of Commons decides in terms of taxation. So, it caused a huge stir when the House of Lords defeated a bill which would cut tax credits. Strictly speaking, the House of Lords can defeat any bill it wants. Yet, it is widely accepted that the House of Lords has no say on taxation. So, when the House of Lords voted down a bill on taxation which had been passed by the House of Commons, was it acting constitutionally? There isn't really an answer to this question.

Second Powhatan Uprising

While the governorship of Berkeley had made a promising start, disaster hit the colony in 1644 in the form of Opechancanough. Yes, the great man was still around, and he still hated the English, over 20 years since he last launched a great assault. He was old by this point, we have no way of knowing exactly how old, but it seems he was over a hundred. We're also told that he needed other people to raise his eyelids so that he could see, and that he was carried around in a litter. While he was physically weak, mentally he was as vibrant as ever. He was still determined to push out the English. Perhaps he saw how much weaker his people had become in the last twenty years, how much more entrenched the English were becoming, and that he was about to die. This was his last chance to try and reclaim his land. So, on Thursday, April 18th, 1644, an attack was launched on the English settlement.

500 were killed in the initial attack. While the 1622 uprising had nearly destroyed Virginia, and had brought about a return of the 1609-1610 Starving Time, the English were incomparably more secure. Even back in 1622 only the frontier settlements were destroyed. Ones further east, such as Jamestown, remained largely intact. By 1644 everything was better fortified, and there were too many English to force them all out.

Berkeley led a spirited defence of Virginia, leading counter attacks personally. This was successful and Opechancanough was captured. He was to be taken back to England to take before the king, but a soldier shot him instead as vengeance for the damage he had caused. Without their spirited leader, Powhatan resistance collapsed and peace was made. With this defeat, the Powhatans ceased to be an important factor in history. Disease had decimated their population, the English outnumbered them as well as having superior firepower, and they had lost their two great leaders, Wahunsonacock and Opechancanough. They would not be the first, and they would not be the last, people to be crushed by the European advancement.

Miscellaneous 1640s

This is a particularly difficult period of history to construct a narrative for. There isn't really an important event between the Powhatan uprising of 1644 and Baron's Rebellion in 1676. Life just sort of carried on. Rather than skipping thirty years into the future, in this section we shall discuss some interesting stuff going on in the meantime.

The English civil war was going on throughout all of this, and Berkeley was a royalist, loyal to Charles. Many of those royal supporters, the Cavaliers, moved to Virginia to escape from the growing power of the parliamentarian roundheads. This migration would form a core of about 100 families who would intermarry and help create the Virginian aristocracy. I'm not going to throw a hundred different family names at you, but I'll give one example. Two of these families would intermarry in the mid-1670s, William Randolph and Mary Isham. Direct descendants of these two include President Thomas Jefferson, Chief Justice John Marshall, and Confederate General Robert E. Lee.

Royalist leanings turned into open rebellion in 1649 when Charles was executed and Berkeley pledged his loyalty to the monarchy. He said that anyone who disagreed with him was guilty of treason. This, unsurprisingly, earned both Berkeley and Virginia the ire of parliament. The colony was instructed to stand down, something peacefully done in 1652 when Berkeley resigned. The rule of the Commonwealth of England was hard on Virginia due to the first of a series of laws, the first of which was created in 1651, the Navigation Acts.

The British Empire is, to economic historians, a huge proponent of laissez-faire policies, such as free trade. But this would not be for some time. At this stage in its history the English supported mercantilism. We shall explore mercantilism in due course, but we shall introduce the idea now. Basically, mercantilism desired free trade, but only within the empire. The loss of bullion to other empires was minimised by setting up high tariffs on foreign imports. As part of this colonies were not allowed to trade with other states, all their goods had to go back to the home country. This is what happened with the Navigation Acts.

Tobacco from Maryland and Virginia was shipped back to England, rather than being allowed to sell directly to the continent, and a special duty was also imposed. The Navigation Acts, would be hugely important over the next hundred years or so. The extra costs involved with this caused economic depression in the colony, which only got worse. In 1660 the monarchy was restored with King Charles II, and Berkeley was reappointed governor, but the Navigation Acts remained in place.

I've spoken before about how land and wealth were being concentrated, and this process continued. When income dropped, the farmers were left with few options. They could either reduce expenditure, or they could go bankrupt. The poor free holders, who were suffering already as we've previously discussed, faced a sudden loss of income at the same time as they were struggling because the tobacco had exhausted the soil. The wealthier land owners reduced costs by expanding slavery, something which was legalised in 1661.[15] Again, we'll have a lot more to say on slavery. In 1671, when the colony was said to have had a population of 40,000, 2,000 of those were slaves. The seasoning was brutal. At least half of all Africans died within three years.

So, there were harsh trade impositions and slavery going on. In 1667 Virginia was hit by storms hurricanes and floods which destroyed between ten and fifteen thousand houses and two thirds of crops. There was also plague which killed half the animals which survived the floods, some 50,000. Then the English and Dutch went to war in 1673 and the Dutch started capturing Virginian ships transporting whatever worthless tobacco the slaves had managed to grow. That's pretty much sums up what was going on in mid-seventeenth century Virginia.

The colony continued to grow, the aristocracy continued to develop, most lived bleak miserable lives. Colonial life was hard. But, a notable middle

---

[15] This followed the lead of Massachusetts which had done so in 1641, and Connecticut, which had done so in 1650.

class was developing, and other things developed around them, such as an interest in horse racing. Honestly, the speed with which Virginia developed is remarkable. There was also work on the fringes of society in these years. While Jamestown and the heartland of Virginia began to develop an element of sophistication, the more primitive aspects of the colony moved to the frontier, to places such as Fort Henry. This was a base for fur trading, and for figures such as Abraham Wood who made it all the way to the site of the modern City of Radford, some 200 miles into the interior, and not too far from what would become the state of Kentucky. This brings us to the 1670s in Virginia.

Chapter 6 – Bacon's Rebellion

Bacon's Rebellion is one of the less well-known pieces of American history. It is, however, rather important. Bacon's Rebellion marks a turning point in our story. The point where England felt the need to really stamp its authority upon its American colonies. It marks a point where we can really begin to cover the colonial era. It was something between a version of the English civil war playing out in Virginia, and a test run of the American Revolution, and is something I have really enjoyed researching. So, we'll just get into it.

The Decline of Berkeley

As we brought Virginia into the 1670s, we noted the miserable conditions for the vast majority of people. Governor Berkeley, who had by this point been in office for some 25 years, was becoming out of touch. He hated the spread of education and printing, thinking that it bred trouble makers. This put him woefully out of touch with the new men of Virginia, the educated cosmopolitan gentlemen who often leaned towards parliament in the civil wars (something which earned them the ire of the fiercely royalist Berkeley). As much as Berkeley may dislike it, the world was changing, preparing to enter the Enlightenment. The new generation wanted such novel concepts as competent government, and when they travelled to the new world they did not find it in Virginia.

While Virginia was in severe economic depression, Berkeley had ridiculously high tax rates. Tax was collected in the form of tobacco, and was assessed at half market value, and then double the amount required was actually collected. This meant that the Virginian government was collecting 4 times as much as it supposedly needed. It was also a poll tax.[16] The Virginians were struggling to grow tobacco due to bad weather and worn out soil, to get across the Atlantic because of the war with the Dutch, and to sell tobacco because of the Navigation Acts and the dropping rates due to the increased volume of tobacco on the market. The Virginians were livid. To compound this, it wasn't clear what exactly the Virginian government was doing with the money. It said it was for defence. They were, after all, at war with the Dutch. The government said it would construct sea-forts along the coast, but all it did was build a few out of mud. Then, there were issues with the Natives.

As Virginia expanded, the English came into contact with more and more Native Americans, the most important of which were the Iroquois. These were more warlike than the comparatively peaceful Powhatans had been. When King Philip's War broke out in New England in 1675, trouble made its way down into Virginia and attacks began on the frontier settlements. The frontiersmen were outraged, and wanted to kill every Indian that they could find. Berkeley would not allow this. He would not consent to open war on all Native Americans. He had diplomatic treaties and trade to think about. None of this was the concern of people being killed. All they knew was that they were being attacked, and weren't allowed to attack back. Berkeley told them to expand into enemy land by creating

---

[16] A poll tax is a tax in which the same amount is collected from every person. This meant that the poorest had to hand over half of their crop.

plantations. This was how Berkeley had won the war in the 1640s, and he saw no reason why it wouldn't work again.

There were, of course, many reasons why the same tactic would be completely useless 30 years on. The most of important was that they were no longer dealing with the Powhatans, a comparatively peaceful group of Algonquian Native Americans. When dealing with mostly settled farmers, expanding the plantation network worked well. However, building a plantation in the land of raiders is just going to lead to that plantation being raided. Plus, there would need to be taxes to fund this new project. Considering that taxes were already four times higher than they should have been, it is understandable why this would be frustrating. Berkeley wouldn't even allow the accounts to be made public when it was questioned just where the money from these extra taxes was going. Virginia was a powder keg, just waiting for a match to set the whole country alight. It would come in the form of one Nathaniel Bacon.

Nathaniel Bacon

Nathaniel Bacon was born to an upper-class family in East Anglia in 1647. This was during the period of the English Civil Wars. Following the restoration of Charles II, Bacon moved with his father to Cambridge where he studied for a few years and gained a reputation as a bright but inattentive young man. He went on a tour of Europe with his teacher, the scientist and linguist John Ray, but he was recalled by his father to Cambridge and he completed his Master's Degree before reading law at Grey's Inn, London. He then courted and married

Elizabeth Duke, daughter of Sir Edward Duke, in 1670. Bacon was not one to settle down. He was still excited by travel, and had a less than dignified side of him. Sir Edward was fiercely opposed to him, and disowned his daughter because of the marriage. Bacon became something of a con-artist, and was exiled to Virginia in 1674, aged 27. He stayed with his cousin and namesake, Nathaniel Bacon, who set him up with some land and Bacon moved to the frontier. He quickly rose up the ranks in the colony, and in March 1675 Berkeley named him to the council, even though he didn't take much interest in proceedings and rarely showed up.

When trouble really began with the Native Americans, Bacon was not happy with Berkeley's timid response. If Berkeley wouldn't help them, they would have to just help themselves. An army was set up. This was, to Berkeley, treason. He knew that Virginia needed to trade with the Native Americans, and that attacking tribes which had nothing to do with the raids would only make the situation worse. To frontiersmen, this reeked of cowardice. They rallied to Bacon. This was civil war.

Skirmish at Jamestown

Bacon was declared a public enemy, and his army was ordered to disband in May 1676. The men of property did so (they weren't going to disobey a command from the governor) but many stuck with Bacon, who was then elected a Burgess in the assembly. Bacon went to take his seat and sailed, with plenty of bodyguards, up the James with the intention of going to Jamestown. However, they were fired at by the canon, and so he landed very late by the house of one of his allies, Richard Lawrence.

The next morning, June 7th 1676, he made to flee the Berkeleyan forces by water, but he was very quickly surrounded by the firepower of the tobacco fleet. A shot was fired, forcing Bacon to stop. It was realised that they were stuck, and Bacon surrendered that afternoon.

3 days later, on June 10th, the general assembly gathered. It was surprised to learn that, once Bacon confessed to being a rebel, Berkeley pardoned him. Berkeley even restored Bacon to his seat on the council. This was very generous. Too generous. You see, Berkeley was well aware that Bacon's army had not disbanded, and was at that moment surrounding Jamestown. If he punished Bacon, he would pay, and so Bacon was to be forgiven for just long enough for his army to disperse. Once it did, Berkeley ordered his arrest the very next night. Before dawn the next day he raided Lawrence's house to seize Bacon, but Bacon had gotten word of the plot and fled. Virginia was about to be engulfed by civil war.

General Bacon

Berkeley set about defending the capital, but he had limited force at his disposal. On the morning of Friday, June 23rd, it was announced that Bacon was within 2 miles of Jamestown. Berkeley could do nothing to stop the attackers. At 2PM Bacon's 400 infantry and 120 cavalry entered Jamestown, garrisoned it, and within half an hour ordered the assembly to gather. Bacon asked for a commission as a general to attack the Native Americans.

Berkeley was outraged. Berkeley demanded Bacon to shoot him, Bacon refused. Berkeley wanted single combat to decide things, Bacon refused. This was quite a desperate gamble from Berkeley (Bacon was 29 and he was 70). Bacon refused this too. He said he only wanted to attack the Native Americans. He would not harm Berkeley. So, Berkeley left, and then Bacon threatened to shoot the men of the general assembly unless they voted him his commission, which they promptly did. This is how Nathaniel Bacon became General Bacon. This reminded many of Cromwell, leading to people calling him Oliver Bacon to his face.

Bacon's Commission

General Bacon had a few political goals before he left to attack the Native Americans. He wanted to ban some of Berkeley's favourites from office. He demanded that the letters Berkeley had sent back to London with his wife (which called Bacon a rebel and asked for military aid) be contradicted. He also intended to punish the captain who had shot at his ship during his arrest. These were hastily agreed to.

Berkeley wanted no part of this, but he adopted a Yossarianesque attitude that he couldn't do the king any good if he were dead, so he might as well acquiesce to Bacon's demands and live. With this agreed, war was declared "against the barbarous Indians". This would not be Berkeley's expansion of plantations. All trade was stopped, and the war would be financed by selling captured slaves and land to the gentry who had sided with Berkeley in an attempt to get them on side.

There was also administrative reform, as the county sheriffs were limited to a year in office, and the tax system was fixed so that tobacco would be collected at market value. There was also a change in voting law. Berkeley had restricted the vote in 1670 to landed men, excluding the freemen. This was undone, and freemen once again had the vote. Before he completed the full extent of his political revolution, General Bacon was forced into action by a reported attack that 8 colonists had been killed in New Kent County, a site only 23 miles from Jamestown.

General Bacon moved north and began gathering recruits, offering an escape to indentured servants and to slaves. Small freeholders were resistant. They feared that their lands would be attacked if they departed, either by the Native Americans or by encroachment from the landed gentry. Bacon's support was further to the north, and one man of note he attracted to his force was Colonel John Washington. Washington had a reputation for hostility towards the natives, to put it very mildly.[17]

Within a month, General Bacon had gathered together an army of 600 infantry and 700 cavalry, along with two months' worth of provisions. As soon as he set off west out of Gloucester County, heading towards the James falls, the notables of Gloucester rushed to Berkeley and delivered to him the Gloucester Petition. The Gloucester Petition was a list of complaints about Bacon's political, economic and military actions. His men had taken whatever they wanted, they had drafted whoever

---

[17] In case you were wondering, yes, John Washington was the grandfather of the more famous George.

they wanted, ignoring draft exemptions, and they showed no respect.[18]

Berkeley immediately went to Gloucester County to assess the situation, and told the inhabitants that Bacon did not have a commission from him. Bacon had forced the comission out of the assembly. He then gathered the militias of both Gloucester County and Middlesex County, supposedly to fight the Native American threat. This force was some 1,200 strong. Berkeley then told the men that they would not be fighting the Native Americans, they were to go defeat that rebel scoundrel Bacon. But the soldiers gathered thinking they were fighting the natives, exactly who Bacon was fighting. They began muttering, 'Bacon, Bacon, Bacon', and then started to just leave. Berkeley was mortified, and he actually fainted. When regained consciousness, all 1,200 men had gone. He was stood in a field with fewer than a dozen officers. It was hard to see how that could have gone any worse for Berkeley.

---

[18] Honestly, when dealing with the gentlemen of yesteryear, I love these opinions on respect. We saw it very early on when John Smith was to be hanged in the Caribbean. He was more upset about being hanged instead of shot than he was about the fact that he had been sentenced for execution. Gentlemen were shot, commoners were hanged, and he was supremely offended by this insult to his honour. We have the same situation here. These men were of course annoyed that this Bacon and his men were stealing their stuff, but what really made them angry was that they were rude about it. They didn't show the proper amount of deference, while they were stealing their stuff. I mean, come on! Sure, you can be a thief, you gotta do what you gotta do, but at least be polite about it.

When Bacon learned of this he travelled to the Middle Plantation,[19] only 7 miles from Jamestown, and from there he sent out officers to every county to secure loyalty. He wanted to secure his position, rather than allow Berkeley to continue with his counter revolution. Those who were not sufficiently loyal were proscribed as traitors to the people. This was at the end of July. When he heard that Bacon had turned around, Berkeley fled. Only four loyalists travelled with him, and he went into hiding. He sailed across the Chesapeake and waited on Virginia's Eastern Shore. The counties of Accomack and Northampton were holdouts for the old families, and remained untouched by war. 20 more joined him over the course of August. These men brought with them arms, supposedly to be used for the campaign against the natives. It benefited the Berkeleyans from a military stand point, but it did damage them in terms of PR. Bacon was able to allege that Berkeley was putting the needs of himself above the needs of the many by harming the campaign against the natives.

With Berkeley out of the picture, Bacon could control the council and called a Revolutionary Council to meet on August 3rd at the Middle Plantation. Berkeley was declared a traitor, loyalty was pledged to Bacon, and a new assembly elected by all free men was to be created which was to convene at Jamestown on September 4th. After the convention broke up, Bacon spent August taking land held by royalists and capturing what ships he could. Giles Bland was given the commission for

---

[19] What would become Williamsburg.

capturing Berkeley and bringing the revolution over to the Eastern Shore of Virginia.

Giles Bland

Bland was not a supporter of Bacon, but he detested Berkeley. He represents something of a third side in this civil war. Berkeley, who it must be remembered was in his 70s, was part of the old order. He liked the traditional way of doing things. If anything, he was the representation of Charles I in the English civil war, in opposition to Bacon, a republican who opposed the monarchy and who could be compared to Cromwell. Bland, if anything, represented Charles II. He was a royalist, but he was a new man too. He wanted to see the imperial power of London expanded at the expense of old governors such as Berkeley.

Bland had spent his past few years in Virginia writing to London of how corrupt Berkeley was, estimating than corruption and evasion in the colony was losing the crown £100,000 a year. Bland sided with Bacon's force not because he supported them, but because he thought any government which opposed Berkeley should be given a chance. He would not go so far as opposing the monarch.

His campaign against Berkeley began with an attack against the merchant ships which were still around Jamestown, and then he advanced to the Eastern shore. In addition to Bland, this force was led by Captain William Carver, an able seaman who had joined Bacon because of his hatred for Native Americans. They managed to find Berkeley, and while there were very few loyalists remaining, Berkeley still commanded respect. Therefore, they negotiated. While Berkeley kept them busy talking on land, he used this opportunity to recapture the flagship of the Virginian navy, the Rebecca, on September 2nd. This gave the Berkeleyans control of the Eastern shore, the bay, and the rivers, and it was also the first reversal that Bacon had suffered. Carver was hanged and his men surrendered to the loyalists, even though they greatly outnumbered them.

Berkeley Fights Back

With this victory, support began to grow for Berkeley. He was able to gather a mercenary force, which we estimate was between 200 and 600. Berkeley set sail with his little fleet, and managed to find another force of 100, and they all made their way to Jamestown. News of this was enough to scare away most of the 500 rebels garrisoning the town, and when Berkeley arrived and demanded surrender, the rest fled that night, September 7th. They landed on the morning of the 8th, and then spent a week plundering Jamestown while the rebels regathered. This more than anything else highlights just how out of touch Berkeley had become. This was supposed to be the re-imposition of order, but it spiralled out of control.[20]

---

[20] You know what I noticed? Nobody panics when things go 'according to plan.' Even if the plan is horrifying. If tomorrow I tell the press that like a gangbaner will get shot, or a truckload of soldiers will be blowing up, nobody panics because it's all 'part of the plan.' But when I say that one little old mayor will die, well then everybody loses their minds! Introduce a little anarchy. Upset the established order, and everything becomes chaos. I'm an agent of chaos. Oh, and you know the thing about chaos, it's fair. Wait, I may have gotten a bit

Bacon had been attacking the remnants of the Powhatan Confederacy, but he returned with 136 revolutionary soldiers. They put Jamestown under siege having total control of the land, while Berkeley's ships were used to control the James River and to plunder rebel plantations.

On September 16th, the loyalists launched a raid out against the besieging forces, but it was botched and they were easily pushed back. While Bacon's forces captured what had been left on the battlefield, they defended themselves by using a human shield of loyalist wives. The next day, Bacon paraded Indian prisoners. This heightened his appeal to the country folk, and highlighted how little Berkeley had done.

It was a grim month, the rain kept falling, Bacon kept firing cannonballs at the city, and the loyalist garrison lost moral, fleeing on the night of the nineteenth ready for Bacon to enter Jamestown the next day. While Berkeley had been scared off for the moment, Bacon realised that he could not hope to hold on to Jamestown without ships. He set fire to the town that night. The key buildings, the symbols of Berkeleyan oppression, were destroyed, along with most of the wooden warehouses.

Jamestown was really taking a beating in this war. I understand that it was a smart move, and that controlling manpower was more important to this war than control of Jamestown, but burning the settlement you're trying to rule just seems like quite a step. Although, perhaps Bacon is man it's impossible to fully understand. Some men aren't

---

carried away there. I love Nolan's writing.

looking for anything logical, like money. They can't be bought, bullied, reasoned, or negotiated with. Some men just want to watch the world burn.[21]

War Beyond Jamestown

The revolution moved from Jamestown to seizing Berkeley's plantation at Green Spring, and the rebellion got a lot more serious. They had already taken some pretty radical steps, such as mass manumission. Former slaves were the most loyal elements of Bacon's force. But, now there was something more serious to discuss.

There was a disagreement between the moderates and the radicals in the rebel camp. The moderates wanted to reform Berkeley's administration, or at the very most remove him as governor and replace him with another member of the executive who would be more open to reform. There was precedent for this. They argued that it would be foolish to try anything more forceful. The crown had more power than they did, if they were too open in their rebellion against Berkeley they may break free for the moment, but this just ensured that England would send a more powerful force over and crush them.

This ignored some key points. Most of the population sided with Bacon. England was a long way away. Would England be able to suppress a revolt on the other side of the world? Plus, they didn't have to stand alone. The Dutch would certainly be interested in helping. It was decided

---

[21] Sorry, I'm doing the Nolan thing again, aren't I?

that they had already gone this far, so they might as well try for independence. It should be becoming clear why Bacon's Rebellion is sometimes viewed as an early version of the Revolutionary war, except with the Dutch taking the place of the French.

The Independence Bid

Following this bold step, they sounded out other colonies. Massachusetts was the ally the revolutionaries really wanted, but Bacon was confident that Maryland and Carolina would both join too.[22] There were, however, some differences. The protestors in Maryland opposed to their government saw the solution not in independence, but in tighter control by England. They wanted a stronger imperial system since each colony was pretty autonomous, aside from New York. They wanted a royal commander in chief for North America so that the colonies could work together more, and so that they would be less at the whims of the colonial oligarchs.

This brought them into opposition against Bacon who was preparing to resist royal troops, even though their initial enemies were the same, Berkeley in Virginia and Baltimore in Maryland. The leadership was certainly in communication, although sadly for historians these communications were later destroyed. Bacon tried to convince the Marylanders that he could be victorious. His men knew the country, his men were acclimatised. They could ambush the English soldiers who would be sick with disease. They would use the tobacco they

---

[22] These two sides sent representatives to the Green Spring meetings.

grew to defy the navigation acts and sell to the French and Dutch for support. This was overly ambitious. As big as Virginia was, it was still reliant on economic support from England, and it could not ignore the trans-Atlantic trade system just yet.

His words were not enough to convince the Marylanders to join Bacon, and why they didn't join explains why the United States of America became independent in 1776, not 1676. Bacon expected 2,000 redcoats to land in Virginia, and the Marylanders believed that 500 would be enough to crush the rebellion. There was no rebel navy to defend the coasts from landing. Virginia was very coastal, and so was easy to raid. It would be easy for the English to starve the Virginians out. Plus, many of the Virginians were recent immigrants with strong connections in England. They would not abandon them as easily as Bacon wanted them to. Bacon's radicalism was also an alienating force. While Virginians were prepared to attack redcoats, men they didn't know, Bacon wanted a radical social revolution. He wanted to kill county officials and tear down the administration. These were people's friends and neighbours. No one really wanted that. The Marylanders believed that Bacon had misunderstood his revolution. This was a racial issue against the Native Americans, and annoyance at Berkeley. This was not, for most, a desire to turn the world upside down with executions of the grandees and independence from England. Bacon wasn't able to distinguish between the oppression of Berkeley, and royal authority, as most did. Bacon was driven to republicanism out of anti-Imperial logic, he was in some ways a century before his time.

While Maryland would not join in open rebellion, Bacon expanded his control of Virginia throughout September and October until he controlled about two thirds of the colony. He administered it by a series of revolutionary councils. The population was approximately 15,000, and Berkeley estimated that only 500 remained loyal. At this point disaster struck. Bacon had been weakened by an illness he caught during the wet camps while campaigning in the forests and outside of Jamestown, and he died on October 26th.

With Berkeley once again in exile on the Eastern Shore, the rebels needed someone to lead them, and so they made Lawrence Ingram their general. He was the most important of the rebel leaders. The troops dispersed to winter quarters, which is why the winter campaign had a very different nature to it.

The rebel forces spread out into small garrisons. Aside from their main base which held 800 men, none of their bases held more than 200. Most held less than 40. This gave the advantage to the loyalist forces centred on the coast, and which also held the sea due to the support of the tobacco ships. An amphibious war started along the James and York Rivers. They slowly wore down the rebels, and by November Berkeley allowed pardons to those who would renounce the rebellion. It took some time, but by the end of November/early December the rebels started to go back to Berkeley, one by one, county by county. 1676 turned into 1677 and Berkeley's forces continued pushing into the interior, reaching Jamestown by the end of January. The rebels found were hanged. The advance continued, Berkeley's home of Green Spring was recaptured.

Suddenly, now that he was once again in a position power, Berkeley reneged on his promised pardons. Admiral Morris, the man in the field who had issued the pardons, was far more decent that Berkeley, and warned those he had pardoned to flee when he got word of what was happening. It is at this moment, the end of January 1677, that the royal forces finally arrived.

1,300 redcoats arrived and began to settle things. Most of the rebels were to be pardoned, and peace was brought. The captains of the Virginian Navy were credited with the victory by the royalists, something Berkeley was too arrogant to do. Berkeley and his allies had not won the war, even though they might think it. They had just caused an awful lot of trouble through misrule.

If you'll allow me to quote from 1676: The End of American Independence by Stephen Saunders Webb:

> "Doubly convinced of oligarchic incapacity, either to fight or to govern, the officers of the crown imposed direct royal government on Virginia, backing it on occasion with military force. Thus they displaced the Berkeleyan regime as well as repressing the Baconian revolutionaries by substituting royal military occupation for English naval patrols... Two bids for Virginian independence therefore

failed in in 1676. The autonomy of the Berkeleyan regime had left it free to provoke the revolution, which, in turn, justified the crown's termination of the oligarchical rule of the old assembly system. The radical effort of the Baconians to secure independence had failed because of colonial underdevelopment, but had nevertheless provoked royal reform of Virginia's government. Ironically, the failed revolutionary effort combined with obvious oligarchical excess to excite an unprecedented imperial presence in Virginia."[23]

Berkeley had to tear apart his life's work. He had spent the greater part of the last 35 years, half his life, working on creating a system of oligarchical rule in Virginia which was almost independent of England. Powers were transferred from the governor to the king. Attempts were made to clean up the whole governance system, to reduce inequality, and make things farer. It was acknowledged that Berkeley had failed to defend the province, the king promised that he would orchestrate a defence, but made clear that there would have to be taxes in order to do pay for it. However, expenditure was to be more transparent. There were also attacks and executions of Native Americans in order to garner favour. Eventually, Berkeley was dismissed. The masses were bought off with popular polices such as these, while voting restrictions were reintroduced and power was

[23] Webb, S. (1984)

concentrated with the richer of the Virginians to gain their support. The former slaves who had been Bacon's loyalist support were oppressed, as they would be for two more centuries. The imposition of imperial authority was complete.

This ends the first stage of our narrative. Our first chapter. We have taken Virginia from the foundation of Jamestown which set off in 1606 to the end of Bacon's Rebellion in 1677. It has been 61 years in which has seen the population of Virginia go from less than 40 in 1607 to some 15,000. It had mostly reached the form it would take for the remainder of the colonial era.

What's Next?

When this part began Virginia was the only English presence in North America. Virginia is no longer in isolation. We also have, in 1677, Massachusetts, New Hampshire, Rhode Island, Connecticut, New York, New Jersey, Delaware, Maryland, and Carolina. Pennsylvania wouldn't be founded until 1681, Carolina wouldn't split into North and South until 1712, and then Georgia would be created in 1732 to bring us to 13. So, now we need to catch up. Next time we turn to New England as we begin to tell the tale of the Pilgrim Fathers.

Part 2

The Birth of New England to 1677

Chapter 7 – The Pilgrim Fathers

Who would true Valour see
Let him come hither;
One here will Constant be,
Come Wind, come Weather.
There's no Discouragement,
Shall make him once Relent,
His first avow'd Intent,
To be a Pilgrim.

Who so beset him round,
With dismal Storys,
Do but themselves Confound;
His Strength the more is.
No Lyon can him fright,
He'l with a Gyant Fight,
But he will have a right,
To be a Pilgrim.

Hobgoblin, nor foul Fiend,
Can daunt his Spirit:
He knows, he at the end,
Shall Life Inherit.
Then Fancies fly away,
He'l fear not what men say,
He'l labour Night and Day,
To be a Pilgrim.

The Pilgrim, by John Bunyan, 17th Century Poet.[24]

---

[24] Some of this poem is used to start Chapter 4 of The
Penguin History of the USA by Hugh Brogan, The Planting
of New England 1604-c.1675. This book was the catalyst
for my own work.

We now begin the second strand of American life. The first was the Virginian Company centred on Tobacco with its origins in Anglo-Spanish rivalry, but the second came from somewhere both very different and very similar. This is the story of the Pilgrims, their voyage on the Mayflower to found Plymouth and what would become New England. This colony would have a very different culture, and history, to that of Virginia. In a lot of ways we need to go back, lay some groundwork, and restart the narrative. If I started the first introduction with Columbus sailing across the Atlantic in 1492, this thread has its origins in 1517 when Martin Luther nailed his Ninety-Five Theses on the Power and Efficacy of Indulgences to the door of the Castle Church in Wittenberg, Saxony. This kick-started the Reformation. If we are going to understand the Pilgrims, we need to understand the Reformation.

A Brief History of Christianity

Christianity is a religion which has suffered from a tremendous amount of infighting, and is pretty diverse. This reflects its early scattered nature in the Roman Empire when it was forced underground due to persecution. Although current theories are that the persecution of Christians was on a much smaller scale than popularly understood.

Once Constantine converted to Christianity, he tried to unify the theology of the religion, but it could not be done. Schisms kept popping up, such as Arrianism, and then as soon as that was dealt with another would appear, such as Monophysitism. Eventually the church broke into two main branches, Roman Catholicism and Greek Orthodoxy.[25]

As time passed and the Catholic Church became such a dominant feature in western European life, there were arguments about whether what the Church had become was positive. It was certainly a very different creature to the one that had existed before Constantine. There were efforts to reform the Catholic Church in the fifteenth century by those who opposed how decadent it, and in particular the papacy, had become. A notorious example is the Borgia pope Alexander VI, who bribed his way to the top and had 8 children by 3 different women by the time he had done so. Not what you think of when you think of the Pope. This tradition was condemned by the late medieval theologians William of Ockham, John Wycliffe, Jan Hus, Lorenzo Valla, Johannes Reuchlin and Desiderius Erasmus to name a few. Erasmus, who was a Catholic, supported a return to looking at the bible rather than focusing on medieval superstition, an approach which would greatly influence Luther.

Luther agreed with many of the pre-reformers, but where he differed was in his opposition to the doctrine of the Church rather than reforming the institutions. He disagreed that salvation could be earned through indulgences, performing good deeds and convention to reduce time in purgatory. While the Church said that specific sins could be forgiven, Luther believed that man committed so many sins that he must be sick, and that the only

---

[25] There were other smaller branches, such as Coptic Christianity, and local variants, such as the Armenian Orthodox Church and the Ethiopian Orthodox Church. But for the purposes of this book, all we need to know is that Christianity had a tendency to argue with itself.

salvation to this was in faith alone. This led Luther to his Ninety-Five Theses which had three central themes, 1) the Church was too decadent. It should spend its money helping the poor, not building fancy churches. 2) The Pope had no jurisdiction over purgatory. 3) The Church was not gospel, only scripture was. This was just Luther expressing himself, he did not intend what happened next.

Luther was declared a heretic, and he was certain to be destroyed were it not for a fluke of history. It was time for the election of the Holy Roman Emperor, and there were three prime candidates. Henry VIII of England, François I of France and Carlos I of Spain. Pope Leo X did not want to upset the balance of power in Europe, and so instead backed Frederick the Wise of Saxony, Luther's protector. It did not stop Carlos being elected Charles V of the Holy Roman Empire, but the Pope's distractions would allow Luther to live. He turned further and further against the Catholic Church, even labelling the Pope as the Antichrist. I won't discuss all the theological matters since if you were desperate to know about the doctrine of transubstantiation you would not be reading a book called 'A History of the United'. But, while all this was going on, Luther made probably his most important work, a translation of the New Testament into idiomatic German. While many were not convinced, Erasmus recoiled from Luther's break with the Catholic Church, many were. Many variants of reform broke out across Europe, the five most notable being Lutheranism, Anglicism, Calvinism, Baptism, and Methodism. I won't go into all their different histories, but our pursuit of setting up New England takes us to England and Anglicism.

While Protestantism and the Reformation swept across Europe, it entered England for a different reason. Henry VIII wanted to divorce his wife Catherine of Aragon so that he could marry his mistress, Anne Boleyn. The Pope wouldn't allow this, so Henry just decided to go found his own church. With blackjack. And divorces. So, England began a transformation into a protestant country. The pope was no longer the head of the church, instead the monarch would be. The monasteries were dissolved. There was no more mass, and a common book of prayer was introduced. It would start under Henry and Edward the VI, go back to Catholicism under Mary I, but Elizabeth I's long reign would solidify Protestantism's hold over England. The reformation was complete. Or, wasn't it?

Puritans

This brings us to the Puritans, a religious force which immerged in the late 16th century. During the brief rule of Mary I, Protestants went into exile, and many found themselves in Geneva where they were influenced by Calvinism. When they returned to England they found the reformation only partly complete. They wanted to remove Anglican ritual, considered by the Puritans to be remnants of popish idolatry. They wanted to strip away the role of the Church and stressed the primacy of an individual relationship with scripture, similar to Presbyterianism. This created problems between the Puritans and Elizabeth.

The Tudors were fond of imposing their rule, and the church was a way to do this, and the idea of religious unity also appealed to Elizabeth. The individualistic tones of the Puritans were troublesome. They tried to get Elizabeth on their side, but Elizabeth was a conservative religious figure, and so appointed conservative bishops who would enforce her views. This really ticked off the Puritans who began forming their own congregations, and ending dreams of a united English Church. This is why groups who started their own congregations are referred to as Separatists.

They preached and spread pamphlets, and just got on with their business. This was the golden age of Puritanism. They have a reputation as dark and drab, but that wouldn't reflect Puritans at this point in history. They were cheery and hardworking folk. John Bunyan's Pilgrim's Progress, with which we began this chapter, is probably the best way of putting across their perspective. Puritan ideas have had a very large impact on the American church in particular. Prior to the reformation sermons and preaching played a very small role in religious life, but in the modern American church the Sunday sermon is the centrepiece of the religious week. Ministers are often referred to as 'preacher' in the states, another Puritan tradition. But this did not last long. Everything changed when Elizabeth died. The new King James was a Calvinist rather than an Anglican, and it was hoped by the Puritans that he would be more sympathetic to their views. These hopes were dashed in 1604 at the Hampton Court Conference. The complaints were dismissed by the line 'no bishop, no king.'

Following this, the Archbishop of Canterbury took things a step further in 1607 and began a persecution of separatist groups in the villages around Lincolnshire, Yorkshire and

Nottinghamshire. These people were not going to just sit around and be persecuted, so they fled in small groups throughout 1607 and 1608, eventually settling at Leyden in the Netherlands. Their members would vary over the years, and there were other English radicals in the Netherlands too. Some of the more senior figures in this group were Pastor John Robinson and Elder William Brewster. Robinson was a graduate of Oxford, forced out of the country for his radical views, while Brewster had studied at Cambridge and was the only one of the group with political and diplomatic experience, having served under senior court official William Davison. These are the people who would become known as the Pilgrims, although that name would not be used until the nineteenth century.

The Pilgrims

The Pilgrims spent the next decade in Leyden. It would not be particularly happy though. The Dutch were Calvinists like the Pilgrims, but it must remembered that so was the King in England who had forced them to flee. Most Puritans were not as cold as they are portrayed in pop-culture, but these separatists were the extreme. They found the Dutch too happy, they didn't keep the same gloomy Sunday of self-reflection as they did. They also were worried about spending too much time there, in case the children and the more impressionable become Batavianised. Plus, Leyden was an urban centre, and the separatists had come from small villages in eastern England. There was also the threat of war. There was an uneasy truce in the Netherlands between the Dutch and the Spanish, and there was no idea when conflict would flare up again. It could be any year. When telling this chapter of the American story we are lucky to have William Bradford's Of Plymouth Planation, a history of the early years of the colony written by one of its governors. Bradford stresses the rationality of their unhappiness. It was, "Not out of any newfanglednes, or other such like giddie humor, by which men are oftentimes transported to their great hurt and danger". In short, the separatists missed England and wanted to go home. But they couldn't. There was only one logical place for them. America.

This makes complete sense. It was these years that saw the Dutch begin to take serious interest in the Americas with the creation of New Netherland. The Hudson river was explored, New Amsterdam was founded, later to be renamed New York, and in Upstate New York a trading post was established called Fort Nassau, later renamed Fort Orange, which would become the state capital of Albany. You have only to look at the flags of New York City and Albany to see the Dutch influence. They both contain the orange, white, and blue stripes of the Prince's Flag (the flag of the Prince of Orange).

The Dutch were interested in sailing the Separatists across, but one of the conditions would be that they would have to join a Dutch colony. The Pilgrims were too homesick for that, and so they tried to see if they could go to Virginia. This would also give them the opportunity to spread their faith. As it was put by Bradford, "The place they had thoughts on was some of those vast and unpeopled countries of America, which are frutfull and fit for habitation, being devoyd of all civill inhabitants, wher ther are only salvage and brutish men, which range up and downe, litle otherwise then the wild beasts of the same." If they couldn't go home, this was the next best thing.[26]

In 1617, two of the more senior figures, Deacon John Carver and Robert Cushman, both travelled to London to see what they could do. Sandys was excited to get them to go to Virginia. While King James would not formally agree to consent with their religious freedom, he agreed informally for the process to advance. There was some delay, but finally a patent was issued allowing them to set up a colony. They also attracted the attention of the Plymouth. It was the Plymouth Company that set up the ill-fated North Virginia Colony at St. George's Fort, and this would give them legal jurisdiction over New England. The only issue was financing the expedition. All these delays led a backer to become interested, Thomas Weston, a London merchant. Weston agreed to pay for the expedition on the condition that they work for him for a period of 7 years, with a division of profits at the end. Each colonist would have one share of stock in the company, and would be given 10 pounds worth of supplies per stock they had. While the Separatists wanted individual ownership, the merchants in London would not agree to this and insisted on the join-stock model which raised around £7,000, and an agreement was finally reached on July 1st 1620. Bradford preserves the terms of the agreement.

---

[26] I will note, as a curiosity, that one of the other places considered was Guiana in South America, next to Venezuela. Just imagine how differently things could have turned out had New England been set up in South America.

"1. The adventurers and planters doe agree, that every person that goeth being aged 16 years and upward, be rated at 10li., and ten pounds to be accounted a single share.

2. That he that goeth in person, and furnisheth him selfe out with 10li. either in money or other provisions, be accounted as having 20li. in stock, and in the devission shall receive a double share.

3. The persons transported and the adventurers shall continue their joynt stock and partnership togeather, the space of 7 years, (excepte some unexpected impedimente doe cause the whole company to agree otherwise,) during which time, all profits and benefits that are gott by trade, traffick, trucking, working, fishing, or any other means of any person or persons, remaine still in the commone stock untill the division.

4. That at their comming ther, they chose out such a number of fitt persons, as may furnish their ships and boats for fishing upon the sea; imploying the rest in their severall faculties upon the land; as building houses, tilling, and planting the ground, and makeing shuch commodoties as shall be most usefull for the collonie.

5. That at the end of the 7 years, the capitall and profits, viz. the houses, lands, goods, and chatles, be equally devided betwixte the adventurers, and planters; which dome, every man shall be free from other of them of any debt or detrimente concerning this adventure.

6. Whosoever cometh to the colonie herafter, or putteth any into the stock, shall at the ende of the 7 years be alowed proportionably to the time of his so doing.

7. He that shall carie his wife and children, or servants, shall be alowed for everie person now aged 16 years and upward, a single share in the

devision, or if he provid them necessaries, a duble share, or if they be between 10 year old and 16, then 2 of them to be reconed for a person, both in transportation and devision.

8. That such children as now goe, and are under the age of ten years, have no other shar in the devision, but 50 acers of unmanured land.

9. That such persons as die before the 7 years be expired, their executors to have their parte or sharr at the devision, proportionably to the time of their life in the collonie.

10. That all such persons as are of this collonie, are to have their meate, drink, apparell, and all provisions out of the common stock and goods of the said collonie."

It had taken them 13 years, but the Pilgrims were finally going to get a new home. Why did it take them so long? The Separatists, frankly, made life very hard for themselves. This was the extreme fringe of Puritanism, it must be remembered. Most Puritans had just gotten on with life in England, and would go on to play a very prominent role in the English Civil War, but these couldn't take it. That is the first indication of making life hard for themselves, then they refused to get too friendly with the Dutch meaning that they couldn't settle there. Even now while they were appealing to help in London, Elder William Brewster, one of the two main figures within the colony along with Pastor John Robinson, decided to, rather than letting a sleeping dog lie, decided to just go ahead and... not even poke it with a stick, more scream down its ear. He openly condemned King James' religious policy in Scotland. This royally annoyed King James. Brewster had to go into hiding for a while, which is an issue when you're trying to convince the people you're hiding from to let you form a settlement in their land. That's my take on the matter anyway.

One of the classics when studying the settlement of New England, The Pilgrim Republic by John Goodwin, first published in 1888, takes a very different approach. "In 1619 the English Government complained that Brewster's books were 'vented underhand' in their country, and asked that he be delivered up for trial in England. Strange it is that the Dutch should have descended to such a violation of the rights of asylum. Brewster for eleven years had been an industrious and peaceful present of Holland, and was still pursuing a calling useful and entirely lawful there. But the Dutch, anxious to strengthen their English alliance against Spain, promptly sacrificed principle and self-respect." Goodwin to me seems a bit too in favour of Brewster here, but feel free to agree with him if you want to. I'm only here to tell you what happened, not what to think. The mood was also dampened when another group of 130 separatists who were sailing to America from Amsterdam died in a storm. Not the best of omens.

The Pilgrims managed to secure a ship, the Speedwell, which was only small at 60 tonnes. This would take them from Leyden to Southampton where they had managed to secure a larger 180 tonne ship to carry most of the passengers, the Mayflower.

The Voyage of the Mayflower

Most of the settlers were unable to organise their affairs in time to make the journey, and they only had two ships. There was no way they would all be able to travel. A small group was to make the initial journey, led by Brewster, while the large majority would stay behind to be led by a bitterly disappointed Robinson. Families were divided, in many cases never to see each other again, despite the pledge that they would make the journey as soon as they could.

There was almost a last-minute hiccup when Weston decided that he wanted to wait until a New England Company could be chartered, but there were too many cogs in motion for the expedition to be halted. So, on July 22nd 1620, the Separatists left the Netherlands and set sail for Southampton.

They were joined by some more religious dissidents, but mostly they met the crew and others gathered by the merchants. Indentured servants and craftsmen the merchants thought would be useful to the colony. I'm sure you'll be interested to hear that our old friend John Smith offered to join the Pilgrims on their expedition, but they boldly refused. Considering that for all Smith's brilliance he left the new world almost dead after his colleagues tried to assassinate him, I don't entirely blame them for not wanting him along. This is the important thing to remember about founders of New England. Of the 102 passengers (plus crew) to travel, only 35 were confirmably separatists. I find that really startling. When you think about the voyage of the Mayflower, it is the Puritans that come to mind. In reality, only a third of those making the trip were of such persuasion.

They set off for America in August, but they very quickly met with problems. Because of the recent shipwreck the other month which had killed the other bunch of travelling separatists, they were really nervous. The Speedwell wasn't the strongest of ships and it began to spring leaks which terrified the separatists. Twice they forced the convoy back to England. Eventually they decided to just abandon the Speedwell and they all crammed onto the Mayflower. On September 6th they finally began their journey to the New World.[27]

Details of the Journey

In September 1620 the Mayflower set sail from Southampton, a port city on the south coast of England, heading out to the New World. It was a cramped journey with over a hundred people on board, of which the Pilgrims were a minority. There is no surviving plan of the ship, and there are no photos, so we can only make educated guesses about what it was like. Bailyn, in his book The Barbarous Years, supposes that it was 113 feet in length, 26 feet wide, with 11-foot depth of hold. Andrews, in his The Colonial Period of America, assuming that the Mayflower was similar to other merchant ships of the era, describes it as a

---

[27] There are some minor disagreements about exactly how many people were on the Mayflower, and when it set sail. I've seen reports that it was September 6th and also that it was September 16th. I can't find a consensus on the matter, but the version which says that the ship sailed on the 6th seems slightly more common, so I've gone with that Just to make you aware, in case you do some reading on the subject and it says that the Mayflower set off on the 16th rather than the 6th, to not think that I'm a bad historian and don't properly fact check. It just goes to show you, historians don't really know anything.

"staunch, chunky, slow-sailing vessel, square-rigged, double-decked, broad abeam, with high upper structure at the stern, the passengers occupying cabins or quarters between decks, or, in the case of the women and children, in rough cabins forward below the poop".

They also learned from the mistakes of Jamestown, they were going to be prepared for this. Furniture, pots, pans, livestock and two dogs would all be taken

The men gathered by the company for the expedition did not get on with the Pilgrims, finding their excessive piety ridiculous. The Pilgrims weren't too fond of these strangers either. Bradford writes some pretty scathing indictments. He was not very fond of the Billingtons, whom he describes as 'One of the profanest families'. One of the children, Francis Billington, aged 8, almost blew up the Mayflower when he shot a gun at a barrel of gunpowder. One Stephen Hopkins, who had been to America before and was of great help to the expedition, was continuously in trouble with the authorities, and two of his servants got on so poorly that they ended up fighting a duel on the ship, but they were both tied up before they could kill each other. It's not what you think of when you think of the Pilgrims and the Mayflower, is it?

It was not all trouble though. There was of course Bradford, aged 30, and Brewster aged 53. There was Brewster's assistant, Edward Winslow, aged 25, a very bright and competent young man. The final of the most important men who we need to introduce was John Carver, a deacon related to John Robinson by marriage who was instrumental in the founding of the colony, and who had been elected the first governor of the colony.

It was a stressful journey, and one that lasted two months, but it was quite healthy. The Mayflower was something known as a 'sweet' ship. This meant that it had been used in the wine trade rather than transporting livestock, so the hold was not befouled by the diseases which they would leave behind. Over the course of the journey, only 5 people died. So, that was the journey, and they reached land on November 11th 1620. It was the Northern most tip of Cape Cod, the site of the modern Provincetown in Massachusetts. Cape Cod juts straight out of the Eastern coast of Massachusetts before turning north to create a U shaped bay, and it was the tip of this extremity that was first sighted by the Pilgrims. It was unsuitable for founding a settlement, but they were able to take on fresh water.[28]

The Mayflower Compact

Bradford describes the situation following their arrival: "And for the season it was winter, and they that know the winters of that country know them to be sharp and violent, and subject to cruel and fierce storms, dangerous to travel to known places, much more to search an unknown coast. Besides, what could they see but a hideous and desolate wilderness, full of wild beasts and wild men – and what multitudes there might be of them they knew not. Neither could they, as it were, go up to the top

---

[28] This is just basic common sense. Any Civilisation player will tell you that you don't just found your capital on your starting space without checking out the surrounding area. It's as basic a mistake as having Ghandi as an ally.

of Pisgah, to view from this wilderness a more goodly country to feed their hopes; for which way soever they turned their eyes (save upward to the heavens) they could have little solace or content to respect of any outward objects. For summer being done, all things stand upon them with a weather-beaten face; and the whole country, full of woods and thickets, represented a wild and savage hew. If they looked behind them, there was the mighty ocean which they had passed, and was now as a main bar and gulf to separate them from all the civil parts of the world."

This was not the original plan; it must be remembered. They had intended to sail for Virginia, but for unknown reasons they changed route mid voyage and wound up here. In fighting quickly broke-out with the crew ordering the Pilgrims to go find a suitable spot to build a settlement or else they would leave them their stranded, while the indentured servants, who were not legally bound to anything since they were not in Virginia, threatened to leave as soon as they landed. The Pilgrim leaders drew up a document, now known as the Mayflower Compact. It wasn't a constitution, but a simple promise to obey the laws of the colony. 41 men signed it, a mixture of Pilgrims and servants. It was not a guarantee of harmony and it did not bring permanent peace to the colony, but for the moment it was enough. It is not a long document, if you'll allow me to go through it:

"In the name of God, Amen! We whose names are under-writen, the loyal subjects of our dread sovereign Lord, King James, by the grace of god, of Great Britain, France, & Ireland king, defender of the faith, &c, having undertaken, for the glory of

148

God and advancement of the Christian faith, and honour of our king and country, a voyage to plant the first colony in the northern parts of Virginia, do by these presents solemnly and mutually in the presence of God, and one of another, covenant and combine our selves together into a civil body politic, for our better ordering and preservation and furtherance of the ends aforesaid; and by virtue hearof of enact, constitute, and frame such just and equal laws, ordinances, acts, constitutions and offices, from time to time, as shall be thought most meet and convenient for the general good of the colony, unto which we promise all due submission and obedience.

In witness whereof we have hereunder subscribed our names at Cape Cod the 11th of November in the year of the reign of our sovereign lord, King James, of England, France, & Ireland the eighteenth, and of Scotland the fifty-fourth. Anno Domini 1620."

Rather than commenting upon this myself, I'll let the sixth president of the United States, John Quincy Adams, have his word: "This is perhaps the only instance in human history of that positive, original social compact which speculative philosophers have imagined as the only legitimate source of government. Here was a unanimous and personal assent by all the individuals of the community to the association, by which they became a nation.... The settlers of all the former European colonies had contented themselves with the powers conferred upon them by their respective charters, without looking beyond the seal of the royal parchment for the measure of their rights and the rule of their duties. The founders of Plymouth had been impelled by the peculiarities of the situation to examine the subject with deeper and more comprehensive research."

This may seem like hyperbole from Adams, and it does look like that in a modern context. There is nothing particularly unique to modern ears, but it had to be remembered that this was written in the context of autocratic Stuart England. While the Mayflower Compact didn't immediately change the world, it did keep the little company together when it looked like everything was going to fall apart, and, it is symbolic as what it is, and what Adams is referring to, is that it is the first expression of sovereignty deriving from the consent of the governed. I don't want to make too much of this.[29] It was a document which kept the men from fighting with each other, they were preparing to leave each other for dead it must be remembered, so this wasn't exactly the model of social cooperation Adams is making it out to be. It also isn't the only democratic ideal being expressed at this time. The House of Burgesses had just been set up in Virginia. But, that said, you can't really ignore the first true example of sovereignty deriving from the consent of the governed. That's pretty fundamental to the whole idea of America, but that line of thought is getting us into abstract revolutionary theory, and there'll be plenty of time for that later.

The First Months

---

[29] It's the sort of thing where, if I were American, I'd probably feel strongly sentimental about this. But I'm not American, and I don't.

While better preparations had been made than when founding Jamestown, things began to go wrong almost immediately. It began as soon as they tried going ashore. The waters around Cape Cod are quite shallow, and to get to land they had to wade through almost half a mile of freezing cold water. People started to get sick. Colds, coughs, that sort of thing. They also made communication with the natives.

These were not as hostile as the Powhatans had been in Virginia, partly to do with the fact that their numbers were extremely low following a bout of plague. They were allowed to dig up some of the supplies the Indians had buried, but there was an issue with this. It wasn't a case of just digging up some top soil. The ground was frozen a foot deep, and when they got it out they had to take it back to the ships, which involved wading back through the half mile of freezing water. Very soon the coughs and colds got worse, they started to get scurvy, and then in December the deaths began. 6 in the first month, then 8 in January. In February the illnesses started spreading and 17 died, 13 more in March, including Governor Carver. And those are just the named deaths, there were others. Bradford writes that over the course of three months half the settlers died. They went from a hundred to around 50. The only slightly redeeming feature was that, while things were bad, they were not as bad as Jamestown had been.

But, life carried on for the people who didn't die. They continued looking for a settlement, and in the middle of a snowstorm on December 11th Bradford led an expedition stumbling into Plymouth harbour, a small bay on the western side of Cape Cod Bay, opposite the landing site at Provincetown. The Mayflower sailed into the bay on December 16th, and it was decided that this would be their new home. According to legend, the first step off the ships onto land was onto a bolder which was named Plymouth Rock.[30]

---

[30] This is almost certainly nonsense. References to the rock don't appear until the eighteenth century when it was discovered, except it was too far up the beach so it was moved to the water's edge to make the site more pleasing for visitors. It's nice to know that tourist traps are an age old tradition.

Chapter 8 - Plymouth

Plymouth was picked as the site for the colony, and construction of the first house was begun on December 25th 1620 (not that the Pilgrims attached any significance to the day, To do so would to be popish).[31] To borrow a line from The Penguin

---

[31] At least goes one version of events. As I aforementioned, the specifics of all this are very much a matter of debate, and so don't be too surprised if you see slightly different dates when reading about the founding of the Plymouth Colony. The dates are seldom more than a week different though, so we can be confident of the broad strokes of what happened. However, I want to explain this date thing in a bit more detail because unless I do the problem won't make any sense to the casual observer of history, who assumes that historians work in a strict linear time progression of cause to effect. But from a non-linear, non-subjective viewpoint, to the historian it's more like trying to untangle a big ball of wibbly wobbly time-y wimey stuff. The issue is all to do with leap days in the Calendar. To explain it we need to go back to the Roman Civil Wars of the first century BC. Different societies struggle to keep the solar and lunar calendars in line, but do so in different ways. A lunar calendar, which is the basis for our months, does not fit into a solar calendar of 365 days, so, how to keep the months in line with the years. Well, this was done in Ancient Rome by the insertion of days, but during the civil wars this was forgotten about and the calendar became all confused, so Julius Caesar decided to bring it to order. He created a regular calendar of 365 days with a leap day inserted every 3 years, although his maths was a little off and it was fixed shortly after to every four years. This creates the Julian calendar we all know and love, aside from the small problem that it doesn't work.

You see, leap years exist because a solar year isn't exactly

History of the USA, "Jamestown had acquired a sister." That is the simple version. However, reality was quite a bit different.

New England has one of the more complicated histories out there, as things go. Virginia was nice and easy. The Virginia company was set up, it founded a colony called Virginia. The colony of Virginia later became a state, also called Virginia. Nice. Simple. Now, things are a bit different with New England. The first thing you'll notice is that there is no state called New England, and there is no state called Plymouth. Why?

In 1620, we have Plymouth Colony, which existed in a state of semi-independence. The Pilgrims, you'll recall, were supposed to settle in Virginia. They did

---

365 days. In school you are taught that a year is 365.25 days, which is why we insert an extra day in every four years to keep the system intact. But, that isn't true. A year is not 365.25 days. It is 365.24. This means that if you insert a leap day every 4 years you are going to insert an extra day every century, sort of. The calendar we current work from, the Gregorian Calendar, has a leap year in all years divisible by 4, unless the year is divisible by 100. The exception to this is if the year is also divisible by 400. This means that 2000 is a leap year, but 2100 is not, 2200 is not, 2300 is not, but 2400 is. So, every four hundred years the calendar would be an extra 3 days behind because there had been 3 too many February 29ths. So, while in the Julian calendar the Pilgrims set off from Southampton on September 6th and began construction of Plymouth on December 25th, on the Gregorian these dates would be September 16th and January 4th respectively. I'm looking forward to the point when the UK adopts the Gregorian reform in 1752, then we end this madness! But, for the moment, we'll just have to work with it.

not have a charter to settle where they did, and Plymouth Colony would be on shaky legal footing until its absorption into the Province of Massachusetts Bay along with the Massachusetts Bay Colony and the Province of Maine in 1692. The Canadian Colonies of Nova Scotia and New Brunswick were also briefly part of the Province of Massachusetts Bay, although that is just even more confusing and we really don't need to talk about that now. So, Plymouth was on shaky legal footing. If not the Pilgrims, who then had the right to found a colony there? Well, that right belonged to the Council for New England.

The Council For New England

What on earth is the Council for New England, I hear you ask. Well, it was a colonial joint stock venture set up in 1620 largely dominated by Sir Ferdinando Gorges. Gorges will play a reoccurring role in our story, most notably in the foundation of Maine, so it's worth briefly introducing him. He was born around 1566, probably in Somerset in England, and would spend the first half of his life in the military. He had a very colourful career, which involved him being knighted in 1591. In the early years of the seventeenth century he developed what proved to be a lifelong infatuation with setting up a colony in the New World. He would finally make progress in 1620 by gaining the charter for the Council of New England, which had the right to all lands between forty and forty-eight degrees north, and a monopoly of trade and fishing in that region.

Considering the Plymouth Colony set itself up on his land, it's ironic that the colony they were setting up was about as far away as possible for what Gorges wanted. Gorges wanted to set up New England on aristocratic, Anglican lines. He, and his other principal aristocratic investors, did not plan on emigrating to New England themselves, or doing anything as base as setting up the colonies themselves. They would distribute the land as a series of manors and fiefs, just like England. There were a few problems with why this wouldn't work.

The first is an observation of my own, namely that attempts to force the structure of the old world on the new rarely went well. The key to success was adaptability. Such an archaic adventure was almost doomed to failure, even if it had been run competently. But, as you often find when aristocrats simply decide to do things, it tends to be a confused mess. Hesketh Racing, I'm looking at you. This was the case with the Council for New England. The land was not properly surveyed, and so the same bits were handed out multiple times. This would lead to a lot of squabbling between the various claimants and colonies, which would contribute to the confusion of who owns what. Plus, there was already an extant colony on the land with a sort of legal claim to it, Plymouth, and the Council was in no position to do anything about that. You won't be surprised to learn that the Council was dissolved shortly hereafter and its Charter given to the Massachusetts Bay Company which would colonise the land directly, removing the confusing middle man nature of the Council for New England.

Founding of Plymouth

The Pilgrims had settled at Plymouth. It was a rather good site. They began to explore the area and found a good verily of trees, including cherry, plum, grape vines and even sassafras. There were plenty of Strawberry plants, watercress, leeks, onions, flax and hemp, and there was also easily accessible clay. As you can imagine from the name of Cape Cod, fish were also plentiful. Cod, obviously, but also herring, and something they called turbot, but which was more likely some sort of flounder or halibut. There was an abundance of sea food, mussels, clams, crabs, and lobsters.

Food wouldn't be too hard to get hold of, but drinks were more of a problem. Water was not great. Tea, coffee, and cocoa were not yet available, and the Pilgrims didn't have access to other drinks such as cider. Their choices were water, or beer. When the beer was cut off shortly after Christmas it is described as an incredible hardship. There was a storm which followed, interrupting things, but on December 28th they got back to work on the construction of the settlement and a plan began to take shape.

There were to be 19 families. Several of these were already extant, but the remainder were created by assigning the single men as would be most convenient. Each family would have a house on a plot which was 3 rods long and half a rod broad for each person in it. The location of each of these houses was determined by lot. The village would be built with houses either side of a street which ran from the shore to a hill on which a fort would be constructed. This street, interestingly, still exists in Plymouth today. Originally known as just The Street, it would go through several names, First Street, Great Street, Broad Street, until in 1823 it received the name of Leyden Street, which it has retained.

We're able to work out what the street almost certainly looked like.

There were more rain delays while they got on with working, then, on January 2nd 1621, they noticed some fires while collecting dry swamp-grass to thatch their roofs. So, the next day, one of the men, Standish, went into the wilderness with 5 others, hoping to establish contact with the natives. They found Wigwams, but no people. January carried on, and they continued to work on building their town and exploring the area. One of the Billingtons explored a small lake now known as Billington Sea, and they were quite disappointed that this wasn't connected to the Hudson.[32]

The walls of Common House, which they had been working on since Christmas, were finished on January 9th and then they began work on thatching the roof. This was a traditional English construction technique, particularly in the east of England, which is where the Separatists had originally come from all those years ago. It's quite simple. A long grass or reed is used; swamp-grass in this particular case. These are waterproof, and 5 or 6 bundles are placed on top of each other until they were about a foot thick, held in place by a mortar. It is warm in the

---

[32] It's strange to think of the thought processes going on here, since, well, we know the geography of the region inside out, but these first explorers really had no idea what they were looking for. Remember how in Virginia the settlers kept looking for the sea route to China? A similar thing was going on here. It was thought that this body of water was connected to the Hudson River, and if they could find this then they could prove that New England was an island.

winter, and cool in the summer, and can be made very easily from local materials.[33]

The first common house was finished, meaning that the workers finally had a sheltered place to sleep on land. The entirety of the common house was filled with beds for twenty men. They could now begin working on individual houses for the families.

The First Mouths

The January of 1621 was a cold and wet month, and working was difficult. There was an issue where two men got lost, and the rest of the Pilgrims thought that they had been captured and so they returned to the ship for safety. The next morning, on the 14th, they found that the thatch on the roof of the common house caught fire and was severely damaged, although the walls and structure of the house were saved. The next day must have been depressing. The sky turned black like a perfect storm, rain came pouring down, and they stood there in their one roofless house. I wonder whether they got drunk on jealousy thinking about their families back in Leyden. There must have been some points when they wished they hadn't bothered. That's not how it comes across in the material though. They stayed focused on their

---

[33] Indeed, it would be the most common roofing material in England until into the nineteenth century. The only thing that would displace thatch would be the commercial production of Welsh slate which began in earnest in the 1820s, and the increased ease of transportation following the industrial revolution. The invention of combine harvester also led to the development of shorter stemmed wheat which was less useful for thatch.

work. They had some mild days in the next week and they were able to repair most of the damage, enough that on the 21st they were able to have an uninterrupted church service for the first time.

January turned into February, and the little group began work on construction of the individual houses. This was the bad time discussed above as the deaths mounted up. The Pilgrims were lucky to have with them a surgeon named Fuller who seems to have been unusually competent for the time, but they lacked medicine and about four a week died.

The other development was that they kept seeing natives, but aside from the initial engagement they weren't able to make contact. This concerned the Pilgrims, and their thoughts began to turn towards their own defence. It's quite surprising that it took this long when you think about it. For the Virginian settlers, setting up Jamestown's defence was one of their first priorities. You'll recall the almost immediate construction of the triangular shaped fortification with a cannon at each corner. The Pilgrims moved their cannon on to land on February 21st, almost four months after they arrived in the New World.

February was probably the hardest month for the Pilgrims. The sickness which was plaguing them was at its worst. At one point, only seven of the colonists were able-bodied. But, as they entered March 1621, there were signs of spring in the air and the pestilence began to dissipate. On the 7th they began planting some garden seeds, although we don't know exactly this means. Goodwin notes that pumpkin, bean and squash were all indigenous to the surrounding hills, and that the potato wouldn't be grown in Plymouth until the 1700s. If I'm understanding his footnotes correctly (Goodwin is fond of long footnotes), he seems to imply that it was probably carrots and turnips that the Pilgrims planted, but don't quote me on that.

Samoset

On Friday March 16th an event of note took place. Out of the woods they saw another group of Native Americans standing on a nearby hill. The Pilgrims were jumpy, expecting an attack, when they were completely caught off guard. One of them walked down the hill, and entered Plymouth walking along First Street. And then he spoke. "Welcome!" He wanted to enter the common house, but the Pilgrims wouldn't allow this in case the man was a spy, but he began to speak to the amazed colonists in broken but understandable English, and he told them about himself. His name was Samoset, and he was a sachem of Monhegan, an island about twelve miles off the Maine coast. And with this we can finally introduce the native Americans of the region.

We know less about this confederacy than we do of the Powhatans, but the tribe we are dealing with here is the Abenaki, one of five tribes which made up the Wabanaki Confederacy. The Wabanaki lived primarily in the area of Maine, Nova Scotia and New Brunswick, but also controlled some of Quebec going down the St. Lawrence River, and New England. Like the Powhatans, they were also of the Algonquian-speaking tribes. The sachem was something which translates as the Great Chief, and so Samoset was quite an important figure. Think of him as an equivalent of Wahunsonacock. Samoset had been dealing with English fishermen for years and so had picked up the language, and was quite familiar with them.

They grew crops, but also hunted the local game. Smoking was common. They were polytheistic, and the Puritans found them highly superstitious. The had priests, powahs, and the most important of their gods was Kiehtan, the creator god, although Abamacho, an evil spirit, was worshiped for his healing abilities. They were warlike, the Europeans seem to have believed that they would have killed themselves through infighting even if they had never arrived in the Americas. In addition to the Abenakis in Maine, other neighbouring tribes and confederacies were the Nipmucks, the Mohawks, the Pequods, the Narragansets, the Pawtuckets, the Tarrantines, the Pokanokets, and the Massachusetts, who gave their name to the region. It is hard to estimate numbers, partly because our sources were not ones for precision. After the plague 40,000 wouldn't be an unreasonable figure, though we have no idea concerning pre-plague numbers.

Of this first meeting Goodwin writes: "Samoset was entirely naked, except for a leathern girdle, which, with its fringe, was about a foot wide; he had straight black hair, short in front and long behind, with no beard. His only weapons were a bow and two arrows, of which one had no head. He was quite talkative, and of good presence. The wind arising, a horseman's cloak was put around him, and upon his asking for beer, he was taken to dinner; and here we get a glimpse of the Pilgrim larder at that time. In the lack of beer, Samoset was given some strong water, followed by biscuit, with butter and cheese, pudding, and mallard. All of these he liked well, and had been accustomed to them on English ships. After dinner he resumed his conversation."

Samoset provided the settlers with a great deal of much needed information. For instance, why they hadn't seen any natives. The Algonquian name for Plymouth was Patuxet, and the place had been abandoned four years previously due to a plague which had decimated the population. Estimates are that 95% of the population died. No one had since claimed the area, which is why it was empty. He told them of their neighbours, to the west was another sachem, Massasoit, who had about 60 warriors at his disposal. Massasoit would visit a few days later, and a treaty was established, Bradford preserves the terms of it.

"1. That neither he nor any of his, should injure or do hurt to any of their people.
2. That if any of his did any hurt to any of theirs, he should send the offender, that they might punish him.
3. That if any thing were taken away from any of theirs, he should cause it to be restored; and they should do the like to his.
4. If any did unjustly war against him, they would aid him; and if any did war against them, he should aid them.
5. He should send to his neighbours confederates, to certify them of this, that they might not wrong them, but might be likewise comprised in the conditions of peace.
6. That when their men came to them, they should leave their bows and arrows behind them."

This peace treaty would remain intact for over 50 years. It is also a mark of their quasi-independence that this little colony made a treaty. But, to return to Samoset, he told them about the tribe to the east, the Nausets. It was by this point getting late and the Pilgrims were not comfortable enough to let him stay in Plymouth, so they compromised and he stayed on the Mayflower. Samoset set off to visit the Wampanoags promising to bring them back beaver fur, something the English had no knowledge of at this time. He returned the next day with 5 tall Indians, hoping to entertain the English with singing and dancing. They brought with them 4 beaver skins, but it was a Sunday so the Pilgrims would not trade, therefore the skins were left with the English until next time. There were attempts to arrange a meeting over the next few days, but it kept being disrupted. On Wednesday March 21st the last of the settlers left the Mayflower, and they were now based on the mainland.

On Thursday, Samoset returned with a Patuxet man who would be invaluable to the Pilgrims, Tisquantum, although he is more commonly known as Squanto. He could speak English a lot better than Samoset. Bradford has been where almost all of my information for the colony so far has been coming from, and he has been writing an almost day by day account of what happened in the colony, and with March 25th he concludes this. This is what we've been working with, but now everything has changed. What follows are a series of narratives, a formal history, which is useful but far less valuable than his detailed journal.

As entered Spring 1621, the first thing the Pilgrims had to deal with was the Mayflower. The ship wasn't supposed to stay around in the New World this long, it had been there about 5 months by this point. The captain didn't want to still be there, but he hadn't really been able to argue. It had taken some time for a site suitable for settlement to be found, and then once that was done houses had to be constructed, and then there was an issue with the fire. By the time it was possible for the colonists to leave the ship and live in Plymouth itself the sickness was well underway, and it wasn't possible for the ship to just abandon them. They needed the refuge, and the extra help, since there was no guarantee that the Pilgrims wouldn't all fall ill. But, now it was spring. Conditions were improving, the health of the colonists and the crew returned. On April 5th the captain felt ready to leave, and the Mayflower set sail on her 31-day voyage back to England. While she would return to the New World, she would never go back to Plymouth. It must have been a sad and terrifying sight for those left behind, watching the little ship go over the horizon. That ship was their one way to communicate with the outside world, with the old world, with the only world they knew. They had no idea when they would next see a friendly face. Plus, you have to disregard hindsight in situations like these. We now know that Plymouth would be highly successful, but in 1621 there was no way to guarantee that. The only other English colony to have survived on the mainland of North America was Jamestown, and that was about to fall victim to the 1622 Powhatan Uprising. Who was to say whether or not Plymouth would be a Jamestown or a Roanoke? Certainly no one at the time knew, all they do was try and prepare for the future as best they could.

This involved planting crops. Some crops they tried planting by themselves. They had taken English wheat and peas with them, but both these failed to grow. The Pilgrims themselves weren't sure why, wondering whether they had some bad seeds, or if they had planted their crops in the wrong season. But, luckily, they weren't on their own. Squanto, a Patuxet whom Samoset brought to Plymouth, moved to the colony.

Squanto was invaluable to the Pilgrims. Maize would be the stable crop of the Pilgrim diet, and Squanto was able to teach them how grow it. He showed them an area of good land, about twenty acres, on which they would grow their crops, and told them that the correct time to plant it was when the oak leaves were as big as the ears of a mouse. This time would soon arrive, so the Pilgrims needed to begin preparing the land. The land had to be broken up with a hoe, they lacked animals for a plough. He also told them how to fertilise the land, they would have to dig holes and bury alewives, a type small fish, in them.

A Change in Leadership

Disaster struck the colony in April when their governor, John Carver, suddenly died. He had worked extremely hard, leading by example, during all stages of the colony's founding. He collapsed on a hot day and didn't recover. Bradford was elected as his replacement, even though he was ill at the time, which shows his standing within the community. He was given an assistant, Isaac Allerton, to help him while he recovered, although this became a feature of the Plymouth constitution. Essentially, these two were the government, although they consulted with the other leading men, such as Brewster. This was modified in 1624. From this date there would be a governor and 5 assistants, sometimes referred to as magistrates, forming something like an executive council in which the governor had a double vote. This strikes me instantly of the board of councillors in Jamestown, with the President who had a double vote. The difference though, between Jamestown and Plymouth, was that the executive council in Plymouth was almost completely powerless.

One of the reoccurring themes of American political culture is the dislike of a powerful executive branch. The most obvious example of this is found in the constitution. While the presidency is often considered the most powerful branch of American governors (particularly, I've noticed, by non-Americans) this is not what the founding fathers wanted. They deliberately made article one of the constitution about the legislative branch, Congress. I don't need to go into any more detail here because we'll obviously have a tonne to say about constitutional theory when we get to revolution, but it's interesting to note that this quirk was present in America from the beginning. It was the job of the governor to enforce the will of the people, and to occasionally act as a judge, but whenever he and the other magistrates did so, appeal could be made to the people. There are a couple of examples of this from 1621, but my favourite is where a duel was fought, and the Pilgrims wouldn't have any of that nonsense. The two were sentenced to be tied together by their heads and feet for twenty-four hours without food or water. The two didn't even make it an hour before they were begging for a pardon, which was duly granted. It worked, this was the last duel fought in the old colony.

As time passed, life got on with its business. On May 12th the first marriage at Plymouth took place, between Edward Winslow and Susanna White, both of whom were widowed. The Pilgrims took a Dutch-Calvinist approach to marriage, and they believed that marriage was a strictly civil affair, to be conducted before a magistrate rather than a clergyman. This may have partly been down to the fact that they didn't have a clergyman in their colony. The closest thing they had was Elder Brewster, but he had been a lay officer within the church. It is also noticeable to have widowers getting remarried in this period. Such a thing would have been scandalous in the Old World, the very height of impropriety. Yet, in such a small community, this was highly desired.

Massasoit Expedition

This brings us into summer. The newly married Winslow, along with Stephen Hopkins and Squanto, went on an expedition to visit Massasoit. The date is debated. Bradford writes that it began on July 2nd, while Winslow writes that it began a few weeks earlier on June 10th.[34]

---

[34] Since June 10th 1621 was a Sunday I find Bradford's date more believable than Winslow's, given how strict the Puritans were about the Sabbath. You'll recall one of their principle complaints about the Dutch was that while they were Calvinist and kept the Sabbath, they were too cheery about it. Therefore, it seems a bit odd that they'd send an embassy on a Sunday.

They headed into the interior, and the first place they found was the town of Namasket where several of the natives attached themselves to this little group. Bradford doesn't paint a pleasant image of the journey, writing that the countryside was filled with bones of dead Indians following the plague. About 40 miles west of Plymouth, they found the land of the Wampanoags, Massasoit's tribe. It comprised of the modern Bristol County in Rhode Island, as well as a bit of Massachusetts.

They met with Massasoit, and said that since his people often visited Plymouth, they hoped they would be allowed to visit him. They gave him a gift of a coat, and asked that the friendship between their peoples continue. They also exchanged corn, so that the settlers would be able to experiment with different types of grain. They then spent the evening talking and smoking together. Massasoit was eager to learn about the Old World, and he asked the Pilgrims to inform the French that they would not be allowed into his territory, since he was now King James' man. They stayed for a few more days, building friendly relationships, and they received a warm reception when they made their way back to Plymouth. This was the first of several expeditions to neighbouring villages as the Pilgrims became versed in the regional politics, and their place within it. They would stay allied to Massasoit, and would be hostile to tribes which opposed him. The Pilgrims quickly gained a reputation as a powerful force, their guns were very amazing to the Natives.

As the summer came to a close and autumn began, we have one last matter to address. I'm going to quote Bradford, and then explain what he's talking about.

> "They began now to gather in the small harvest they had, and to fit up their houses and dwellings against winter, being all well recovered in health and strength, and had all things in good plenty; for as some were thus imployed affairs abroad, others were excerised in fishing, about cod, and bass, and other fish, of which they took good store, of which every family had their portion. All the summer there was no want. And now began to come in store of fowl, as winter approached, of which this place did abound when they came first (but afterwards decreased by degrees). And besides water fowl, there was great store of wild Turkies, of which they took many, besides venison etc. Besides they had about a peck a week to a person, or now since harvest, Indean corn to that proportion. Which made many afterwards write so largely of their plenty here to their friends in England, which were not fained, but true reports."

What Bradford is describing here is the first thanksgiving. Plymouth now had along the street 7 houses and 4 public buildings. It was a good first crop. The peas failed, but the Indian corn was bountiful, along with the natural houses. They had spent every day working since they landed, aside from Sundays on which they worshiped. Therefore they took advantage of the plenty to have their first real celebration. They captured enough food to last for a week, and sent an invitation out to Massasoit. They had three days of feasts. The Pilgrims entertained the natives with military drills, while they entertained the Pilgrims with dancing. This is the origin of thanksgiving. Sort of. The word doesn't appear until 1623 when there was decreed a day of thanksgiving, and then it would take some time for the holiday to gain steam. It spent about 200 years as a tradition celebrated only by the east coast, but during the 19th century it spread into the gulf coast and the great lake region and became the national holiday we[35] know and love today.

New Arrivals

A couple of days after the thanksgiving feast the Nausets sent word to the Pilgrims that they had sighted a ship around Cape Cod. This put the English on edge, expecting this to be a French ship looking to attack. They readied themselves, but this wouldn't have been particularly intimidating since their military force, commanded by Standish, was around 20 men strong. The next day the ship came within sight, and then startled the colonists by putting up an English flag. It turns out that this ship was the Fortune, commanded by one Robert Cushman who had come over to investigate how things were going, and brought 35 new colonists.

---

[35] Well, Americans. And Canadians. Although Canadian Thanksgiving is celebrated in October, and according to some historians marks the failed attempt to find the North West Passage by Martin Frobisher in 1578.

This may seem like a good thing, the Pilgrims would be reunited with some of those they had been forced to leave behind in the Netherlands, but, practically speaking, it was a disaster.

After the sickness had thinned their numbers, at this juncture there were around 50 settlers. They had enough food stored up to see themselves through the winter. What they did not have was enough food for 85 people. It was very much a mixed blessing to have these extra mouths to feed. The arrival of the Fortune was the first contact the Pilgrims had had since the Mayflower had departed, and it contained communications from London, notably from Weston. Weston wasn't happy that the Mayflower had returned without a full cargo, and asked that they stock up the Fortune on its return. Bradford wrote an elegant reply, but bizarrely Weston withdrew from the enterprise before the Fortune could return. It also informed the Pilgrims of the developing legal situation, that the London Merchants had been able to gain a patent for the colony from the Council for New England.

The Fortune didn't have the best of return voyages. The Pilgrims had duly filled up the ship with a mixture of sassafras, lumber and beaver pelts with a collective value of £500, and it set off back to England after a few weeks. Once it was off the English coast it was taken by a French privateer who took the cargo, but did allow the crew to leave along with their papers.

The pressing issue for the Pilgrims was sorting out the food supply, Bradford estimated that if they went on to half rations they would be able to survive for 6 months. The winter was fortunately quite mild, so the Pilgrims were able to stay healthy and active. Bradford was very proud that by March each family had its own garden plot. There is an anecdote Bradford includes about the Christmas of 1621 which I would describe as quite interesting, so if you'll allow me to quote.

> "On the day called Christmasday, the Governor called them out to work, as was used, but the most of this new-company excuse themselves and said it went against their consciences to work on that day. So the governor told them that if they made it matter of conscience, he would spare them till they were better informed. So he led-away the rest and left them; but when they came home at noon from their work, he found them in the street at play, openly; some pitching the bar and some at stoole-ball, and such like sport. So he went to them, and took away their implements, and told them that was against his conscience, that they should play and others work. If they made the keeping of it matter of devotion, et them keep their houses, but there should be no gaming or revelling in the streets. Since which time nothing hath been attempted that way, at least openly."

The Pilgrims did not celebrate Christmas. So, that brings the narrative into 1622. There were stirrings of trouble from the Narragansets, but they were not prepared to do anything serious due to their fear of firearms. The Pilgrims made moves to defend themselves, and spent 5 weeks constructing a palisade throughout the winter, while Standish got underway training his forces, which with the new recruits was about 50 men strong which he divided into four companies. One of these had an extra function where it was trained what to do if the Indians set fire to one of the buildings.

As spring 1622 arrived they planned an expedition to Boston Bay to trade with the Massachusetts. One of the Indians living with them, Hobomok, tried to dissuade them, claiming that the Massachusetts were in league with the Narragansets. The leadership was not convinced, and believed that withdrawing from the expedition would show cowardice. Considering their small numbers, much of their negotiating position came from perceived power rather than any attack they had made. If they made a single action to highlight their actual weakness it would break the illusion. They couldn't not go. So they set off, but as soon as they left Squanto reported that the Narragansets and Massasoit were attacking, and so the expedition immediately returned. Hobomok said that the rumour was false, and an embassy was sent to Massasoit, and it was found out that he was in no way preparing an attack. There are suspicions that Squanto was trying to manipulate the situation to exaggerate his importance to both sides. Massasoit was extremely annoyed with him, causing Squanto to never leave the English again. Massasoit demanded that Squanto be handed over to him, but he was too valuable. The English came up with excuse after excuse about why they couldn't hand him over. Massasoit was so annoyed that he ceased to visit Plymouth. The journey to deal with the Massachusetts could finally get underway, some trade happened, but nothing particularly important.

They were unable to secure a supply of food, when at the end of May they saw another ship on the horizon, the Sparrow, which had been sent by Weston and had been fishing off the Maine coast. On board were a some letters, one of which informed them of the massacre that had taken place in Virginia, and then there were a series of letters from Weston, the first of which pledged his support for the colony, but then as they went on they announced that he had sold his shares in the company, and then that he was planning on launching his own colony and had seven men on this ship who would form an advanced guard for this possible rival colony, and then had no food for said men so he asked if they could look after them. He promised he would send food in future, but he didn't. The Pilgrims were not impressed. In Bradford's own words:

> "Thus all their hopes in regard of Mr. Weston were laid in the dust, and all his promised help turned into empty advice, which they apprehended was neither lawful nor profitable for them to follow. And they were not only thus left destitute of help in their extreme wants, having neither vitals, nor anything to trade with, but others prepared and ready to glean up

what the country might have afforded for their relief. As for those harsh censures and suspicions intimated in the former and following letters, they desired to judge as charitably and wisely of them as they could, weighing them in the balance of love and reason; and though they (in part) came from godly and loving friends, yet they conceived many things might arise from over deep jealousy and fear, together with unmet provocations, though they well saw Mr. Weston pursued his own ends, and was embittered in spirit."

Starving Time

As the Pilgrims entered June with seven extra mouths to feed, they ran out of food. Completely. They had no more supplies. Finding food proved difficult. The wild-fowl was out of season, as were the ground nuts. There were also difficulties with fishing. There were fish in the bay, but getting them out of the water was the problem. They didn't have nets which were strong enough to catch bass, and they didn't have bait which could be used in the deep water to catch cod. There was only one option left. Sea food. They found mussels, clams, and lobsters, which were available, although they required plenty of effort. They were very lucky in that hot summer to survive on an entirely sea-food diet, with no bread or vegetables.

The Sparrow returned to Maine shortly afterwards, and Winslow travelled with them in an attempt secure food. The Pilgrims had constructed two shallops (a type of small boat), and he took one of them. The fishermen didn't have much by way of food stores, but gave what they could spare to Winslow and wouldn't accept payment. He brought back enough bread for four ounces per day per person, which would be enough to tide them over until the harvest. When he returned he found that, while disease had not broken out, the Pilgrims were visibly weaker.

The summer was very hard. On so little food, it was a struggle to tend to the crops (60 acres being grown this year as opposed to the 20 of twelve months previously). They also worked on building a fort on the nearby hill, Fort Hill. The other event of the summer was the arrival of two more ships from Weston, the Charity and the Swan, carrying between them 60 colonists for the new settlement. Much like the Pilgrims and the men chosen by the merchants for the initial expedition did not get on, the Pilgrims and these men were at loggerheads too. The new arrivals stayed at Plymouth for about six weeks throughout the summer. They sheltered there, they took food from Plymouth and severely damaging their crops, they left their sick there, and then they departed to go found a colony in Massachusetts Bay. In return, they did nothing. They didn't allow the Pilgrims access to their food supply. What lovely guests.

These 60 then ventured north and founded Wessagusset Colony, on the site of the modern Weymouth in Massachusetts. Plymouth is now no longer alone in New England. Where there was one, now there was two.

A Tale of Two Colonies

It was the best of times, it was the worst of times, it was the age of wisdom, it was the age of foolishness, it was the epoch of belief, it was the epoch of incredulity, it was the season of Light, it was the season of Darkness, it was the spring of hope, it was the winter of despair, we had everything before us, we had nothing before us, we were all going direct to Heaven, we were all going direct the other way – in short, the period was so far like the present period, that some of its noisiest authorities insisted on its being received, for good or for evil, in the superlative degree of comparison only. There were a governor with a large jaw and an assistant with a plain face, residing in Plymouth; there were a governor with a large jaw and an assistant with a plain face, residing in Wessagusset. In both colonies it was clearer than crystal to the lords of the town preserves of loaves and fishes, that things in general were settled for ever. It was the year of Our Lord one thousand six hundred and twenty-two.

The former captain of the Mayflower returned to Plymouth in September, this time commanding the Discovery, stopping off on its way from Virginia. He drove a hard bargain, but the Pilgrims were in a desperate position. Their own harvest was very small, damaged by the Wessagusset colonists and starving Pilgrims. Jones had spare supplies and items for trade with the Indians which he was more than happy to part with... for double its value. He would also be very happy to buy up their beaver skins, for a fifth or a sixth of what they were worth.

In October, a ship arrived from England and Weston, with a winter's worth of supplies for Wessagusset. Wessagusset was led by one Mr. Richard Greene, the brother-in-law of Weston, with John Sanders as the second in command. While the government of Plymouth was quite stable, it wasn't at Wessagusset. The grain supply was wasted, and there was immediately a panic over a foreseeable famine in their near future.

Greene proposed that there be a joint expedition to the south side of Cape Cod to trade with the goods Plymouth had recently acquired. This was agreed. Standish would command, and Squanto would be the guide. Greene travelled to Plymouth, but while there he died of a fever. There was a ceremonial burial, as befitting the leader of their sister colony, and then they set off. Twice storms pushed them back, and then a third time Standish fell ill, but finally, on the fourth attempt, Bradford and Squanto set off to sail around Cape Cod. It was quite successful, and the Pilgrims managed to secure some food. Eight hogsheads of corn and beans.[36]

---

[36] I should clarify that a hogshead isn't a literal hogshead, but rather a type of barrel. Funnily enough Goodwin describes a hogshead as being able to carry 191 beaver-skins. As though this is a unit of measurement that the reader will be intimately familiar with. I don't know about you, but when either I or my friends are buying a car I always ask the dealer how many beaver-skins I can fit in it. How big a hogshead is varied, with different measurements in place depending on what it was carrying, but a full hogshead could fit something in the region of 60 gallons, around 230 litres, or in terms of weight around a thousand pounds or 450 kilograms.

When they were preparing to continue their journey, they met with trouble as Squanto caught a fever, and died. It was a huge loss. Bradford personally looked after him as his health faded, and he asked Bradford if he could pray that he go to the Englishman's God in Heaven. Faced with this disaster, they decided not to continue to sail southwards, but instead sailed back to Boston harbour. There they bought 10 hogsheads worth of food, although the Pilgrims had trouble with bringing it home, so this was stored and brought back to Plymouth at a later date.

Bradford was curious about the country, and so he decided to walk home rather than sail. He travelled around visiting the other neighbours, stopping off to see Massasoit. This brought to an end 1622. Things were not looking promising. There was a growing uneasiness amongst the Native American tribes of the region, and they hadn't secured anything like enough food. Partly due to the activities of the Wessagusset colonists, the value of the goods they were able to trade had diminished to a quarter of what it once was.

The Pilgrims made their way through the winter, struggling, and collecting the corn that Bradford had been able to purchase towards the end of the previous year. It was difficult, since Standish, who recovered from his illness, was met with numerous attempts on his life.

As they entered spring, word came that a Dutch ship was in the region, and the Pilgrims were very excited about this. The Dutch and the English were on very friendly terms. The ship happened to be stranded with Massasoit, which represented the perfect opportunity for the English to visit. They had, after all, been on rocky ground with Massasoit ever since the Pilgrims refused to hand over Squanto, but Squanto was now dead. It was an Indian tradition to visit a person of power when they were ill, so the Pilgrims decided to try and repair the relationship between themselves and Massasoit, and to make contact with the Dutch at the same time.

Winslow's Expedition

Winslow would head the expedition as he had visited Massasoit before, and he was familiar with the Dutch language. He was joined by a man described as 'a gentlemen of London' who was visiting the country, one Master John Hampden. We have no way of knowing for sure, but some historians suspect that this John Hampden is *the* John Hampden, esteemed parliamentarian and frequent source of trouble for King Charles until his death in 1643. It would not be difficult to imagine that this is the sort of thing Hampden would do, and it would be odd to allow someone who was just visiting the colony on such an important embassy unless he were someone of importance, and it is impossible to prove that he was elsewhere at this period of time. The matter will never be resolved, but it's certainly an interesting theory.

They very soon met with difficulties. Once they arrived in Indian territory, they found out that the Dutch ship had sailed away and that Massasoit had died. Hobomok was very uneasy with this turn of events and encouraged Winslow and Hampden to leave because he could not be sure that they would be safe. Winslow didn't agree though. The man most likely to succeed Massasoit was a chief named Corbitant, who ruled the Pocassets. Winslow wanted to make contact to establish a friendly relationship with him. It was uncertain what sort of reception they would receive; they had previously had conflict with Corbitant before. The other two were hesitant, but eventually they relented and went along with Winslow's plan.

They travelled to his home at Mattapuyst, but found that he was not there. He had gone to see Massasoit. They were instead warmly received by his wife, and a messenger was sent to go find Corbitant. When the messenger returned he said that while the Dutch had left, Massasoit was very much alive, but would certainly be dead by the time they reached him. They raced there, a found him still alive.

His sick bed was crowded. If you're dying, suddenly everybody loves you. He was told he had visitors, and he raised his hands into the air, grasping to see if he could find someone for he had gone blind, and breathed, 'Keen Winsnow? Keen Winsnow?' Translated, 'Are you Winslow? Are you Winslow?'.[37] Winslow replied 'Ahhe!' 'Yes'. 'Matta neen wonckanet namen, Winsnow!' 'I shall never see again, Winslow!' Winslow had to resort to a translator, Hobomok, who passed on sympathy from Bradford, and said that he had brought with him some confection. He placed it on the tip of his knife, and fed it to Massasoit. The confection dissolved in his mouth, and he was able to swallow it. The spectators were astounded; it was the first

---

[37] They had some trouble pronouncing certain European sounds, the l, n, and r sounds in particular.

food he had swallowed in two days. Winslow proceeded to clean his mouth, which is described as 'furred', and he scraped some foul matter off his tongue. Indeed, we can live with dignity, but we can't die with it. Winslow gave Massasoit some much needed water with more confection dissolved in it. Within half an hour he began to noticeably improve, and not long after that his vision returned. Winslow continued to tend for him while sending a messenger to Plymouth asking for advice from Dr. Fuller, as well as some chickens for a broth.

Massasoit's appetite soon returned, he ate some broth, and fell into a sleep. When he awoke he asked Winslow to tend to the sick in his village. It was not only a nice thing for Winslow to do from a moral point of view, but it also gave him some political goodwill to work with.

I am able to write in great detail about this particular incident since we have Winslow's own account of it. I've been summarising, but there really is nothing quite like the primary sources, so I want to include some of the account. The next bit is pretty good, so in Winslow's own words:

> "After dinner he desired me to get him a goose or duck, and make him some pottage therewith, with as much speed as I could. So I took a man with me, and made a shot at a couple of ducks, some sixscore paces off, and killed one, at which he wondered. So we returned forthwith and dressed it, making more broth therewith, which he much desired. Never did I see a

man so low brought, recover in that measure in so short a time. The fowl being extraordinary fat, I told Hobbamock I must take off the top thereof, saying it would make him very sick again if he did eat it. This he acquainted Massassowat therewith, who would not be persuaded to it, though I pressed it very much, showing the strength thereof, and the weakness of his stomach, which could not possibly bear it. Notwithstanding, he made a gross meal of it, and ate as much as would well have satisfied a man in health. About an hour after he began to be very sick, and straining very much, cast up the broth again; and in overstraining himself, began to bleed at the nose, and so continued the space of four hours. Then they all wished he had been ruled, concluding now he would die, which we much feared also. They asked me what I thought of him. I answered, his case was desperate, yet it might be it would save his life; for if it ceased in time, he would forthwith sleep and take rest, which was the principal thing he wanted. Not long after, his blood stayed, and he slept at least six or eight hours. When he awaked, I washed his face, and bathed and suppled his beard and nose with a linen cloth. But on a sudden he chopped his nose in the water, and drew up some therein, and sent it forth again with such violence, as he began to bleed afresh. Then they thought there was no hope; but we perceived it was but the tenderness of his nostril, and therefore told them I thought it would stay presently, as indeed it did."

While 17th century writing can be difficult to understand at time, there is something very poetic about saying that he cast up the broth. Anyway, at this point the messengers returned with the chickens, having made a hundred-mile round trip in 24 hours, but since Massasoit had mostly recovered the chickens were kept for breeding. Many had come to visit Massasoit during his illness, but the English had truly won his respect. He saw them now as true friends. The three of them, Winslow, Hampden, and Hobomok, were treated with every honour, and then were sent on their way. There was one more thing. Hobomok was taken aside before he left by Massasoit and he passed on a secret message to be given to Winslow on the journey back, and then to Bradford once he made it back to Plymouth. There was a conspiracy in the works.

Wessagusset Conspiracy

While they had gotten on just find with the settlers at Plymouth, the Wessagusset colony was a completely different matter. They had not gotten on well with the Indians, and so the Indian tribes had decided to terminate them. The Massachusetts were the instigators, and by this point it involved the Nausets, the Paomets, the Succonessets, the

Neponsets, the Mattakees, the Manomets, the Agawaywams, and those from the isle of Capawak, today known as Martha's Vineyard. The initial plan had just been to attack Wessagusset, but it was realised that this would provoke a reaction at Plymouth. So, while none of them had anything against Plymouth, soon the Pilgrims would have a problem with them, so they needed to kill the Pilgrims first. The tribes tried to recruit Massasoit to the conspiracy while he ill, but he would have none of it. It is an insight into Native American political systems that while Massasoit was their king, he was unable to stop his subjects from doing this. Massasoit should not be considered an absolute monarch for the region. He still cared for his people, they were his people, but he couldn't support them in this, which is why he had to warn the Pilgrims.

As a historian I'm trained to not believe anything. Everybody lies. But, some people are more deceitful than others. So, while they are richly detailed, the histories of the Pilgrims are remarkably unsatisfying. When you want to know the truth about someone, that someone is probably the last person you ask. Everything we know about the Pilgrims was written by the Pilgrims, therefore it shouldn't be remotely surprising that they always appear so faultless in the narrative. This is, though, conjecture. I can speculate, but I can't prove anything, and you should know that. Humility is an important quality. Especially if you're wrong a lot. Of course, when you're right, self-doubt doesn't help anybody.

So, Massasoit gave advice to the Pilgrims. He told them to be active. He heard that the Pilgrims would not attack unless they were themselves attacked, but they couldn't do that. Not this time. They needed to take the initiative. If they waited, the first sign of attack would be the complete destruction of Wessagusset, and then they would be at a huge disadvantage for mounting their own defence. So, what had the Wessagusset colonists done exactly that had provoked such a reaction? You might say if nobody hates you, you're doing something wrong, but wiping out the English is taking matters to extremes. Let's diagnose this.

When we last left Wessagusset, they had received a winter's worth of supplies from Weston who had sent the Pilgrims nothing. They managed to use it all up by the middle of March. Even their seed-corn. They began stealing corn from the Indians, and they were punished for this. But, the practice became more common. Once they stopped selling corn to Wessagusset, stealing their corn practically became policy. Plymouth disproved, saying that the Indians were not selling corn because they didn't have enough to spare, not out of some malice. It was expected at that time that a governor would be sent over from England to take command of the region, and Plymouth warned John Sanders, the leader of Wessagusset, that such actions would be punished. Sanders is depicted as a good person, even though he was unable to control his colony.

A settlement had been constructed with a palisade, but most of them had abandoned it and moved into the forest to scavenge for food. They had sold their clothes to the Indians, so they were wondering around the New England woods half-naked with no food. The sources also report that the natives took advantage where they could. This was the situation when Bradford got word of the plot.

On March 23rd 1623, there was a town meeting and it was time for the annual elections. Bradford explained the situation to citizens of Plymouth. They, and the neighbouring colony of Wessagusset, were in grave danger. There was a vast conspiracy of the Native American tribes in the region to destroy them, and Bradford made the case that if they wanted to survive then they would need to make the first move. The Pilgrims were not comfortable at all with this suggestion. The Indians had been hospitable to them, and they did not want to attack unless they were assaulted first. But, they valued Massasoit's opinion. He warned them that the first news they would hear of aggression would be the destruction of Wessagusset, so they would need to move before that happened. The plan of action was endorsed, and Bradford had his authority to make war.

This is, at least, how the Pilgrims tell the story. I'm sceptical. The Pilgrims insist on their jovial relationship with the Indians, and that the attack was entirely down to the behaviour of Wessagusset, but this really doesn't make sense. There have been skirmishes and fights between the Pilgrims and the Indians from as soon as they landed. The threat of attack has always been there, so I'm not satisfied with the explanation that this was a sudden break. Something must have been going on. Likewise, if it was just Wessagusset that was the problem and the Massachusetts really didn't want to attack or provoke Plymouth, you get the feeling they could have allowed the Wessagusset colonists to starve to death. At this point they had mostly abandoned their own settlement, and were half-starved, half-naked, hiding in the woods. It doesn't seem like a threat to require a grand conspiracy. It all doesn't quite add up.

Anyway, Standish, the Pilgrims' go to military man, was selected to handle the matter. Firstly, Wessagusset needed to be warned. Standish would travel to Wessagusset under the guise of the trading mission, warn the colonists, and then punish the conspirators. He didn't want to give the Indians any reason to suspect he knew what was going on, so in addition to this being a trade mission he only travelled with 8 men. It was a gamble, but a necessary one.

Standish set sail on March 25th. When he arrived at Wessagusset he found a happy Sanders who told him about how friendly the Indians were being. He told them how he allowed Indians to stay with him, and trusted them so completely that he did not keep his weapons with him. Most of the population was quite dispersed. Standish ordered him to recall his men, and they were ordered to stay at Wessagusset on pain of death. They were given some of the precious Plymouth seed-corn supply as an incentive for them to remain.

In the next day or so an Indian appeared at Wessagusset supposedly to trade, but he was a spy. Based on Standish's demeanour, he suspected that the plot had been found out. This provoked resistance. Those Indians present threatened Standish, wielding knives. Standish wasn't provoked, wanting to get all the conspirators together before doing anything. He soon realised that this was impractical, and he gathered those present in a room with his own men, a fight broke out and most were killed.

That same day, there is a report from one of the English who was living with the Indians. They received a messenger, and all grew sad and then left. This unnerved one of them, who hastily returned to Wessagusset, probably saving his life.

The next day, Standish's fourth in Wessagusset, a skirmish broke out with a nearby tribe, although the Native Americans hastily withdrew and there were no deaths. Following this, a youth who had been friendly with the English came over, and divulged some details about the plot. The Wessagusset colonists had been constructing 3 boats for the Indians, and the plan had been to commence the massacre as soon as they were finished. Had Standish arrived 3 days later, he would have been too late.

Standish encouraged the Wessagusset colonists to return to life as normal now that the Indians had been scared off, and the colony saved. They would no longer have to fear for their lives. But, it was not to be. The experience had not been a pleasant one, and they just wanted to escape. They took most of Standish's precious corn-seed and set off for the fishing-vessels off the Maine coast. They were going home. Wessagusset was abandoned. Plymouth was alone again, naturally. However, not everybody left. A few would join the Pilgrims at Plymouth.

Standish returned home with his men and the new additions from Wessagusset. There was a celebration at their return, at the fact that they hadn't lost a soul. The head of one of the conspirators was placed on a pike above Fort Hill, an old European tradition.[38]

While Standish was at Wessagusset, a Neponset spy had made their way into Plymouth, but they were seized and placed in Fort Hill. They were broken when they saw the Indian head, and they confessed the whole plot. This scared many of the Neponsets into staying away from the English. They withdrew into swamps, but they struggled to find food there and many died. The tribes of the cape were now subdued. They would side with the English during King Philip's War. Massasoit himself acted very conciliatory with those involve in the plot.

Soon after this the colony received a surprise visitor. Weston. He had been sailing over to visit Wessagusset, but had been shipwrecked off the Maine coast, and only made his way to Plymouth with the help of some Indians. They helped him, despite their own poverty. They loaned him some beaver skins which allowed him to fit out one of their ships and start a trade. He never repaid the loan, and threatened to expose the leaders of Plymouth for going beyond their authority in lending him the furs in the first place. Weston doesn't come across very well in this tale.

While Weston was certainly a pain, the other backers of the colony were a bit more supportive. One the London merchants, one John Peirce, finagled a way of securing the patent for himself, and planned to set himself up as a the sole-proprietor of the company. He decided to sail to the new world with the Paragon in December 1622, but was forced back by storms. He regrouped, and set

---

[38] King Philip will get the same treatment when we make it to King Philip's War, but that is quite a ways away.

off once more in February 1623, but he never made it. The Paragon was caught up in a tempest in the mid-Atlantic and the ship was horribly damaged, but it managed to make its way back to England somehow. The voyage had cost the London merchants something in the region of over £600, but because of Peirce's legal situation with the patent to the company he bore the brunt of the loss and was ruined. To cover his losses, he was forced to sell his shares and his patent to the company, but the rest of the debt wasn't received.

A New Approach

The Pilgrims, now on their own, were in serious trouble over food shortages. They realised that they needed to make this crop a good one if they were going to survive. Something radical would need to change, and indeed it did. The nature of Plymouth was fundamentally changed, and it is really hard to not see this as a sign of the America that would emerge from these early roots. Plymouth had operated on a completely communal system, but it wasn't working. Whatever anyone grew would end up in the common store, and those who produced little corn and a lot of corn received the same. There was a general discontent with this system. It was noticed that some were not showing the desired effort, since they would get the same amount of food as people who did. So, how to change it?

The common field was abolished. The land would instead be divided by household, each receiving one acre per person. Most of what was grown would be kept by individual families, but a common store would also exist, which a proportion of the food would go into. It had a radical effect. People were more invested in their own farms than they had been in the communal field, and it was not improper for women and children to work on a family farm in the way it was to the Pilgrims for them to in the communal field. A far greater area was cultivated, and things were looking very promising. But.

There is always a but. In this case, the but is draught. It began in early summer, and lasted weeks. Because of the fish fertiliser, the soil was in better condition than it might have been, but still. The younger plants became dry, and the older plants wilted. If the corn-crop failed, it would be a disaster. They would be ruined. In July they held a day of prayer during which the Pilgrims prayed, sang, chanted, and went through scripture for 9 hours. When they went home a fine rain began which continued for fourteen days. Winslow wrote: "It was hard to say whether our withered corn or drooping affections were most quickened or revived, such was the bounty and goodness of our God." A Thanksgiving service was held for this, and the event made a great impression upon Hobomok and the other Indians.

The famine lasted three or four months, during which the Pilgrims had no idea where their next meal would come from. Some of their hunters were stationed permanently in the woods looking for food. Miraculously, despite the growing weakness amongst the population, they once again remained healthy.

As we move into summer of 1623, several ships arrived in Plymouth. It's funny how quickly the

European world followed their pioneers. A few short years ago, Plymouth was the very edge of the 'civilised world', now there was regular travel across the Atlantic. In July, a ship called the Plantation arrived, bringing within it an old friend, one Francis West.[39] He was appointed admiral for the New England Coast, and was placed in charge of securing the monopoly of fishing the Council for New England held in the region. The Council held the rights to fish in the region, and then fishermen would have to pay a rather expensive licence fee in order to fish in the region.

The operation met with mixed success. Francis West was unable to do anything about the stubborn fishermen from the west of England. The size of the fishing-fleet shrank from four hundred ships down to a hundred and fifty. The matter was taken to parliament, who sided with the fishermen and passed a bill to make fishing free in the region, but the king wouldn't ascent to the decision and it did not become law.

Another ship arrived carrying food, but once it realised how desperate Plymouth was it dramatically raised the amount for some peas. The Pilgrims refused to pay, and the ship sailed for Virginia instead.

Before we move into autumn there is one more thing to cover, yet more ships. The 140 ton Anne, and the 44 ton Little James. These two ships brought with them a hundred new settlers to the

---

[39] You should remember him for the prominent position he had in the Virginia colony. He was the younger brother of Thomas West, the Baron De La Warr.

colony, greatly increasing its size. Many were from Leyden, and were friends and relatives of the earlier settlers, and they included the ones that Pierce had failed to bring over in the Paragon. We know that 97 of them stayed, for a few were so completely ill-suited to the colony that Bradford paid to return them back to England on the next ship back. We have Bradford's own description of the reunion.

> "These passengers when they saw their low and poor condition ashore, were much danted and dismayed, and according to their diverse humours were diversely affected; some wished themselves in England again; others fell a weeping, fancying their own misery in what they saw now in others; other some pitying the distress they saw their friends had long been in, and still were under; in a word, all were full of sadness. Only some of their old friends rejoiced to see them, and that it was no worse with them. For they could not expect it should be better, and now hoped they should enjoy better days together. And truly it was no marvel that they should be thus affected, for they were in a very low condition, many were ragged in apparel, and some little better than half naked; though some that were stord before, were well enough in this regard. But for food they were all alike, save some that had got a few peas off the ship that was last

195

here. The best dish they could present their friends with was a lobster, or a piece of fish, without bread or anything else but a cup of fair spring water."[40]

Plymouth and Jamestown

When we think of colonisation efforts, it's standard practice to view to think of it as countries acting, and to a certain extent it is. We have England, Spain, France, and the other European heavyweights staking claims to the New World, but this strand of imperialism is very different from the version of it which exists during the Victorian era, the height of the Second British Empire.[41] That empire will not exist for some time. What existed in the seventeenth century was not the English state colonising North America, but rather the English state giving out licences to companies which would colonise North America on the state's behalf.

At this point in history, both Jamestown and Plymouth were controlled by two different companies, each with a different set of investors back in London. They operated the colonies, they sent officials over, and they funded the operation. If

---

[40] I should clarify that while lobster is now considered a luxury food, this only developed towards the end of the nineteenth century. They were extremely common along the coast, and were considered trash food. Fit only for the lowest of the low. This is the point Bradford is trying to make. It's not a humblebrag.

[41] The First British Empire is the one we are currently witnessing the construction of, centred on the United States, the Second British Empire is the one which would be centred on India.

a colony needed supplies, it would be the merchants doing it, not the state. So, while there were two English colonies on the North American continent, they had very little to do with each other legally. They might share some abstract patriotism, but they would both have little reason for helping out the other. This is part of the reason for why Jamestown did not help Plymouth with its food issues.

There was also a more practical element. Virginia had been in existence for about 15 years, and hadn't yet reached a point of maturity where it was self-sufficient. Most of its crop was not food, but tobacco, which was sent back to London to secure supplies. Part of the reason that Virginia did not break free of British control in Bacon's rebellion was that it still hadn't reached maturity to the point where it didn't need British supplies, and it couldn't yet fend for itself. Plus, the whole 1622 Powhatan uprising. It only had around a thousand or so inhabitants at this point in history, so it couldn't support the establishment of another colony, even if it wanted to. It's not unreasonable to think that the early Virginians would have resented Plymouth as a distraction in England from their own colonisation efforts. That's exactly how they felt about Maryland.

Weymouth

The summer of 1623 was quite busy at Plymouth, not least of which was the arrival of a hundred more Pilgrims we discussed previously. It takes us to September, and another arrival into New England. Robert Gorges, son of the founder of the Council for New England. He was going to re-found the colony of Wessagusset, but he gave it a new name, Weymouth. He was to be the governor general of the region, and formed an executive council made up of Admiral West, Christopher Levett, a key figure in the New England colonisation effort, and the governor of Plymouth.

Gorges would spend a couple of months in Weymouth, but he did not enjoy the colonial experience. He would be embroiled in a legal battle with Weston that ultimately came to nothing. He decided to return to England, leaving behind to represent him Mr. William Morrell, an educated clergyman. Morrell spent a year at Plymouth, observing the region. It was only when he eventually left that he revealed he had the authority to force the Pilgrims to conform to the Church of England, but had not.

Meanwhile, at Plymouth, attention was primarily on absorbing the new settlers. There was an issue over food at first, but it was decided that the older settlers would keep the grain they had grown, while the new settlers would use the food they had brought with them on the Anne . The Anne was filled with furs, and on September 10th it set sail back to England along with Winslow, who was to communicate with the London merchants to secure needed supplies for the colony.

This was shortly followed by the harvest, which was bountiful. The food supply was finally secure, and we'll no longer be talking about famine when dealing with Plymouth. On November 5th there was a small fire when a bonfire got out of hand. The sailors had set up a bonfire while celebrating Guy Fawkes Night.[42]

In in December there was a note in Bradford's notebook about a law which was enacted, that "all criminal facts, and also all matters of trespasses and debts between man and man, should be tried by the verdict of twelve honest men, to be impanelled by authority, in form a jury, upon their oath." Plymouth Colony is really beginning to take shape.

In March 1624 it was time for the annual elections. Bradford decided to step down, not wanting one person to monopolise the governorship. He had held the office for the past three years. The Pilgrims wouldn't allow it though, and he was forced to stay in command. It was at this point that the colony's administration changed as we discussed previously. The council was introduced, giving Bradford more help in governance than just Allerton. There would be 5 of them. Bradford, with his double vote, Allerton and Winslow, and it is likely that the other two were Standish and Fuller. This would be the state of affairs until 1633 when the council was increased to 7.

The Charity

A fishing vessel arrived around this time from London, sent by the Merchants, known as the Charity. It brought with it a series of letters from Europe. One of these was from James Sherley, who had replaced Weston as the head of the

---

[42] The important piece of information here is that a few houses burned down, but I'm personally more amused at the description of those celebrating. It tickles the American Football fan in me to read about patriots in Massachusetts when the source is describing English patriots, rather than, you know, Tom Brady and Gronk.

Adventurers, the London Merchants. Bradford includes a lot of letters in his account, most of which I just summarise, but I think you'll find it interesting for me to include these.

"Most worthy and loving friends, your kind and loving letter I have received, and render you many thanks, etc. It hath pleased God to stir up the hearts of our adventurers to raise a new stock for the setting forth of this ship, called the Charity, with men and necessaries, both for the plantation and the fishing, though accomplished with very great difficulty; in regard we have some amongst us which undoubtedly aim more at their own private ends, and the thwarting and opposing of some here, and other worthy instruments, of Gods glory elsewhere, than at the general good and furtherance of this noble and laudable action. Yet again we have many other, and I hope the greatest part, very honest Christian men, which I am persuaded their ends and intents are wholly for the glory of our Lord Jesus Christ, in the propagation of his gospel, and hope of gaining those poor salvages to the knowledge of God. But, as we have a proverb, one scabbed sheep may mare a whole flock, so these malcontented persons, and turbulent spirits, do what in them lyeth to withdraw mens hearts from you and your friends, yea, even from the general business; and yet under show and pretence of godliness and furtherance of the plantation. Whereas the quite contrary doth plainly appear; as some of the honester hearted men (though of late of their faction) did make manifest at our late meeting. But what should I trouble you or my self with these restless opposers of goodness, and I doubt will be continual disturbers of our friendly meetings and love. On Thursday the 8th of January we had a meeting about the articles between you and us; where they would reject that, which we in our late letters pressed you to grant, (an addition to the time of our joint stock). And their reason which they would make known to us was, it troubled their conscience to exact longer time of you than was agreed upon at first. But that night they were so followed and crossed of their perverse courses, as they were even wearied, and offered to sell their adventures; and some were willing to buy. But I, doubting they would raise more scandal and false reports, and so diverse ways do us more hurt, by going off in such a fury, then they could or can by continuing adventurers amongst us, would not suffer them. But on the

12th of January: we had another meeting, but in the interim diverse of us had talked with most of them privately, and had great combats and reasoning, pro and con. But at night when we met to read the general letter, we had the lovingest and friendliest meeting that I ever knew and our greatest enemies offered to lend us 50 pounds. So I sent for a bottle of wine (I would you could do the like,) which we drank friendly together. Thus God can turn the hearts of men when it pleaseth him, etc. Thus loving friends, I heartily salute you all in the Lord, hoping ever to rest, Yours to my power, James Sherley. January 25th, 1623."[43]

Also on board the ship There was a letter too from Robert Cushman, who was in London as the chief-agent of the colony, and he explained the nature of the decision to Bradford. Basically, Cushman felt that a fishing vessel would be of more use to the Pilgrims than comforts such as butter and sugar. This seems fair, but their attempts to get fish out of Plymouth had not met with much luck before this.

---

[43] I think you can see why I normally don't include them, given the language, length, and style, but coming from the world of ancient history with so little sources, I love having documents written by the people I'm describing, rather than ones written hundreds of years after they died. It's good to include stuff like this occasionally. Let's go over just what was included in that, in case it wasn't clear. The language really takes some getting used to.

Goodwin views it as an obsession, writing that the London merchants had 'fishing-mania'.[44]

It also had on board a ship-maker who was very well respected, and who would build two shallops and a lighter. He was in the process of building a forth ship for the colony when he died of a fever. It also brought a saltmaker who was... incompetent. The less said about him the better.

The Charity came with a patent for some land at Cape Anne, and the ship was sent there with some of the settlers in order to construct a fishing stage. Should the reader not be familiar with the process of how exactly the New England 17th century fishing industry worked, a fishing stage is a type of wooden building which would be constructed on an elevated platform either at the edge of the water, or at the landwash, which can roughly be considered the area between high and low tide. It was a place used during the summer months for the fish to be salted and dried. So, it was with the intention of building one of these the Charity set sail. It didn't go particularly well. This was partly to do with the time of year that they set sail, but Bradford reserves primary blame for the captain who spent the whole voyage drunk, and most of the men followed his lead. No good came of this mission.

The Charity also brought with it the first cattle to Plymouth, 3 heifers and a bull. It would have been a great home comfort for the Pilgrims, to have a feature of the landscape there which felt natural.

---

[44] Which sounds exactly like the title of the next History Channel 'documentary'.

They were carefully watched, given the fact that wolves roamed the area, but the grass of the area was good for them, and Bradford pleasingly notes that they soon grew nice and fat.

Also on board was a letter from Pastor John Robinson (who was leading the flock back in Leyden) writing to Elder Brewster. This mainly complained about Standish's actions with Wessagusset, but given that Robinson was in the Netherlands and Standish was on the scene, and had had a resounding success, I'm sure you'll forgive me for not going into this. It is however an important moment. Robinson and Brewster were the early leaders of the colony, back from its time in Leyden, and Robinson would die in 1625 while still in his 40s. It was a shock, and means that this letter is the last contact Robinson would have with the colony he had been so instrumental in setting up.

Divisions in Plymouth

The Charity was an unwelcome arrival for some who had not gotten on well with the Pilgrims, a faction led by Master Oldham. It was believed that they would be placed in control of the colony, and they were disappointed to find both this wasn't the case, and that their complaints had been revealed. Bradford addressed the concerns which they raised, and the matter was quickly smoothed over.

The greatest complication made by the arrival of the Charity was the arrival of Master John Lyford along with his family. He was a preacher in the Church of England, but was a Puritan, and he had been selected as an agent by several Adventurers. Winslow and Cushman both opposed him going, but relented in order to keep the peace. Lyford was housed, and was well respected. Shortly after his arrival he appeared to convert to congregationalism, and offered to renounce his membership of the Church of England, although Brewster made it clear that this wasn't necessary. He was not to be made a pastor, but was allowed to preach along with Brewster. The council regularly consulted with Brewster, Lyford and Oldham. It seemed that all was going well. At first.

Suspicions were raised when it was noticed that Lyford was spending a lot of time with Oldham, in addition to other malcontents, such as the permanent source of trouble that was John Billington. When the Charity was getting ready to sail away, it was also observed that Lyford was writing a lot of letters. Bradford was very uneasy about this. From the letters he had received from Sherley, he knew who precarious the colony's position was back in London. He feared that if the letters contained anything slanderous it would greatly weaken their position. Bradford and the council asked to see the letters. The master of the ship, one William Peirce, was a friend of the Pilgrims and was happy to oblige.

Bradford set sail on the ship along with Winslow and the letters were opened. It was discovered that the letters were full of slander about the colony. Bradford returned to Plymouth that night while Winslow and Peirce sailed back to England. The conspirators, Lyford and Oldham, were very nervous, but Bradford did nothing for a few weeks, and they eventually assumed that he had just gone on the ship to speak with his old friend Pierce before returning to Plymouth. What they didn't know was that Bradford was waiting so that he would be able to catch them in the act of treachery.

He didn't have to wait too long. They soon began to cause trouble, and Oldham at one point refused to obey his captain when it was his turn to take watch. Bradford was scandalised that Oldham actually called his captain 'a beggarly rascal'. He then brandished a knife. Bradford sent men to quite Oldham, but Oldham cursed them all to high Hades and had to be imprisoned. No doubt, Oldham was expecting some sort of popular reaction against this. When none manifested he came to his senses and was released. After this aborted uprising, the conspirators resorted to the plan they had written about in the letters.

Lyford and his accomplices waited until a Sunday when they set up an alternative congregation. We don't know what about this exactly caused offense, but we do know that there was something about it designed to tear apart the colony. It was exactly what Bradford had been waiting for. He called a town meeting which the whole colony was to attend. Lyford and Oldham were both charged with treason. They denied it, and demanded proof. He referred to their actions in public. Lyford's issues with the church, and the previous issues Oldham had had with the colony.

They thought that this was all the evidence that Bradford had. Lyford denied the charges. At this point, some of the letters were produced. Lyford was speechless. Oldham raged, furious that they had opened his letters. He called upon his friends for revenge, and then was mortified when not a single person leapt to his defence. Bradford asked

Lyford his opinion on the opening on his letters, but Lyford didn't reply. Next, all the letters written by Lyford were revealed by Bradford. He doesn't include the letters as there were too many of them, but in his notes he sums up the charges and answers them.

It would be impractical to go through the full version of Bradford's summary, but to condense the matter, Oldham and Lyford said that the Pilgrims were ruining the colony with their religion and incompetence, and encouraged the London Merchants to allow no more separatists from Leyden to go to Plymouth, and for them to send over as many Englishmen as possible so that they could outnumber the Pilgrims before things got any worse. My favourite bit is a rather funnily worded complaint by Lyford. He asks the London merchants for a better general, "for this Captain Standish looks like a silly boy". Considering how well Standish has handled the military responsibilities of Plymouth so far, I really wish I could have seen his face when that letter was read out.

The letter was read out, and Bradford asked Lyford for a response. Everyone in the town was present. If he needed witnesses, they were all here. What was his defence? What were his thoughts on these letters? Did he have any other complaints about the Pilgrims he hadn't written down? Bradford said that Lyford claimed he now realisedthat he had been misled by some of the people he had listened to, such as John Billington, and that this caused him to exaggerate other issues. Billington and the others denied any wrongdoing, and the Pilgrims believed him. This was a huge blow for Lyford. His standing with Bradford, Standish, Brewster, and the other men of note was below that of John Billington. He burst into tears, wailing that he feared not even God would forgive his sins.

The votes were cast. Oldham was banished with immediate effect, although his family were allowed to stay for a while until he found another home for them. Lyford was given 6 months, but with an eye towards lifting the punishment if it turned out he had actually repented. He confessed his sins afterwards at the church, and the Pilgrims began to trust him again. He was once more allowed to preach. Samuel Fuller and some others amongst the company began to ask this punishment to be lifted. The Pilgrims were then completely caught off guard when two months later Lyford packed up and left the colony in floods of tears, saying that he felt the need to take his punishment. He did not deserve to have it lifted for making up such lies. Thus ends the tale of Lyford and Pilgrims.

Except not quite. There is another twist in the tale, for Lyford wrote another letter in secret which he sent back to the London merchants.

> "Worthy Sirs,
> Though the filth of mine own doings may justly be cast in my face, and with blushing cause my perpetual silence, yet that the truth may not hereby be injuried, yourselves an longer deluded, nor injurious dealing carried out still, with bold out facings, I have adventured once more to write unto you. Firest, I do freely confess I dealt very indiscreetly in some of

my particular letters which I wrote to private friends, for the courses in coming hither and the like; which I do in no sort seek to justify, though stirred up there unto in the beholding the indirect courses held by others, both here, and there with you, for effecting their designs. But am heartily sorry for it, and do to the glory of God and mine own shame acknowledge it. Which letters being intercepted by the Governor, I have for the same undergone the censure of banishment. And had it not been for the respect I have unto you, and some other matters of private regard, I had returned again at this time by the pinass for England; for here I purpose not to abide, unless I receive better encouragement from you, than from the church (as they call themselves) here I do receive. I purposed before I came, to undergo hardness, therefore I shall hope cheerfully bear the conditions of the place, though very mean; and they have changed my waged ten times already. I suppose my letters, or at least the copies of them, are come to your hands, for so they here report; which, if it be so, I pray you take notice of this, that I have written nothing but what is certainly true, and I could make so appear plainly to any indifferent men, whatsoever colours be cast to darken the truth, and some there are very audacious this way; besides many other matters which are far out of order here. My mind was not to enlarge myself any further, but in respect of diverse poor souls here, the care of whom in part belongs to you, being here destitute of the means of salvation. For how so ever the church are provided for, to their content, who are the smallest number in the colony, and do so appropriate the ministry to themselves, holding this principle, that the Lord hath not appointed any ordinary ministry for the conversion of those that are without, so that some of the poor souls have with tears complained of this to me, and I was taxed for preaching to all in general. Though in truth they have had no ministry here since they came, but such as may be performed by any of you, by their own position, whatsoever great pretences they make; but herein they equivocate, as in many other things they do. But I exceed the bounds I set myself, therefore resting thus, until I hear further from you, so it be within the time limited me. I rest, etc. Remaining ever yours, John Lyford, Exile. Dated August 22nd. 1624."

Lyford didn't return to England on the pinass as he wrote in the letter, instead he joined Oldham at

Nantasket. Bradford writes that nothing else of interest happened that year.

In the spring of 1625 it was time for the annual election of the governor. Oldham broke the conditions of his exile, and returned with some friends. He ranted in a mad fury. It wasn't a particularly threatening incident. It was unsettling. You get the feeling that the Pilgrims were rather embarrassed that they had to see this.[45]

He was imprisoned while he calmed down, and then was forced out of the colony once more. Oldham was marched between two rows of musketeers who each hit him with the butts of their guns as he passed, and before placing him back on his boat. While all this was going on, people didn't notice that a ship had arrived, bringing with it Winslow and William Peirce, who had returned to Plymouth in the Jacob after leaving on the Charity last year. They were furious at all the problems Lyford and Oldham had caused for them back in London, where Lyford had such a good name. There had been a huge scandal where past acts of Lyford came to light. It was decided to take no further action, but such ill feeling had been caused that many of the London merchants gave up the venture. Plymouth was too much hassle and they could do without it.

Oldham and Lyford will both have cause to reappear in our story further down the line. They were both invited to join a colony in Massachusetts which died before 1625 was over, and then would

---

[45] I'm sure anyone who has witnessed such a tirade on public transport at 2AM can relate to this. I sure know I can.

have very interesting lives. Lyford would become a pastor at Salam (yes, that Salam) while Oldham had a prominent role in the Massachusetts Bay Company.

While things were falling apart in London, the merchants still invested in the colony sent over some goods to be sold on. But, more importantly, more cattle were sent, bringing the total of the herd up to 9. The Jacob then sailed on to Cape Ann with Standish, where the Pilgrims had constructed the fishing stage the previous year. When they found it, another group of Puritans had seized it. Fighting almost broke out, but peace was made and the stage was expanded to make room for the Jacob.

Speaking of Standish's adventures, in the summer of 1625 Standish set sail to London to deal with matters there. Most of the adventurers had pulled out of the agreement they had made for the colony, and he wanted to clarify what their legal position was. He hoped to buy out the adventurers with help from the Council for New England. Standish ran into difficulties. Firstly, there was a change in government. James I died and was replaced by Charles I. The Pilgrims had always had a tricky relationship with James. They disliked his authoritarian style, and they had partly fled to the Netherlands and then to the New World, in order to escape him. Charles was even worse. You have only to think of what Charles relationship with the Puritans back in England would be, and then to remember that the Pilgrims were extreme Puritans, to know why this would be the case. But we don't need to repeat the details of Charles' ascension here.

A Brief History of Plague

The other complication was plague. Plague is one of the more famous diseases to hit the world, arguably the most famous, although Malaria and Smallpox also have to be up there. It is caused by a bacteria known as Yersinia Pestis which primarily lives affects wild rodents and is spread by fleas. This is how the disease can pass to humans. A bubo, a swelling on the lymph node draining the flea bite site, is a primary characteristic of the disease. It's how it gets its name of bubonic. Flu like symptoms develop between 3 and 7 days, fever, chills, aches and vomiting. A real problem is caused if the bacteria reaches the lungs as this will give the victim pneumonia, allowing the disease to spread through infected droplets while coughing. This is pneumonic plague. Infection can also spread directly through the blood stream, septicaemic plague. If it is untreated, the disease has a fatality rate of between 30 and 60 percent.

So much for the disease. Now, on to outbreaks. There have been three major outbreaks of plague, these are categorised as the three plague pandemics. The first of these broke out of Egypt in the mid-sixth century during the reign of the Byzantine Emperor Justinian, and it would haunt Europe until the eighth century, breaking out with frequent regularity. The Second Plague Pandemic originated in China, and spread into Europe along the Silk Road in the fourteenth century. The initial outbreak of the Second Plague Pandemic is often referred to as the Black Death. It killed 50 million people in Europe during the fourteenth century. This was not the end of the Second Plague Pandemic. It haunted Europe until into the eighteenth century. These outbreaks are less famous, but still deadly. In the UK the Great Plague of London is particularly famous which lasted between 1664 and 1667, killing perhaps a hundred thousand, but this was one of the smaller outbreaks. Half the population of Naples, some 150,000, died during a plague outbreak in the 1650s. The Great Plague of Seville saw the death of half a million people c.1650, as did the Great Northern War plague outbreak in the early 1700s. There was also a third Pandemic which began in the 1890s in China. This outbreak was largely contained to the east, but ravaged India and China, killing perhaps 12 million people. Tangent over, there is your brief history of plague.

Back to Standish in London, while he visited in 1625 there was an outbreak of the second pandemic. In this particular occurrence, 40,000 people died. What this meant was that those who could, i.e. the wealthy, fled the city. Standish was in London, but he couldn't complete any business. The whole voyage was a bit of a waste, and Standish returned to Plymouth in April 1626.

1625 was a rather dull year at Plymouth, which I suspect the Pilgrims probably enjoyed. There was no starving, no conspiracy, just getting on with life. They had a good crop, and used the surplus to trade for furs. Winslow led the expedition, and was able to get hold of £700 worth of beaver and other skins.

Standish reception upon his return was mixed. The Pilgrims were happy to see him, obviously, but not so happy at his news. The mission had been a failure, and he had to report back all the deaths. King James, Prince Maurice, who had led the Dutch government during their time in Leyden, Robert Cushman, their agent back in London who had been the colony's right hand, always fighting for their interests. These were all tragic, but the hardest to accept was the death of Pastor John Robinson.

Without the interference of London trying to force fishing on them, the Pilgrims spent 1626 farming. They were able to sell their corn at 6 shillings a bushel. There was an issue with other English colonies devaluing the crop, therefore the Pilgrims decided that it would be more profitable for them to trade further afield. They only had a house-carpenter, but he had worked with the ship-maker before the ship-maker's death. He was employed to expand one of their ships by inserting about 6 feet of waist after chopping the ship in half. It was a success, giving them better trading options. They were beginning to become more and more established in the New England trade network. That mostly covers events in Plymouth. The other thing to happen that year was that another voyage was made to England, this time by Allerton. It was hoped that things would be more settled than they had been the previous year. The government should be more stable, and the bout of plague had run its course.

Allerton returned in 1627 with some more goods, but the real piece of interest here was that he had made a contract with the adventurers to buy them out of the colony which received the hearty approval of those back in Plymouth. They would buy the colony for £1,800, which would be paid in instalments of £200 every September 29th, which was chosen as Michaelmas, the day of Saint Michael the Archangel. I'm sure the Pilgrims were somewhat relieved that they were now the owners of the colony, but there was a bit of an issue.

Legal Ownership of Plymouth

The shaky legal position of the colony was once again coming back to haunt them. Plymouth was unchartered. It had a government based solely on the consent of the governed, rather than a contract giving it authority from a sovereign force. It was what made the Mayflower Compact important, authority coming from the consent of the governed was such a novel idea, but it made things complicated for the Pilgrims. The issue was that because of these factors, Plymouth didn't legally exist. It wasn't a legal entity. This meant that it wasn't possible for the colony to buy itself, the only way out of the mess was if someone bought the colony for them.

This was a legal technicality. The funds could come from the colony itself, but someone would need to legally represent it. This wouldn't be an issue if no problems occurred, and they were able to pay off the £1,800. The problem was over securities. If the colony ran into disaster, and was unable to pay off the debt, what would be taken as collateral? Well, the individuals who represented the colony would likely be thrown into prison as debtors. They would be ruined. But, being a leader is not all about power and glory. There are real responsibilities attached.[46] Eight men were willing to put their names forward to shoulder this particular burden: William Bradford, Miles Standish, Isaac Allerton, Edward

---

[46] Insert your own political commentary here.

Winslow, William Brewster, John Howland, John Alden and Thomas Prence.

From this point, legally, these 8 men owned the colony, and they were free to do with it whatsoever they wanted. They were no longer bound by the whims of the London merchants. Now that they had the final say, the first thing they did was hold a meeting to discuss whether or not they wanted to introduce a restriction on who was allowed to live there. While the core of the colony was made up of Puritan separatists, the London merchants had provided a collection of characters. Not all of them respected their church, and not all respected their civil government. A proposal was made to remove them from the colony, this was then rejected. This can be spun both ways. The Puritan separatists who were so closed minded that their first independent action was to propose to remove anyone who did not share their beliefs from the colony, or that they were so tolerant that this measure was repressed. I think that both of these spins are counterproductive, and only shed light on the prejudices of the author. The proper thing to do is note that both things took place. The measure was proposed, and it was rejected. The fact that both of these things happened tells us more about the Pilgrims and their view of the world than any moralised viewpoint which only distorts the account. You need to take events in history together, you can't just abstract single incidents to make points. It doesn't work like that.

With this proposal having been rejected, they could begin organising the colony on new lines. It was decided that Plymouth would be an equal partnership. The heads of all the families, and the self-supporting single men, would each receive one share in the public holding as purchasers, and would have the right to take additional shares, one each for a wife or child. There were about 156 purchasers, 57 men, 29 women, 34 boys and 36 girls. There were also a number of servants who did not receive shares numbering between twenty and thirty.

It was decided not to alter their farming methods, or their trade. Each person would pay their share of the debt towards buying the colony which was not covered by trade. The cows, goats, and pigs were divided evenly between people. Land was divided 20 acres per share, in addition to what they already had.[47]

A Dutch Message

In March 1627, Bradford was pleasantly surprised to receive a letter from the new Dutch colony which had been set up on Manhattan Island, at the mouth of the Hudson.[48] It said that since the Dutch and English motherlands were friendly, that they were happy to trade whenever they might wish. A reply was made, and the friendliness was reciprocated. They told the Dutch that they would never forget the Dutch kindness they had received during their years in Leyden. Bradford asked them to avoid trading with the natives in Buzzard's Bay, and not to

---

[47] This is the simple version. Should you want to know the exact system for determining lots, and where land plots were, the information is out there, but I don't think we need to trouble ourselves with it.
[48] The settlement which will become New York, whose establishment we will of course give plenty of attention to down the road.

settle in the lands claimed by the Council for New England.

The Dutch responded in August that while the King of England could claim the land, the Dutch States-General claimed them too. Some English patent would not stop them trading in the lands around Plymouth if they wanted. The tone was pleasant and polite, even if the content wasn't. Bradford replied, likewise with every curtesy, that they would expel any Dutch they found in their land breaking the patent. An invitation was made to a trade summit to arrange the details, and a threat was also made about the Virginia fleet and the New England fishing ships. No guarantee could be made over what would happen should the Dutch come into contact with either of them.

This summit was when Bradford received a notification from Secretary De Rasieres that he was in the area, and a trade agreement was struck which would last for several years. It was useful for the English, as they learned quite a bit about the region from the Dutch. For instance, they learned about Native American money. The Indians used as currency something called either wampum or sewam, a type of bead made from the shell of the quahog.[49] The clam shells were broken into small pieces, tidied up into regular round shapes, and then polished. Interestingly, to me at least, the most valuable colour of bead was purple. This was because only a small part of the quahog shell was purple, making these beads the rarest.[50]

---

[49] No, not the fictional town in Rhode Island which is the home of a certain Simpsons rip off, but a type of hard clam that the fictional town is named after.

219

The Dutch sold £50 worth of wampum to the English, although it would be two years until they were used. While wampum was common among the east coast, and indeed, also into the interior, they had not spread further east than Narraganset. Once they started using it, the benefits of it became obvious. Indeed, to the Europeans too. It was an issue that in the New World they were short on liquid capital in the form of coins, which is why most trade took place through battering. Corn in exchange for furs, and other such deals. But the wampum filled this gap in the economy, and would be widely used throughout the seventeenth century, at one point even becoming legal tender. It did not last into the eighteenth century. By then, coinage was more common in the Americas, and the Europeans, with their advanced production techniques, were able to produce wampum on a far greater scale than the Indians could manage. The result was such inflation that it became impractical to use as. In the 1620s, the amount of effort required to produce the beads was not worth as much as the wampum was worth. The exchange rate was 6 white beads per penny, and then purple beads had twice the value of a white bead, but it was more profitable for the England to work in other ways. One effect of this increase in trade was

---

[50] I'm going to describe the wampum as a form of currency, simply because that is an easy translation, but as linguists know, translation causes problems because a lot of the time it doesn't capture the full sense of what is going on. Wampum was traded, and exchanged for goods, so it was sort of like money, but it had a spiritual and ceremonial use too, and could be even used as a way of recording information.

that the Native Americans started illegally buying guns.

The other important event in Plymouth in 1627 was the shipwrecking of the Sparrowhawk, a ship which was sailing from London to Virginia. The people were saved though, and jointed Plymouth, but they did not stay long. There was a scandal, involving a servant of one of their leaders, and the group were shortly after moved along.

Undertakers

In 1627 eight leading figures of the colony, Bradford, Standish, Allerton, Winslow, Brewster, Howland, Alden, and Prence bought out the London merchants from the colony. They would be responsible for the trade which was to be responsible for financing this operation, and their taking of responsibility is how they became known as the Undertakers. Allerton was sent back to London during the autumn to represent the Undertakers as they made their business, new issues had to be dealt with.

Other colonies were springing up on the New England coast, e.g. the Dutch, and this greatly change the dynamics of the colonial operation. We saw the same thing happen in Virginia with the arrival of a group of German settlers. It greatly altered the relationship between Jamestown and the Powhatans. The Pilgrims started to take decisions based on the increased trade competition, trading further afield. For instance, they had started trading with the people along the Kennebec River, and they wanted to receive a grant for this land.

This was the primary reason Allerton needed to go to London.

Allerton received the support of 4 Londoners in their endeavour, attaching themselves to the Undertakers. These were James Sherley, who we have already met, in addition to John Beauchamp, Richard Andrews and Timothy Hatherly. Gathering their support and winning the patent for the Kennebec took time. He wouldn't return until 1628, when he brought back with him someone to be a pastor, seemingly at the desire of his friends, one Mr. Rogers. However, isn't really known why. Mr. Rogers was insane, and had to be sent back immediately. Allerton would return to London later that year to expand the Kennebec patent.

Mount Merry

During 1628, Standish had another one of his little adventures. A number of small colonies were popping up along the English coast, but they generally had nothing to do with the Pilgrims. They were Episcopalians, not Congregationalists. But despite a subtle hostility to the Pilgrims, Plymouth did have an aura of authority over the region. It was the first English colony in New England, and it was particularly well organised. So, in June 1628, when the English colonies of the region had a problem, it was to Plymouth they turned. What was this threat, that was so able to alarm the English? Was it Indians? Was it a European power? No. It was a group of drunks. True story. History is the just the best sometimes. So, let me tell you the story of how a bunch of drunks almost destroyed New England.

In 1625 a colony was set up at the sight of the modern Quincy in Massachusetts, just south of Boston, by one Captain Wollaston, a rather highly esteemed man. He found it tough, and moved on to Virginia, but a few were left behind including a certain Thomas Morton, who had been an attorney in London. Morton roused up the servants, and promised to make them partners in the plantation. He did this after they forced out Lieutenant Fitcher, who had been left in command. What follows is one of the stranger incidents I've come across in my studies. The settlement was reorganised along the lines of fraternity and equality. They traded with the natives, and used the profits to buy rum in large quantities. They planted a maypole and renamed the settlement Mount Merry.

This couldn't go on for much longer. The settlement began to attract trouble. The other colonies of the region worried about what having this little slice of freedom would do. Would the criminals and fugitives of the region flock there, eventually making it strong enough that it could be a threat to them?[51]

There were also practical complaints made about Mount Merry. The settlers had trained Native American hunters on how to use firearms, and they swiftly abandoned their bows and arrows in favour of the advanced technology. The settlers traded these weapons to the Indians in large numbers.

---

[51] I particularly enjoy the irony of this. When you think of all the rhetoric that surrounds the founding of the United States of looking for freedom from the oppression of the Old World yada, yada, yada, how funny is it that these new colonies immediately sought to destroy the one that wanted to operate differently? It's a fascinating curiosity.

Having access to firearms was one of the key advantages the Europeans had, so important that King James had forbidden the sail of such weaponry to the Indians in 1622. And now, a bunch of drunks throwing this precious advantage away! They had to be stopped, before they could destroy New England.

So, the colonies of New England looked to Plymouth, and Plymouth, as always, looked to Standish. Standish led a group of musketeers to Merry Mount where they found the men held up in a bunker. It's possible that they could have put up a serious fight, you know, if they weren't a bunch of drunks. They were drunk when Standish arrived. When Standish ordered them to leave, they just hurled abuse at him and then stumbled outside to meet him. Morton overcharged his gun and pointed it at Standish, intending to kill him, but Standish, who is quickly becoming one of my favourite historical figures, just pushed the gun out of the way. Morton was arrested, but the rest of the colony was left in peace, having been brought to heel.

Chapter 9 – The Disorganisation of Massachusetts

Having spent the last 68 pages dealing with the Pilgrims, from their roots in the European Reformation to Plymouth Colony in 1628, from the starving few freezing to death in the wilderness to a healthy colony about 300 strong, it is now time to pause that narrative and turn towards the colony which would eventually absorb Plymouth, The Massachusetts Bay Colony.

Plymouth was the first and most successful of the early New England plantations. While it found success, it wasn't the type of immediate riches those back in London were looking for. They didn't trust the Pilgrims, and there had been too many problems. Other colonies began to spring up. We've already looked at Weston's attempt to found Wessagusset, which was a disaster, and the whole fiasco at Merry Mount. But, on the fringes of the narrative, I hope that I've been able to put across the point that things were beginning to get more organised.

I've mentioned the foundation of Weymouth previously, and indeed Sir Ferdinando Gorges of the Council for New England and Captain John Mason were key figures in setting up legal claims along the New England coast. There were other colonies being set up too. Reverend William Blackstone on the Shawmut peninsula, the site which would be the home of Boston, and Samuel Maverick settled at Noddles Island in Massachusetts Bay.

There is another settlement I've mentioned a couple of times in the narrative, Cape Ann, which is on the northerly limit of Massachusetts Bay. It was founded in 1623 with the involvement of Plymouth. It was funded by a group of merchants from Dorchester, the leading figure of which was Richard Bushrod, although the spirit of the enterprise was Reverend John White, an Anglican rector of the Church of the Holy Trinity in Dorchester. Merchants were interested in the fishing opportunities on the New England coast, while White hoped that he could make it a religious settlement too.

Like many of the expeditions to the region which harboured dreams of growing rich off the fishing potential of the settlement, it was unable to prosper despite the efforts of a number of important individuals, including Roger Conant, and it collapsed in 1626 with most of the settlers returning back to England. Conant stayed though. He believed that the colony could work. In the autumn of 1626 he moved southwards from Cape Ann and founded a settlement at the mouth of Naumkeag River, this settlement was the town of Salem, although it wouldn't receive that name for a couple more years.

Conant was very optimistic about Salem, and spread word of this confidence back to England where it greatly excited Reverend White. Conant had also come around to thinking that Salem could be a refuge for those who were growing unhappy with the religious state of affairs in England. A lot of this had to do with William Laud.

Religious Persecution

Laud, born in 1573, came to prominence first under James I and then under Charles. He was fiercely devoted to Church unity, and opposed Puritanism.

He supported national uniformity of the church, all under the Book of Common Prayer. He was a close advisor of Charles, and was made Archbishop of Canterbury in 1633. He held this office until he was executed by Parliament in 1645.

In these years, persecution of Puritans increased to a greater scale than that which forced the Pilgrims to flee to Leyden. It must be remembered though that these were a different sort of Puritans than those at Plymouth. While the Pilgrims left the Church of England to found their own congregation, which is why they are called both Separatists and Congregationalists, Reverend White wanted to take the reformation to its logical conclusion from within the Church of England, purifying it from within. While similar to Plymouth, it was also different.

Based on this, White made his appeals to the businessmen of London and the Puritans of Eastern England. He was able to gather together some support, enough to found a new company, The New England Company. The company appealed to the Earl of Warwick, the president of the Council for New England, for a land patent, which they received in March 1628. The grant stretched from three miles north of the Merrimac River down to three miles south of the Charles River, and from the Atlantic Ocean to the Pacific. There are two problems with this. There is the obvious problem, which isn't that important, and then there is the less obvious problem which is very important.

The obvious problem is with the sea to shining sea nature of the grant, but this isn't a realistic issue since nobody was sure how big America was at this point. At the initial foundation of Plymouth, the early explorers suspected New England to be an island. This was still the case in 1628. It was thought that the Hudson was connected to the Saint Lawrence, so this wasn't as huge a claim as it might seem. Not that, once the full extent of America was discovered, it would stop states from claiming such huge tracts of land. Virginia, Massachusetts, New York and Connecticut would all claim huge tracts of the mid-west which it would take until the end of the eighteenth century to fully resolve. But, as I say, this wasn't a real issue. The more pressing problem caused was that the grant overlapped with prior patents given to Gorges and Mason. If you think they are just going to sit back and let another colony take their land without causing a fuss, you would be mistaken.

Land Patent Complications

When the New England Company sent over John Endicott to replace Roger Conant as the man on the ground, they realised just how much opposition they had, and that a legal challenge would be mounted. The solution for the New England Company was to go around the backs of the Council for New England to the source of all legal authority, the king. They appealed to Charles for a new patent, and this was granted in March 1629. The land grant remained the same, but the company had greatly expanded powers. It was, as part of this process, renamed. It became known as The Governor and Company of the Massachusetts Bay in New England, or, in short, the Massachusetts Bay Company. This grant overruled the other grants which had been given in the region by the Council for New England.

Our focus has been on Plymouth for the 1620s in New England, but I have been trying to keep the narrative of the Council for New England in the background, just plodding along, and I hope it has come across in this narrative just how unorganised the whole thing was. It was a mess. A real mess. It was also a bizarre set up, with the Council holding the grant and then giving other grants to a medley of different investment groups. There was no real plan at work, and what had resulted was a confused shamble of criss-crossing land claims within English territory, not to mention the claims other Europeans, such as the Dutch, had to the region, or, heaven forbid, the people who were already living there, the Native Americans. The Massachusetts Bay Company would directly manage the region, eliminating the unnecessary middle man. This is a rather significant moment in the history of the region.

And, not just for the history of Massachusetts. Mason and Gorges were not happy with how all this had gone on, and they were not going to abandon their efforts, even though they hadn't really done anything to populate their territories beyond a few token settlers. This challenge forced them to get a bit more serious about their colonisation efforts. These odd little settlements were divided between Mason and Gorges. Gorges would take the land between the Kennebec and the Piscataqua Rivers, while Mason took the land between the Piscataqua and the Merrimac. Gorges' land became the Province of Maine, and Mason's became the Province of New Hampshire. So, almost out of nowhere, we have gone from having Plymouth colony in New England, to also having Massachusetts, New Hampshire, and Maine. The histories of these four colonies are heavily intertwined, and Massachusetts will at one point or another absorb the other three. We won't have much to say about Maine and New Hampshire for a while as they were only a few small settlements, but just know that they do sort of exist at point. I say sort of, because neither of them have the same strong set up and charter which would define Virginia and Massachusetts.

The colony would have a governor and a board of 18 executive assistants which were elected by freemen or stockholders. The government could make laws, appoint officials and punish wrong doers, in short, all matters which were necessary for orderly government. John Endicott was named as governor, and it was decided that the colony would make their primary settlement the one on the Naumkeag, which now received the name of Salem, meaning house of peace. It was funded by a mixture of merchants from London and Dorchester, while the settlers were mostly Puritans, and in 1629 several hundred of them prepared to set off for Salem along with all the supplies they would need to set up a colony, such as tools, goods for trade, and cattle.

A City on a Hill

One of the many excited by the possibilities was John Winthrop. Born in 1588, he was a country gentleman from Suffolk who took up work as an attorney in order to support his growing family (he had 16 children). Winthrop, and the other Puritans, felt that England was about to feel God's wrath, and was thrilled at the potential of unexploited land just waiting in New England. It wasn't an easy decision.

Winthrop felt like he was abandoning England and all his friends there when they needed him most, but it was not enough to change his mind. Winthrop thought he would be better able to do the Lord's work in the New World, where he could build something great, free from the interference of the royals and the Anglican church, which could serve as a shining example to decadent Europe. In Winthrop's own words, 'We must consider that we shall be as a City upon a Hill, the eyes of all people are upon us.' As Winthrop got involved with the colony and brought other Puritans with him, events sped up pace, and he found himself elected governor of the company in October 1629.

Winthrop was part of a group of great men, members of the gentry, who would define their generation, along with John Pym, John Hampden, and, of course, Oliver Cromwell. He was reasonable, and intelligent. His religion reflected his character rather than defining it. He was known well by Puritan gentry, merchants, lawyers and ministers, and it isn't that surprising that once he was on board for the expedition he quickly became prominent in it. Winthrop was a giant of history. What you'll see, as we tell this story, is that through Winthrop and his associates the mark of Puritanism is, while time may have altered it, still imprinted on American society.

His election took place ready for the expedition which was to be launched the next year. In April 1630, 400 settlers set off from the Isle of White on the south coast of England, heading for the new world. It was a two-month voyage, and they reached their destination in early June, but they were not very pleased by what was waiting for them. What they found was the remnants of the old colony at Salem, and they were not in a good way. It had been selected for their base, but there was little good land and a large population couldn't be supported. 400 settlers was a huge number for the time. Plymouth was almost 10 years old and still only numbered around 300. What little land there was hadn't been cleared, housing hadn't even been build. Most of the population lived in a mixture of tents and Wigwams. It wasn't a very promising sight for Winthrop's City on a Hill.

This could have ended very badly. Jamestown was a bad site for a capital in Virginia, yet it would take decades for the heart of the colony to move inland. Had the Puritans been as obstinate, perhaps I'd be telling you the story of how they settled in a bad location, and all starved to death. But they didn't, so I won't. Winthrop was an intelligent man, and he was able to recognise the problems that would occur, so he moved south. Further down the coast was the land they needed, they initially landed at Charlestown and then set up several small settlements around the bay, such as Newton (which would be later renamed Cambridge), Watertown, Roxbury, Dorchester (named in honour of Reverend White), and, of course, Boston.

The size of the initial colony caused problems. During 1630, 1,000 Puritans made the journey to these new settlements. It was the start of a great migration during which 20,000 would leave the old England for the New. It would take the outbreak of the English Civil War in 1642 to bring the migration to a halt. Considering the difficulties the Pilgrims had in their first few years securing a food supply, you can imagine the scale of the problem facing fledgling Massachusetts. They had, however, some key advantages over Plymouth. While the Pilgrims had been forced to discover everything for themselves as the first Europeans to settle the area, there was now more of an infrastructure in place. Trade was common and the geography of the region was known. It was hard for them to secure food, but not impossible. Winthrop personally dealt with as many tribes as he could in person to negotiate for food in this this first year. June was too late for crops to be planted, as you will know if you recall the founding of Plymouth. Winthrop also sent a ship back to England for more supplies.

The whole operation was done well. It was organised, and they took advantage of the benefits of already having colonies set up in the region, but, you really can't move that number of people to a new colony without suffering problems. Jamestown and Plymouth were both around a hundred strong when they were founded, and many of the smaller settlements we've dealt with along the way were a lot smaller than that. The hundreds and hundreds of people brought there meant that getting enough food for a healthy supply would be a herculean effort, and so while Winthrop did a sterling job, what followed was pretty inevitable.

These first winters have been brutal for the settlements we've dealt with so far, and it would be no different for Massachusetts. They had enough corn to keep them alive, but barely. I doubt you would describe their physical condition as healthy. Then they didn't have any meat, which coupled with a lack of fruit and juice resulted in scurvy. There was freezing weather and frostbite. These factors resulted in an outbreak of disease. At least

200 people lost their lives in this first winter. Given the large number of settlers, this isn't that surprising, and a large percentage of the population did survive. But it was still a huge loss.

Governments of Massachusetts and Plymouth

While the food crisis was going on, there were political developments afoot. I briefly mentioned the structure of the colony, a governor and 18 assistants, but it's worth getting into a bit more detail. Firstly, we need to make a distinction between this and other early colonies, particularly how its government contrasted with Plymouth.

When I first started my investigations into this topic, and untangling the mess that is the early history of New England, I was interested in the role of Plymouth in the story. There had been earlier settlements than Plymouth, and there would be more important settlements, but Plymouth has a very special place. When I speak with friends in the UK about the research I'm doing, a lot of the time they have no idea what I'm talking about. As much as I enthuse about Bacon's Rebellion, it means absolutely nothing to them. Most of my friends are classicists, so I'm not that surprised by a look of perplexity if I talk about anything other than the Roman poet Statius,[52] but Plymouth is different. The Pilgrim Fathers, the Mayflower: these are names which mean something. They've almost left the world of factual history behind, seeping into the world of the American legend alongside George Washington and Abraham Lincoln. Why?

---

[52] Abad del Vecchio, J. (2015)

The idea of American history versus the American legend is one I we'll return to over the course of this series, and I'm sure my ideas will develop with time, but right now I suspect it is due to the significance of their democratic government. Everybody owned a share in the colony in Plymouth, everybody had a vote. When you look towards the idea of America as the land of the free, this makes for a very noble beginning to the story. While Plymouth was absorbed into Massachusetts, this origin story is preferable to the one of the substance of the state.

The Pilgrims were very strange in their democratic approach; I can't stress that enough. Massachusetts had a very strong Puritan character, but it cannot be considered democratic. Puritans revered government. It was held as a divine institution which was given to God following the fall of Adam in order to control the sinful being that was man. Followers of political philosophy won't be too surprised by this. It's not that far removed from the idea of the social contract which would really take off in the 17th century. The idea that government is something used to control man's baser instincts is common to both schools of thought, but whereas the social contract focuses from this start point towards man giving up natural freedom in return for the benefits of society, the Puritans instead saw it as something imposed by God. The Puritans considered themselves to be God's agents, and that they took this burden of governing the world by his rules. They were to build the City on the Hill.

You might think that this doesn't sound very democratic, and you would be right. The Puritans held that democracy wasn't a good thing. A government had no responsibility to the people, it was not accountable to God alone. I hope you're beginning to see why I'm finding this approach so interesting when compared to Plymouth, and why the United States might look towards Plymouth as the first chapter in its story, rather than Massachusetts Bay, when Massachusetts became a state but Plymouth did not.

With no democratic principles, there was no need for the government to be accountable to the settlers. So, who were they accountable to, and who elected them? The shareholders of the company, known as the freemen, were of great importance in Massachusetts, particularly since so few of them travelled over from England. These freemen were supposed to meet four times a year in something known as the General Court. Once a year they would choose the governor, deputy-governor, and the 18 assistants. These would run the colony for the following year. Either the governor or the deputy governor was supposed to attend every meeting of the General Court, along with 6 of the assistants. This government had the power to do anything which didn't go against the laws of England. About a dozen freemen made the journey, so only 7 were needed to function as the General Court. Constitutionally, it would be perfectly possible for this small group to act as the government without any input from the colonists. You can really understand why the Mayflower Compact is a far nicer opening chapter for the colony than this.

That said, the charter was soon changed. The people of Charlestown were invited to the first meeting of the General Court in October 1630. They voted to change the charter of the company, turning it into something of a constitution. The term 'freeman' was redefined so that it now referred to a free citizen, these were eligible to vote and stand for office. However, the oligarchic nature of the settlement remained. The citizens could now vote, but only for the assistants. It was decided that the assistants would then elect the governor and deputy-governor.

This is the thread of the colony's early political tapestry. Democratic overtones, but fundamentally oligarchic in nature. In the next meeting, in May 1631, the colony was made a commonwealth, and 116 of the settlers were made freedmen. These were the men who were not indentured servants. This is, on the face of it, democratic.[53] But, freemanship was restricted to members of the colony's churches. This was to keep the Puritan nature of the settlement from being eroded away. Again, a point I keep coming back to, how interesting is it that this enforced religion into the government of the state is commonly overlooked in favour of the historically smaller and less important Plymouth? What we have here isn't a separation, but rather a fusion of church and state. This is a hugely important event in the story of the United States. The first large scale organised setting up of a state, rather than the haphazard approaches of early Virginia and Plymouth, but one which doesn't enter the American legend because of its support of oligarchy and the fusion of Church and State. It's a fascinating curiosity that this doesn't come up more.[54]

---

[53] Aside from the obviously undemocratic fact that women were not included in the government.
[54] Perhaps I'm pushing the idea to hard. It is an idea of

The next year, in 1632, inevitable political change was brought about. In such a small community, in which the powerful had nothing approaching the resources of the European aristocracy, it would be difficult to permanently establish an oligarchy. It was decided, therefore, that the governor and the deputy governor should also be elected from the freemen.[55]

Two years later, in 1634, the demand for a fairer approach continued and the people demanded that they see the charter for the colony, which had been brought over from England. Winthrop showed it to them, and they learned from this that the freemen had the power to make laws, even though they hadn't been able to so far because of the oligarchic nature of the early colonial organisation. This realisation sparked something of a radical change in the colony's government. It was decided that the General Court would continue to meet 4 times a year, but now that each town would send a representative to the body. This turned the general court into an elected legislature. This was a rather important shift, but you will not be surprised to learn that there was an oligarchic reaction in 1635.

A member of the colony, the Reverend Thomas Hooker, decided to leave Massachusetts along with his flock in order to found a rival colony, Connecticut.[56] When the matter came to the

---

mine, rather than a widely recognised theory, so feel free to disagree. I won't hold it against you.

[55] Remember though, freemen referred to the male members of the church, this wasn't a complete democracy.

[56] We'll cover the specifics later.

General Court, there was a division over whether or not to allow the departure. The deputies from the towns of the province had no complaints, but it was opposed by the magistrates who claimed the right to veto the action. This right to veto would be the major topic of political discussion in Massachusetts for the following decade, and would result in the Court being divided in 1644 into two separate houses, a bicameral legislature. This gave a veto to both houses, the House of Deputies and the Council of Assistants. As there were fewer assistants than deputies, the assistants were more powerful now than when the deputies could just outnumber them in the single chamber.

Social and Economic Life in Early Massachusetts

This pursuit of political developments is now taking the narrative into the 1640s, we shall now get more into the social and economic side of early Massachusetts life. What was it like for ordinary people as they lived and set up the series of villages in Massachusetts Bay?

The defining feature of Massachusetts in the 1630s was growth. Rapid growth. This was due to the large numbers of Puritans making the trans-Atlantic voyage to escape from the repressive policies of Charles I of England and the Archbishop of Canterbury, William Laud. In just over a decade 20,000 made the journey. This volume led to rapid maturity of the colony. Immigration is hugely important in driving economic growth.

The first group of colonists in 1630 had arrived late in the season, which led to hundreds of deaths that winter. But, once they could begin to grow crops, they took to it with great gusto. Much labour was needed to provide food and shelter, but the immigrants were able to do this. The colony didn't have much trouble taking care of itself, in contrast to Jamestown which relied on supplies from England for years. The speed with which Massachusetts reached this position is highly impressive. For instance, by 1634 it was already producing a crop surplus, and was able to send wheat to both the West Indies and the recently established colony of Maryland. This was soon followed by cattle and fish, which were sent to Virginia and the Caribbean islands. But, this was just one arm of the trade network that was being set up.

Goods sold in Maryland and Virginia could be exchanged for tobacco, and in the Indies for sugar. These could be consumed by the New Englanders themselves, or traded back to England. The bulk of Massachusetts' trade was with England, where it would ship back its furs and its fish. This fish was also sold in Spain and Portugal where it could be exchanged for wine, lemons and salt. It's quite easy to see in the early history of Virginia the future of the south, highly agricultural with a land owning gentry. Likewise, there is something of the north here. The commercial nature of the north-eastern ports was present from an early stage.

The initial group of immigrants formed a number of settlements along Massachusetts Bay, but as more and more people flooded into the region they pushed westwards. The sovereign body of the colony was the General Court, and it was this body alone that could issue a grant of land needed to found a settlement. A group of freemen needed to receive such a grant, and then the work could begin.

The settlers would arrive at the site and then set out a detailed plan, but all of these followed a general scheme. Typically, in the centre of the town was a lot sized 3-5 acres for use as a common. The main street would run around it, and on this street were the town's key buildings. These would include the church, the house of the minister, and the school. This would be surrounded by home lots (a lot for a house to be built). Each house came with a plot of land for cultivation slightly further out. Each of the original proprietors was given one of these lots, but there were others kept for future inhabitants. There was also some land reserved for common pasturage, and a common wood.

Religion was highly intertwined in the early political life of Massachusetts. This was reflected in the new. In 1631 freemanship was limited to members of the Puritan church. We previous discussed this in so far as that the vote was restricted, but since only freemen were able to appeal to the General Court for a grant of land, only members of the church were able to set up a new town. In 1635 membership of the church actually became compulsory, but only in certain areas. The religious qualification for citizenship was not universal. Only about 20% of the population were members of the church, but it is thought that the majority of the population was sympathetic towards the world view of the church, even though they were not members. There were even taxes which were used to pay for the church's upkeep. In the towns of Massachusetts, political action took place through the church. The church dealt with local administration, e.g. roads and maintenance of local buildings. Everyone was invited to these meetings, but only church members could vote.[57]

It is important to remember that not everybody emigrating to New England was leaving solely for religious reasons. By 1640 the population was around 14,000, which is rather large, and something of a more complex economy developed, reflecting the nature of these immigrants. Fur was a promising industry which was beginning to develop, and the forests of the region would be used for shipbuilding.

While the focus of the Virginia colony was the tobacco plantation, in New England it was the town. The great landowning aristocracy of Virginia did not develop in New England, and while slavery existed, it didn't reach the same levels here as it did in the south. Instead, the ambitious would set up small businesses, showing yet another trait of American culture, that of enterprise and rugged individualism.

Small business wasn't the primary focus of town life though. That was agriculture. This is because the New England towns were highly self-sufficient, producing what they needed themselves. The soil wasn't particularly fertile. It was cold, and it was rocky. It could provide them with food, but little else. There wasn't a great surplus. Instead, the great industry of New England was fishing.

The relationship between New England and its fisheries is legendary. The industry has declined recently, but is still of cultural importance. One such example is the Sacred Cod of Massachusetts, an

---

[57] And by 'everyone', I obviously mean 'white men'.

242

almost 5-foot-long wooden carving of an Atlantic Cod which still hangs in the House of Representatives chamber of the Massachusetts State House in Boston.[58]

Massachusetts and Gorges

Back in England, problems were being caused for the company by Gorges, whose patent the company had ruined. Gorges still considered New England his. He appealed to the Privy Council in 1632 with the aim of recovering this land, but this went nowhere. He wasn't discouraged, and with the help of others such as Thomas Morton and John Mason, he managed to get an investigation launched. Under the presidency of Archbishop Laud, a committee known as the Commission for Foreign Plantations was set up in 1633. Massachusetts wasn't happy with this, considering they had fled to the new world in large part to get away from Laud, and it isn't that surprising that the committee ruled in favour of Gorges. It was ordered that the company charter be returned to London. This was all well and good, but there was a significant problem with this. Massachusetts was 3,000 miles away from London, and it could just ignore the order. This it did.

Charles appointed Gorges governor-general of Massachusetts, John Mason was made vice-admiral, and they planned to put down this rebellion against the empire. This repression did not go well. They managed to get a ship to sail to America. Yes. One

---

[58] The cod has had a quite adventurous history, including an event when it was stolen by the Harvard Lampoon in the 1930s which I would encourage you all to look up.

ship. To reclaim Massachusetts. One ship. This ship immediately broke when it was launched. While the crown backed them, and Gorges and Mason had legal command in Massachusetts, they were stuck in England and could not do anything about it. Mason then died, leaving Gorges without the money to do anything to enforce his legal claim. Perhaps if he'd have had the backing of a powerful monarch this wouldn't have been an issue, but Charles was anything but a powerful monarch. He was broke and couldn't raise money without parliament. Parliament rebelled, and the English civil war made everybody forget that technically Massachusetts was an illegal colony in revolt against the crown. Being forgotten about was exactly how the New Englanders liked things. England didn't interfere, and they could just get on with business as, to all intents and purposes, a fully independent state. This was the state of affairs for the next half century, and it would not be until after the Restoration that England forced discipline upon her colony.

Chapter 10 – Rhode Island and Connecticut

Rhode Island is a curiosity. I'm not going to play favourites with states throughout this history, but there is something special about Rhode Island. It is the smallest state, only 1,214 square miles, 48 miles north to south and 37 miles east to west. For comparison, this is over 600 times smaller than the largest state, Alaska. It also has a rather unique and radical history. It was the first of the original thirteen colonies to go into rebellion against England, and was also the last to ratify the constitution. I've said previously that you can see states gaining their character from very early in their history, it will not take you very long to work out just how Rhode Island came to take this attitude. To do that, we need to look to its founder. Roger Williams.

Roger Williams

Williams was born in London, we're not sure on the exact date, but 1603 seems most likely. He was not born to a wealthy family. He was not part of the gentry, like Winthrop, but the son of a shopkeeper. He was a smart child, but his family was unable to fund an education. Luckily for Williams, he managed to find a patron – Sir Edward Coke, a commentator on English law. He studied divinity at Cambridge, and then became a chaplain for Sir William Masham. He fell in love with one of Masham's daughters, who rejected his marriage proposals, but eventually married one of the maids in 1629.

Williams was a bright young mind around Cambridge, so naturally his attention was captured by Puritanism. He took to it very passionately, and was critical of high Anglicanism with its Common Book of Prayer. This earned Williams the displeasure of William Laud, and he fled to Massachusetts in 1631.

Once he had arrived in the new world, we are able to get a better perspective of the type of puritan Williams was. Importantly, both for Williams and the future of the United States, he had a rather different perspective than did governor John Winthrop. Winthrop, you'll recall, didn't want to completely abandon the Church of England. He recognised that there were problems with it, but he wanted to fix the church from within. Not replace it. This was in stark contrast to the Separatist Pilgrims in Plymouth. Williams was a separatist too, and this was going to cause some issues.

For instance, when he arrived he was offered the position of minister at Boston, but Williams refused on the grounds that the Boston church wouldn't separate complete with the Church of England. He was then offered the ministry at Salem. Williams accepted. But Winthrop, who had greater power and prestige than anyone else in the colony, put pressure on Salem to withdraw the offer. They complied. It wasn't anything personal. Winthrop liked Williams, indeed, you might say he admired him. Winthrop had to appreciate William's intellectualism. But, he was disruptive. Winthrop was trying to build a unified religious establishment in the colony, and Williams, for all his promise, was an unwanted disruption. Williams was greatly discouraged by this, and decided to leave Massachusetts. He would settle with his fellow Separatists in Plymouth in 1631.

This didn't go particularly well. I've often said that the Pilgrims were the extreme fringe of Puritanism, and this led them to have some very fringe ideas for the time. One of them was tolerance, and this didn't sit quite well with Williams. He assisted the minister there, but he was uneasy with how relaxed the atmosphere was. The Pilgrims were very strict themselves, but they didn't enforce their strictness upon others. So, when people returned to England, they didn't particularly mind if they chose to go to worship in the Church of England. It was their right to do so. Williams couldn't abide by such an impure strain though, and so he left in 1633 and headed off to Salem.

They didn't offer him the position of minister, not wanting to provoke a reaction from Winthrop, but he was allowed to work as an assistant to the minister. This situation was untenable. It couldn't last. His extremism had forced him out once, and he wasn't going be restrained as the senior figures in the colony would have liked. Instead, Williams started making these senior figures rather uncomfortable by saying things they wished he wouldn't.

He mentioned that he thought the colony wasn't technically legal. Considering with how the company got the patent, and the issues of other patents which would mean that the colony ended up in rebellion, technically, for the better part of half a century, they weren't exactly happy about this. But what is really interesting, to me at least, is why Williams thought the patent was illegal. His point was that the patent was invalid because the King had no authority to grant the charter. The lands belonged to the Native Americans, not him.

The King of England was not authorised to give the land away.

The senior figures of the colony managed to get him to quiet down briefly, but not for long. In November 1634 he started to mention these issues again, and actually suggested that the charter should be sent back to England to be altered, and if his issues were not legally resolved that they should all return to England. Eventually, he was persuaded to stop talking about this in public. But, this was just one of many ideas that Williams had. And most of them were not very popular.

Purity is a reoccurring theme in the ideas of Williams. For instance, he believed that nonfreemen should not be given the oath of allegiance. This is because he considered the oath to be a form of worship, and therefore if an official gave the oath of alliance to an nonfreeman, he would be worshiping with a wicked person who was, by not being part of the church, taking the Lord's name in vain. He opposed the laws enforcing church attendance and the church tax, seeing them both as unnecessary interference in church affairs by the state. He was opposed by the elders and magistrates who again encouraged Salem to force him out. But they didn't. Instead, in April 1635, they elected him pastor.

1635 was a very eventful year for Williams. The General Court called him to Boston to explain himself, and force him to relent his claims that the state had no right to interfere with the church. At this particular moment, Salem made a request to the General Court to confirm their ownership of certain lands around Cape Ann. The Court saw this as an opportunity. They denied Salem's request and hinted that if they removed Williams then they could review the case. Williams was, as you might expect, outraged. He called upon all the churches of Massachusetts to condemn the General Court. They didn't. He then accused these churches of impurity, and called for the Church of Salem to separate itself completely. This was a step too far for the General Court, and in October 1635 they put him on trial. He was found guilty, and sentenced to 6 weeks' banishment. He was destabilising the colony, but it was autumn, and he was in ill health, so he was allowed to stay, as long as he kept quiet.

He returned to Salem to find his church divided, but he wouldn't compromise. He instead resigned. You'd think this would help him avoid trouble, but no. He held meetings with his friends, and preached to them, and continued to criticise the administration of the colony. This was the final straw for the magistrates. They decided to arrest him, but Williams was warned in advance by Winthrop and made his escape. In January 1636 he fled overland to Narragansett Bay, which lay just outside of Massachusetts. He lived for a while with the Indians, before moving onwards. It was here that he would be joined by those who sympathised with his cause. It was here that he set up Providence Plantation, which is still the capital of Rhode Island.

Providence Plantation

I'm quite sure he didn't quite intend what would happen as Williams set up his house and the foundations for a town. In many ways, it was exactly like a New England town. The heads of all the families would come together to run the town. However, there were a few differences which reflected Williams' altercation with the Massachusetts church. It was more democratic than Massachusetts. Williams was deeply uncomfortable with the system of power in the churches, which rather than giving authority to the congregation concentrated power in a small group of pastors. To Williams, this wasn't Puritanism, but rather Presbyterianism. Massachusetts was something of a religious oligarchy.[59]

Williams was deeply opposed to the power that these pastors had acquired over the whole colony for two distinct reasons. The first of these was that he felt religion was a private personal matter, and resented the state forcing its way into religious affairs. Church and state should be separated, not fused. The second was that he felt that it violated the concept of sovereignty deriving from the people. On the face of it this sounds very democratic, but it wasn't. Williams did not believe that every person automatically had a vote. He, like many at the time, viewed the state as something like a corporation. A corporation shouldn't be dominated by the men at the top, like was happening in Massachusetts, but, likewise, it shouldn't be run by everybody. What right did some person off the street have to interfere in the running of the company? The only people who had a stake in a company were the owners, the shareholders, the freemen. Every shareholder in the company had one vote, and as much say as any

---

[59] I personally find oligarchic theocracy a more pleasing phrase, but then I'm not director of Pawnee Parks and Recreation Department, so what do I know.

other shareholder. This right was not extended to the wider population of the colony. This gave power to a minority of the male population. This was the extent of Williams' democratic leanings.

There was very little 'government' at Providence. There was a compact which they would "from time to time subject ourselves in active and passive obedience to all such orders and agreements as shall be made... by the major consent of the present inhabitants... and others whom they shall hereafter admit until them, only in civil things." This is similar to the Mayflower Compact, except that it was clear that there was limited scope of government. But still, what was created here was very radical. It has been said that what Williams created was the most enlightened political institution in the world at the time. This was a free, secular republic.

While it was a republic, Williams was the heart of the plantation. He owned the land, and by 1637 was one of the most powerful men in New England. He had a trade with the Indians, and the Dutch at New Amsterdam. Williams didn't personally like politics, and had no real preference other than tolerance.[60] In 1638 he deeded his land to thirteen associates, he was one of them. In 1640 they adopted the Twelve Articles which said that they would be ruled by the 1636 compact, and governed by a group of 5 called 'the disposers', and an assembly made up of the heads of the families who owned land.

Anne Hutchinson

---

[60] which strikes me as odd when you think about how hard he fought to separate himself from the Church of England

251

Now we get to discuss one of the early great American women, Anne Hutchinson. Born in 1591 in Alford, England, Anne Marbury was the daughter of a clergyman and spent her early years in an intellectual atmosphere. In 1612 she married a merchant, William Hutchinson, and she remained interested in religious affairs. She was a follower of Reverend John Cotton, and travelled to Massachusetts in 1634. She was fascinated by Cotton's services, and started holding meetings at her house on every Tuesday to discuss the sermons with her friends, the other women of the colony. Cotton highly approved of this.

Hutchinson then did something rather unique for the time. She started talking about her own opinions. She didn't only talk about what Cotton thought, she had views too. Her meetings quickly gathered an audience as minsters and magistrates came to hear her speak. Her views centred on the individual relationship a person had with God, and that this relationship was far more important than institutionalised beliefs and the opinions of the ministers. This was risky stuff. Particularly in Massachusetts. Hutchinson's opinion that the views of the church were not important when compared to an individual's views couldn't be tolerated. She was a social threat. She quickly found herself opposed, and her enemies accused her of antinomianism, which is the view that God's grace releases Christians from the need to observe strict moral principles.

She found the concept of morality that her opponents were using very narrow, and she was supported at first, but this changed. The person behind the need for social harmony was John Winthrop. Once he opposed her, it was only a matter of time before her support fell away. She was tried by the General Court in 1637 and was sentenced to banishment, although she was held in custody until 1638 when she was tried before the Boston Church, and then excommunicated.

She decided to follow in the lead of Williams and found her own settlement. She went to Aquidneck Island in Narragansetts Bay and founded the settlement of Portsmouth with her supporters, including William Coddington. Unfortunately, her story doesn't have a happy ending. Her husband died in 1642 and she decided to leave Portsmouth. She travelled west to the site of the Bronx in New York City, and then she and most of her children and servants were killed in an Indian attack in 1643. Rather than the grisly end, we should instead focus on the fact that she spoke her mind and went on to found one of the initial four townships of Rhode Island. That's pretty cool. Speaking of which, we've set up Providence and Portsmouth, but we still need to found Warwick and Newport, which is why we now turn to William Coddington.

William Coddington and Samuel Gorton

Coddington was born in England in 1601 and migrated to Massachusetts in 1630. He held high office, being the company treasurer between 1634 and 1636, and he was also deputy in the legislature. However, he sided with Anne Hutchinson in her religious controversy, and so was forced to leave the settlement. He settled at Portsmouth with Hutchinson, not for long. He became embroiled in a dispute with Hutchinson and moved in 1639 to found the settlement of Newport, also on the island of Aquidneck. While he left, relations between the two towns were still friendly, and they unified in 1640 with Coddington elected governor. This makes three, and we must introduce the final player in Rhode Island history. Warwick, and Samuel Gorton.

New England is in many ways a story of people being continually forced out of places because nobody wanted their religious views. Perhaps Samuel Gorton is the ultimate examples of this. Gorton was born in 1593 in my own hometown, Manchester. He was, unlike many of those who travelled to New England, not a puritan, and this led to all his problems. He was inspired by the puritans and their challenge to traditional Anglican thought, but he didn't reach the same conclusions. He believed that the Holy Spirit was inside every person, giving them an inner divinity, and that this divinity should be followed rather than human authorities. A sort of Spiritism. Given the authoritarian position of the Massachusetts Church, confrontation was inevitable. He would never actually identify with a specific denomination, but this ideology was taken up by later groups such as the Quakers. This is easy to see by looking at terminology. A common phrase used by Quakers is to talk about 'Inner Light', or 'the Spirit of God within us'. Gorton travelled to Massachusetts in 1637, but he did this because he misunderstood what Massachusetts was. He believed that it was a bastion of religious toleration, which it most certainly wasn't.

After he arrived in Massachusetts, it didn't take very long for him to run into trouble. His views were controversial, and the magistrates of Massachusetts wanted to avoid controversy, and anything which threatened the unity that they were trying to create. He was very quickly banished, and he fled to Plymouth, hoping to find a better life there. This was, you'll recall, what Roger Williams had tried. However, just like Williams, he wasn't keen on Plymouth either. He found Plymouth too intolerant for him, and so he left and moved to Aquidneck Island, hoping to find the peace he wanted at either Portsmouth or Newport. Gorton soon got into trouble with Coddington, and was whipped, and forced to flee. He found protection at Providence with Williams, but still couldn't settle here. In 1643 he decided that he would just found his own town, since he couldn't get on with anybody else. He moved to the western shore of the bay and set up Warwick, where he was joined by those who shared his opinions. Because literally nowhere else would have him.

By 1643 there were four settlements around Narragansett Bay. Providence, Newport, Portsmouth, and Warwick. These four did not get on. This isn't that surprising. Gorton had been rejected by all three of the other settlements, and with so many settlements that close together, competition is inevitable. These four towns could have very easily fallen to infighting and been absorbed by one of their bigger neighbours. They were after all surrounded by Massachusetts, Plymouth, Connecticut, and the Indians too. They were all lurking, and the four settlements recognised the potential threat that this would cause. They decided that the best way to prevent their liberty being taken by one of the larger states was to cement a legal claim to the territory. Williams returned to London for a year, and returned with the 1644 Charter which he had managed to win against the wishes of the Massachusetts Bay Company.

Charter for Rhode Island and Providence Plantations

This charter was quite similar to the other charters we've seen so far in the story. The Incorporation of Providence Plantations was given the land around Narragansett Bay. They could not make laws contrary to the laws of England, but apart from this they had the right to self-govern as they saw fit, and use the land how they wanted. While this wasn't the optimal solution for the towns, who were very proud of their independent nature, they began to come together in order to best protect themselves.

The government of the four towns was unified in 1647. In May, representatives from the four towns met in Portsmouth and had something of a constitutional convention. It decided that the colony, Rhode Island, would be governed by an assembly made up of representatives from the four towns. While they knew that this assembly had to exist, it was to be kept weak. They disliked the centralised government of Massachusetts, and there were many unique factors of the Rhode Island constitution. Any law passed by the assembly had to be ratified by the towns, and legislation could only be initiated by a proposal from the towns, not by the assembly itself. There was to be a president who was elected by the assembly, in addition to four assistants who were also elected. This would happen once a year. The assembly would be made up of four representatives from each town. It was a federation which had freedom of conscience, and the separation of church and state. This all embodied the beliefs of Roger Williams. The dominant political battle for the following decades would be fought behind the scenes by Williams and Coddington. Coddington opposed the plans, and briefly in the 1650s manage to secure his own patent for Aquidneck Island, but this only lasted a few years before Williams managed to have it revoked. The situation wasn't properly resolved until the Royal Charter of 1663 issued by Charles II, but we will cover all of this later. It's now time to introduce Connecticut.

Connecticut

Connecticut is a rather interesting case, and it marks a turning point the narrative. One of the defining features of the American story is the push westwards. Connecticut is the point in the narrative where the second group of English settlements, New England, begins this move away from the coast. They had previously stayed close to Massachusetts Bay, but as the Puritan migration continued the settlers needed more land, and so they began to expand into the Connecticut valley.

This movement began in 1632 when our old friend Edward Winslow of Plymouth conducting a trading mission. Other ones followed, including one by another old friend, John Oldham. As the valley was explored, it became clear just how fertile it was. The other colonies soon began to view the territory with envious eyes. The Pilgrims and Dutch both began to construct outposts, Hartford and Winsor, but the ones most interested in the area were the poor settlers of Massachusetts. The person who would lead these efforts on behalf of the England was Thomas Hooker.

Hooker had moved to Massachusetts in 1633 and was one of the early leaders, but he disliked being overshadowed by John Cotton, whom you'll recall Hutchinson had followed to the colony. Hooker also had concerns over the colony's government. He disliked the fusion of church and state, how much power had been given to the magistrates, and the effects of the religious qualification for citizenship. He also had economic concerns, finding the lands on Massachusetts Bay not of much use.

The initial movement was setting up new towns with a slightly broader power base, but not very different to Massachusetts. In addition to Winsor and Hartford, the new towns included Wethersfield and Springfield, which would eventually leave this grouping and is today part of Massachusetts. Although, the exact legal status of these settlements was confused early on. I doubt you're surprised. The phrases 'New England Colony', and 'confused legal status', seem to be inseparable.

The colonies were acting under the jurisdiction of Massachusetts, but they desired their own political autonomy and began to make moves towards securing it. They set up a general court in 1637. This was a place where representatives from the towns would meet, and they could discuss matters which affected them all (such as methods of dealing with the Indians). This was a preamble. Matters developed in 1639 with the Fundamental Orders of Connecticut. Connecticut wouldn't receive a royal charter until 1662, which does make sense considering the English civil war. I'm quite sure for the intervening two decades Parliament would have had more pressing matters than formalising Connecticut.[61]

The Fundamental Orders of Connecticut began with a social compact, and then set up the government for the colony. There was a general assembly made up of four representatives from each town. This assembly was to meet twice a year. The qualification for citizenship and voting rights was not religious, as was the case in Massachusetts, but instead was based upon acceptance by the majority of inhabitants in the individual towns. There was a puritan character to the early settlers. The elected delegates had legislative responsibilities, and themselves elected magistrates which formed an upper house of the legislature and an executive. The exact function of the magistrates was vague, but not as murky as the magistrates of Massachusetts.

---

[61] I mean, technically Massachusetts was in rebellion and nobody cared about that.

Part 3

The Dutch

If the sixteenth century, colonialism was defined by the Hispano-Portuguese expansion into New Spain and South America. The seventeenth century was when European attention turned towards North America. The English, forever living on the fringes of Europe, threw themselves into the adventure and managed to set up two colonial groups, one centred upon tobacco growing around the Chesapeake and one with an eye towards fishing in Massachusetts Bay. They were mostly concerned with internal affairs. Matters of religion, matters of voting, matters of securing food. As time passed and they began to develop into actual settlements with characters of their own, their field of vision began to expand. They felt more secure, and abler to see what was going on beyond the horizon. What they found was that they were not alone. Just as important to the history of the United States are the other groups of European settlements popping up. The nucleus of New France was forming along the St. Lawrence, but our attention for Part Three of A History of the United States Volume 1 is located further south along the Atlantic seaboard. We now turn to what was happening along the Delaware and Hudson rivers. A complicated heterogeneous network of colonies was forming made up of Finns, Swedes, Flemings, Frisians, Holsteiners, Danes, Germans, French Huguenots, and, most importantly, the Dutch. Okay. Let's back up a bit. And when I say a bit, what I mean is a lot.

A Brief History of the Dutch

The Low Countries, the lands which would become the modern Belgium, Netherlands and Luxemburg, have a rather complicated past. They first appear in recorded history as on the frontier of the Roman Empire, forming part of the Roman province of Belgica. When the Roman Empire collapsed, it became dominated by a tribal group known as the Frisians, but the Franks always held a strong position and it was soon absorbed into the Frankish Empire of Charlemagne. The Frankish Empire did not long outlive Charlemagne. It broke into pieces. Broadly speaking the Western half became medieval France, and the Eastern half became the Holy Roman Empire, which is nothing at all like a traditional empire. It was more a collection of quasi-independent states who collectively elected an emperor with some power over the whole group. The Low Countries, as a collection of these principalities, were sucked into the Holy Roman Empire. Holland quickly became the most powerful of these principalities, but it was inevitable that a more powerful neighbour would pounce. It finally happened in the later Middle Ages when the region was dominated by the Duchy of Burgundy, one of the more interesting lost states of Europe which I would highly encourage you to research. The Duchy was, in the wider Feudal scheme, a vassal of the King of France, and would spend much of the fifteenth century in an ultimately doomed fight to secure independence from France.

The last Duke of Burgundy, Charles the Bold, was killed fighting the French in 1477, extinguishing the Duchy, but not the line family. Now, things are about to get complicated. Charles the Bold had a daughter named Mary, and Mary claimed the title of Duchess of Burgundy. Mary was married to Maximillian, the son of the Holy Roman Emperor Frederick III, a Habsburg of Austria. Mary died in

1482, passing the title to her 4-year-old son Philip the Handsome, who became the Duke of Burgundy. Fighting took place in the Low Countries about whether they should side with Charles VIII of France, or Holy Roman Emperor Frederick III. Then Frederick died, simplifying the matter. Maximillian became Holy Roman Emperor Maximillian I and Archduke of Austria. In 1493 a council of Burgundian Nobles gave the position of Lord of the Netherlands to the 16 year-old Philip. This is how control of the Netherlands passed into the hands of the Austrian Habsburgs. With me so far? Good.

Okay, Spain. Spain didn't technically exist at this point. What existed was a marriage alliance between Isabella I of Castile, which controlled most of what is today Western and Central Spain, and Ferdinand II of Aragón, which controlled Eastern Spain, Sardinia, and was in the process of conquering Sicily and Naples. This pair had several children. A younger daughter would be Catherine of Aragon, who famously married Henry VIII of England and was the mother of Queen Mary I, but we are really only interested in the oldest 3. Isabella, Juan, and Joanna. Juan was the heir, and married Margaret of Austria, the sister of Philip. Isabella married Manuel I of Portugal, and Joanna married Philip.

Juan died in 1497, making Isabella the heir, but she died the next year while giving birth to a son who was sickly, and shortly died. This made Joanna the heir to Castile, Aragon, and Naples. She and Philip had a son in 1500, Charles, or as I've previously referred to him, Carlos. Now, Isabella died in 1504 making Joanna her heir, and Philip was crowned as king, but he died 1506 to be succeeded by his son

Charles. To recap: Maximillian I is Holy Roman Emperor and Archduke of Austria, 6 year old Charles is Lord of the Netherlands, Joanna is Queen of Castile, and Ferdinand II is King of Aragon and Naples. All good? Good. Let's continue.

Ferdinand II died in 1516, and was succeeded by Joanna, making her the Queen of Castile and Aragon. Although these two titles would never again be separated, so we might as well just call her Queen of Spain. Joanna has a very interesting life story, but she likely suffered from depression and was considered mad at the time. She made Charles co-ruler, and soon after she was placed into forced confinement. While she was technically Queen of Spain until 1555, here she exits the narrative, and to all intents and purposes Charles was now King of Spain, and he came with the rule of Southern Italy, and the title of Lord of the Netherlands. This is how the Habsburgs came to rule Spain. The Habsburgs were the dominant power in Europe, but their power was about to be concentrated.

In 1519 Emperor Maximillian I died. The three contenders for the title of Holy Roman Emperor were Charles I of Spain, Francois I of France, and Henry VIII of England. In an attempt to stop one of these becoming Holy Roman Emperor, the Pope backed Frederick the Wise of Saxony, the protector of Martin Luther, allowing Martin Luther to not be killed. The pope's efforts were not successful, and Charles was chosen, making him Emperor Charles V. This added Austria and the Holy Roman Empire to his already extensive domains, which increased ever more when you factor in the conquests Spain would make in the Americas. Charles V was by some margin the most powerful man in the world. But, we're not talking about that. We're talking about the Netherlands. The purpose of this whole detour was to get here, where we now understand just what the Austrians and Spanish are doing in the Netherlands in the First Place. It took a lot of explaining, but I found this method infinitely preferable to just starting with, 'So the Spanish and Austrians are in the Netherlands.'

But, we are now at that point. The Spanish are in the Netherlands. The Dutch were okay with this, and the situation continued until far into the sixteenth century, but began to run into problems during the reign of Philip II who ascended to the throne in 1556. He was, it's worth mentioning, also the King of England at this point he was married to Queen Mary, the daughter of Henry VIII and Catherine of Aragon.[62] In 1557 we have a report from a Venetian ambassador who wrote that the Dutch nobles were troubled by Philips preference for Spain rather than the Netherlands. He adopted a Spanish lifestyle, and filled his councils with Spanish and Italian advisors. I should note that there is nothing particularly strange about this. Philip did have to administer both Castile and Aragon, and it was only natural that he would have advisors from those territories to help govern them. But the Dutch nobility were annoyed. Philip attempted to impose commercial regulations which the Dutch opposed, and he also tried to force a return to Catholicism. The Protestant Dutch were tolerant, but they did

---

[62] If you are at this point thinking, wait, were Mary and Philip related, you would be correct. Catherine of Aragon was the younger sister of Philip's grandmother Joanna. Just in case understanding all of this wasn't confusing enough.

not want Catholicism forced upon them. In 1568 they started a war of independence known as the Eighty Years War.

The Eighty Years War

This conflict began with an invasion of the Netherlands by Prince William I of Orange, who raised a mercenary army augmented by Dutch irregular forces. The initial attack in 1568 was unsuccessful, as was a second in 1572, but then things began to go right. By 1573 the provinces of Holland and Zeeland were captured and protected against the Spanish. In 1576 the rest of the provinces joined in open revolt and the war for independence was on. The region fragmented during this war into the more hostile north, and the more reconcilable south. The seven northern provinces broke away in 1579, and two years later declared themselves independent as the United Provinces of the Netherlands. The southern provinces, which would become Belgium, made peace as they were reconquered by the Spanish by 1588. It looked as though the independent north was about to be crushed into oblivion. But, it was not to be. Spain overreached. At the same time as it was engaged against the Dutch, it was also fighting the English. 1588 was famously the year of the Spanish Armada. As the Spanish became distracted, it allowed the Dutch to begin a counter offensive, and establish their position. A truce was arranged in 1609. About the time that the Pilgrims were arriving in the Netherlands. You'll recall one of the factors in them leaving was a worry that the war with Spain would restart, which indeed it did, as part of the Thirty Years War.

The war commenced in 1621 with a series of early Spanish successes, but the tide reversed. The Dutch managed to secure their position, and gained an advantage by allying with the French who pushed into Flanders. Eventually peace came about, and the United Provinces of the Netherlands was recognised as an independent state in the 1648 Treaty of Munster. So, that's the story of the Dutch. But, I know what you're asking. This is all very interesting, but what does this have to do with the Dutch founding the New Netherlands? The answer: everything.

Since Philip the Handsome married Joanna and became king of Spain, the Netherlands were sucked into the Spanish trade network. The Habsburg Empire was the most powerful state in the world, so it is only natural that this continued under the reign of Charles. The Dutch were a maratine people, they were traders, so it was only natural that their ships would frequent the ports of the Iberian Peninsula. Cadiz and Lisbon were the most popular destinations as they sold manufactured goods from Northern Europe, and brought back spices from the far east, or tobacco and precious metals from the New World. It was only logical. This was massively complicated by the war with Spain.

The Spanish were not going to trade with a people they were at war with. There was still Lisbon, but in 1580 Spain annexed Portugal and so this was no longer an option. This forced the Dutch, if they wanted to keep trading, to bypass the Iberian leg of the journey, and just go directly to the new world. They started to sail directly to the islands of the Caribbean and the far east to trade for spices directly without the Iberian middlemen, and started to attack Spanish and Portuguese ships. This was very profitable, and the Dutch began to organise themselves, setting up the Dutch East India Company in 1602 for both trade and war. They also began to get more serious about the New World, and the Dutch East India Company contacted an Englishman by the name of Henry Hudson to go search for a sea route around America to the Far East.

Henry Hudson

Henry Hudson was one of the great explorers as the turn of the seventeenth century, and we know almost nothing about his early life. We suspect he was born sometime around 1565, and we cannot get more specific than 'England' as to a location. We know nothing about the first 40 years of his life, and he emerges into the historical narrative in 1607. It seems that his family was connected with the drive towards Arctic exploration, and he probably developed an interest in this early on in his life.

It might seem odd that the Dutch would turn to an Englishman interested in Arctic exploration as a solution to their trade conflict with the Spanish, but if you think about it, it makes sense. The biggest problem for the Dutch traders was that the places they were trading with were really far away. Really, really far away. The world is a lot smaller today than it was 400 years ago. This is partly because of air travel, but also because of the construction of canals, in particular the Suez Canal and the Panama Canal. If you wanted to sail from the Netherlands to the far east, you would have to sail around Europe, around Africa, and then across the Indian Ocean.

That would get you to the Indies. Then there was the extra voyage north if you wanted to travel to China. What everybody was looking for was a shortcut to getting there faster, and that's how Henry Hudson enters the story.

In 1607 the Muscovy Company of London hired Hudson to find the Northeast Passage, a shortcut to Japan via the North Pole. Hudson was convinced that he would find an ice-free sea to the north of Russia, and he was convinced that he was the man to find it. He set sail north and made his way to the Svalbard Archipelago, a collection of islands halfway between Norway and the North pole. He explored the area, but he was unable to make his way through the ice. He was pushed back, and decided to try again. This time he would look for a route between Svalbard and Novaya Zemlya, a large island to the North of the Ural Mountains. This too was a failure as he was pushed back by ice, and he returned to England in August.

Whilst there, he was lured to Amsterdam by the Dutch East India Company. They wanted him to take another voyage to find the Northeast passage, but while he was there he heard reports of another possible route to the Pacific, the Northwest passage. There were 2 theories about where this would be. One came from John Smith who suggested that there was a route at 40 degrees north, and another came from George Weymouth who thought that there was something at 62 degrees north. Hudson was interested in these theories, but he had a job to do for the Dutch East India Company. He told them that he would set sail in 1609 for the Northeast passage, but if he was forced back he would return to Amsterdam and they could look at the Northwest passage.

He set sail in April 1609 and travelled north east, but was soon pushed by heavy winds. He immediately changed his mind about returning to Amsterdam, and simply turned his ship west. He decided to investigate the claims made by John Smith and so travelled to the fortieth parallel north. He found a river which had been originally discovered by the Europeans almost a century before which he named the Mauritius after Prince Maurice, the future Prince of Orange. However, this name would not stick, and it is instead named after Henry himself, the Hudson.

Hudson sailed up the Hudson for a hundred miles to the site which would become Albany, before concluding that, despite Smith's theories, this river did not lead to the Pacific. He bought some furs, beginning Dutch trade in the region, and then sailed back to England where he was ordered to cease and desist exploring for other nations. He sent on his log to the Netherlands, and the Dutch became increasingly interested in the region. But, before we move on to further Dutch action in the region, I'd just like to finish off telling the story of Henry Hudson. He would make one more journey to try and find the Northwest passage, this time using the information collected by Weymouth and sailing to the 62nd parallel north where he did indeed find an inlet to a great body of water which was also named after him. I'm of course talking about Hudson Bay. Hudson sailed around, reaching James Bay (the southerly point of Hudson Bay), and when he realised this he became rather frustrated. The situation on board the ship because troublesome and there was a mutiny in 1611. Hudson was kicked off the ship, never to be heard from again. This would form the basis of English claims to Canada.

Following this initial exploration, Dutch ships sailed to the Hudson for trade purposes almost every year. Then in 1614 Adriaen Block sailed with the intention of exploring. He journeyed along the Long Island Sound, and it is likely that he also travelled into the Connecticut Valley. This expedition was very successful, and a group of merchants in Amsterdam put together something known as the New Netherland Company. This gave them a patent to send out four trade missions in three years. They constructed a fort on the Hudson near the modern site of Albany, but when the patent expired in 1618 the fort was abandoned, and others were free to trade in the area.

While the New Netherland Company wouldn't play much of a role in history, it would be succeeded by a wider group of merchants who were very ambitious in colonial ambitions, it is in this context that the Dutch tried to settle the Pilgrims as a Dutch colony, but as you'll recall this didn't work out. Instead, what was created in 1621 by the States General was the Dutch West India Company, and play a role in world history the Dutch West India Company most certainly would.

The Dutch West India Company

While the New Netherlands Company was based in Amsterdam, the setup of the Dutch West India Company was national. There were regional groups which were all part of the company throughout the Netherlands, each with its own board of directors, which sent delegates to a council of 19 in Amsterdam (18 send by the regional councils, one send by the States General). This council was the governing apparatus of the Dutch West India Company, and had substantial powers. It had a monopoly of all commercial activities along the American coast and in the Atlantic south of the tropic of Cancer. It could create laws, administer justice, raise and maintain armies, make war and treaties with foreign powers, all by itself. This is something completely different to the companies we've dealt with so far, and was effectively a state in its own right. It had three main interests. 1) Establishing colonies in the new world. 2) Trade with North American Indians. 3) Make war on the Spanish. We'll deal with the latter of these first by turning southwards to the Caribbean.

There was a raid against Bahia, a Portuguese port, which was launched in late 1623. The settlement was captured in 1624, giving the Dutch a great deal of plundered profit. This was a very productive start, although they were pushed out by the resurgent Spanish in 1625. However, while this was going on, the Dutch West India Company, began to make their move on the North American continent.

They sent out a colonising expedition led by Cornelius Jacobsen May. It was funding by the Dutch, but the population of this expedition was mostly made up of French speaking protestants from the area which would become Belgium. This first colony was very different to the English colonies, which had focused on founding individual settlements. Jamestown was the focus of Virginia, and then the Pilgrims focused on the settlement of

Plymouth. The Dutch did not want to follow this plan, they had their own ideas.

The Dutch were primarily interested in the fur trade, and so they intended to set up a multitude of settlements from the beginning. They initially landed on Manhattan Island, but soon divided into a number of small groups and set up settlements around the region. One group constructed Fort Nassau in the Delaware Valley, another was created on the Connecticut. But these were only secondary, the two important settlements were founded on the Hudson. A group of colonists travelled up the Hudson where they settled at a sight known as Fort Orange which would become Albany.

A group of the settlers decided to not leave the mouth of the Hudson, and settled at what is now known as Governors Island. This settlement was a brilliant strategic and commercial location, and soon became the heart of the colony. More ships and colonists arrived and it was realised that Governors Island was too small, meaning that in 1625 a permanent fort was constructed at the southern tip of Manhattan Island, Fort Amsterdam, at the current sight of the Alexander Hamilton U.S. Custom House. This is the foundation of New York City.

Fort Amsterdam

Within the original Fort Amsterdam was the office of the Dutch West India Company, in addition to a church, a market, barracks, and the governor's residence. Settlers built farms outside the fort, and the settlement spread along the East River. During the first few years of the colony the governor, Peter

Minuit, would secure land for the colony by buying Manhattan Island. The price was for goods worth 60 guilders.[63]

The structure of this colony was quite different to the English colonies. In theory, all settlers were servants of the Dutch West India Company rather than shareholders. They were told where they had to live, and had to work for the company for six years. This was in exchange for the company paying for their transport, and the land they were given in America. They were also given tools and supplies for two years, and only had to begin to pay this off once their land began to make a profit. Internal trade was allowed, but all goods for export had to be sold to the company, and small industry was forbidden to protect the company's monopoly. The governor had absolute control and required total obedience. It was expected that they be Calvinist, and that they actively try to convert the indigenous population. However, the colony actually contained religious toleration, and it was law that nobody be persecuted for religious beliefs. This was unlike the English colonies which were springing up around Massachusetts bay.

I cannot overemphasise what a perfect location New Amsterdam was in. It was a settlement almost guaranteed to be a success, it just required time. It was the English would be the main beneficiaries, and this period of the history of the region is characterised by growth which while steady, was slow. Perhaps it could have been quicker, but the

---

[63] There is no agreement about what this converts to. I've seen figures estimating $100 and $15,000, and many figures in between.

Dutch had a problem of attracting colonists. While Massachusetts Bay would be filled by religious decedents fleeing persecution, the Dutch weren't really inclined to leave the Netherlands. Most of the free population were Walloons and Frenchmen, not to mention African slaves. To try and encourage migration, the Dutch West India Company tried creating something approaching a feudal set up. A colonist who brought 50 settlers with them would be given a strip of land. They would have a feudal title with this land, and have complete feudal control. This wasn't a great success, and the autonomy of the feudal lords created complications with the ban of foreign trade. This ban had to be sort of listed, and the lords could acquire a licence from the company as long as they paid a customs fee.

While not the main industry, farming was crucial to securing a food supply for the colony. They didn't have any great problems, finding that the wheat and rye both grew well on Manhattan. They settled there late on in 1625, and in 1626 they managed to export 45,000 guilders' worth of grain. By 1632 this amount expanded to 125,000 guilders. While this was an important foundation, the monopoly of the fur trade the colony held was its single greatest economic advantage.

The second most successful industry was alcohol production, to the extent that drunkenness became problem and regulation was needed. They forbade selling alcohol to the Indians, although this didn't work, and in 1638 it was required that all sailors be back on their ships once darkness fell.

As for government, New Netherland supposedly had the same laws as the Netherlands, but in practice it took on a very military character. This stemmed from the first governor, Cornelius Jacobsen May, being the captain of the ship which brought them to the New World, and them keeping ship rules. This is why New Netherland is often described as an amphibian colony. There were other offices of the colony who controlled trade and order, as well as a council with advisors, but the size of this council fluctuated by quite some margin over time. The governor and council were all three branches of government, the executive, legislature and judiciary. They were responsible only to the company. Occasionally, the population was able to influence the government, such as forcing through a change of governor in 1647. As a rule, they had no say in governance. There was a meeting of representatives to hear these protests in 1653, but this didn't result in any meaningful changes. The only thing that altered was that the sheriffs were now appointed from among the local residents rather than from outside, but they were still appointed by the governor. This was as close as New Netherland would ever get to democracy.

The cosmopolitan nature of the settlement gave it character, but it never really developed something you could call culture. The Dutch themselves weren't interested in education, only commerce. It took until 1637 for a school teacher to be sent over, but he couldn't live off teaching alone and had to take a second job. A school wasn't constructed until 1655, and a Latin school was opened in 1658. A fire service was created in 1657, followed in the next year by a police force.

It must be remembered that this was only one aspect of the Dutch West India Company. Arguably, it's priority in these years was its conflict with Spain and Portugal. In 1630 they made a rather bold move against the Portuguese and actually invaded Brazil, capturing the northeastern provinces, an area twice the size of the Netherlands, which was named New Holland.[64]

We are rapidly nearing the point where the colony became New York, but we have an important event New Netherland was involved with, because by the time it became New York it cannot really be considered solely a Dutch colony anymore. This is because of another colony to which we must now turn, New Sweden.

---

[64] New Holland doesn't really have much to do with the USA, but it must be noted that during the two decades or so that it existed, New Holland was the focus of the Dutch West India Company. Not New Netherland. It was far wealthier, more cultural, and it was a more attractive proposition to settlers than a shack on the Hudson. It was too attractive for it to be allowed to exist. The Portuguese were deeply unhappy, and recaptured the territory by 1654.

Chapter 12 – New Sweden

Sweden has a long history stretching back into the murky past, where it is impossible to separate history and legend. Our overview of Dutch history was confusing, and I'm not even going to attempt to chronical how the small kingdoms of Sweden joined together. That would be a complete waste of time in a history of the United States. But, join together the states did, and we know that at some point in the later middle ages a Swedish state came to exist, and that this state managed to gain control of the region which is now Finland, although it is a mystery how this happened.

In the late fourteenth century Sweden was brought together with the crowns or Norway and Denmark in the Union of Kalmar. This lasted for a century until the Union disintegrated and Sweden once again became independent. It would spend the sixteenth century as a regional power, but it only really becomes an important player in history in 1611 with the ascension of Gustavus II Adolphus, a man regarded as the founder of the Swedish Empire. Gustavus was one of the most brilliant generals in world history, and is often considered the first modern general. He within a few years managed to turn Sweden into the third largest state in Europe, behind only Russia and Spain. He, in short, turned Sweden from a regional power into a world power. It ushered in the stormaktstiden, literally, the period of great power, which would last until Sweden lost the Great Northern War in 1721.

Sweden was the ambitious state in Europe, and it was this new found confidence that led them to believe that what they really needed to do was found a colony in the New World. I really need to emphasis just how upbeat the Swedes were about this, because if I don't then their decision to found a colony makes no sense. There were a lot of reasons for it being a bad idea. I suppose when you're wearing rose tinted glasses, all the red flags just look like flags.

Why Sweden Wanted a Colony

It makes sense for England, France, Portugal, the Netherlands, and Spain, to be conducting colonial efforts in the New World. They all had direct access to the Atlantic. This was problematic for Sweden. Their heartland was around the Baltic, meaning that they would either need to go overland across Scandinavia, or through Danish waters, if they wanted to get to America. Both were problematic. The next issue was population size. England's population in 1600 was around 5 million, Spain had a population of approximately 8 million, and France contained 20 million people. These were all countries which could afford to send some of their population to America. In contrast, Sweden was very sparsely populated. Despite being the third largest country in Europe, it only had around a million inhabitants. This problem was complicated by the wars of Gustavus Adolphus.

In the decade before his death in 1632, around 50,000 soldiers lost their lives giving the country a reputation as a nation of soldier's widows. Losing 5% of the population was a massive blow. The modern equivalent would be the UK losing three and a half million people, or the US fighting a war in which 16 million young men would die. It's not hard to see the problems caused by such a gender imbalance would have on the long term population of the country. It was also the loss of a significant part of the tax base. Those left would have to pay a higher rate, not to mention the already high rates to fund the army which employed perhaps 15% of the population. For comparison, the famous military state which is the Roman Empire never exceeded having 2% of the population in the military. And that is at a maximum. It probably never exceeded 1%. That is a huge percentage of the population to be a drain on the economy rather than producing. Partly because of this, Sweden had a very medieval economy. It barely moved beyond the feudal era. They had succeeded in conquering their neighbours, but they were clearly not destined for world domination. But nobody wanted to think about such depressing matters. They were more than happy to dream of a colonial empire on the Delaware River.

There were a group of merchants operating around the Baltic who were involved with Spanish and Dutch trade, the most important of whom at first was Willem Usselinx. He was Flemish, born in Antwerp, a city presently in Belgium. He was a merchant, but was more a dreamer of expeditions than a practical trader. He was very influential in the foundation of the Dutch West India Company, but was shunned by the merchants because of his impractical ideas. Usselinx looked around for an audience which would be more approving of him, and he found it in the ambitious Swedish Empire. Gustavus Adolphus was certainly interested in the idea, and invested quite heavily in it. He commissioned something known as the South Company in 1627 which was to conduct Swedish trade throughout "Africa, Asia, America, Magellanica or terra Australia", to settle foreign lands, and conduct diplomacy, and raise funds by subscription. Gustavus Adolphus thought it was a terrific idea. He invested heavily in the project, and ordered all officials, soldiers, and merchants to do the same. How could this not work?

Well, the huge list of problems I've just mentioned. Sweden was suffering a manpower crisis because an already small population had been diminished by warfare. This resulted in high taxes, and the large military meant there was a lack of investment in the state's infrastructure. The end product of all this issues was that there wasn't surplus wealth to make such a venture feasible. Even if it was a good idea, and I must repeat that it wasn't, Sweden wasn't in a position to create a global empire, no matter how successful Gustavus Adolphus' wars were. The rational thing to do would be for Gustavus Adolphus to not go through with the plan, and instead invest in Sweden. He should have focused on modernising the country and wealth creation, not throwing their surplus away. But if history teaches you anything, it's that people are rarely rational.

Unsurprisingly, the South Company was unable to raise enough subscriptions and the venture fell flat on its face. By 1629 the venture was, to all intents and purposes, dead. Usselinx wasn't one to give up so quickly. The South Company transformed into the United South-Ship Company, which also went nowhere. Then in 1635 it entered its final incarnation, the New Sweden Company. While at this point Usselinx was financially ruined, this venture was hopefully. It had received the support and backing of others involved with the Dutch West

India Company, such as Samuel Blommaert, a well-connected Dutch merchant who, in addition to being a director of Dutch West India Company, had experience of working in the region of the Delaware river. He also had an interest in Swedish markets, particularly brass, copper and grain, and he saw the possibility of trading these goods around the Atlantic. Blommaert was able to form a close relationship with Axel Oxenstierna, the chancellor. They also brought on Peter Minuit, the former director of New Netherland who had made the purchase of Manhattan island. If you will allow me to quote The Barbarous Years by Bernard Bailyn, "Thus tied to and patronised by the highest leadership of the Swedish government, the Swedish West India Company began its short, strange, and well-recorded career."

New Swedish Company

By the time the New Swedish Company was founded in 1635, Gustavus Adolphus had died. He was replaced by his daughter Christina, who was born in 1626. Since she was only a child, real power passed to Axel Oxenstierna, the powerful chancellor. Usselinx had been ruined by his unsuccessful attempts to form a colony, and so the role of lead merchant passed to Smauel Blommaert, one of the chief investors and directors of the company who had formerly been a director of the Dutch West India Company. There was also Peter Minuit, who we have mentioned before as the German born former director of New Netherland who purchased Manhattan, and a few others who we haven't previously mentioned, Admiral Klas Fleming, who would become director of the New Sweden Company, and the Dutch born Politian

Peter Spiring, who would both represent government interests within the company.

After gathering together their resources, an expedition made of both Dutch and Swedes set out for America in 1637. It was made up of sailors and soldiers rather than settlers, and was primarily focused on exploration. The Swedes had not yet travelled to the new world, and the company had the mandate to trade and plant colonies on the North American continent, from Newfoundland to Florida. This is slightly misleading though. As strange as it is to think about, we are only 30 years on from the founding of Jamestown, most of the Atlantic Seaboard had already been claimed by the Europeans. The French were firmly entrenched in the north around the St. Lawrence, the Spanish had long been in Florida and the Carolinas were part of their sphere of influence. The English had bases set up on the Chesapeake and Massachusetts Bay, and the Dutch were on the Hudson. There was only one real place for the Swedes to go, and that was Delaware, which may be why they had already identified that as their best target.

The expedition arrived at the Delaware in 1638. After they had learnt about the area most returned home, but they did leave twenty men, along with an Angolean slave, to set up a base camp. This was Fort Christina, a few miles off the Delaware on a major Indian trade route. It is approximately the sight of the modern Wilmington, Delaware. They remained their two years, and in 1640 a second expedition arrived bringing more settlers. There were 5 expeditions between 1640 and 1644, and during these years the foundation of the colony was built.

A series of settlements were constructed along the shores of the Delaware for a hundred and twenty miles. It was thinly populated, much like Sweden itself. The colony would exist for around 20 years, and it is strange that it lasted so long, and would become part of the American identity. This is because after 1644 the Swedes lost interest in the expedition. Only 4 ships were sent from Sweden to the colony after 1644, and one of them was after it had been absorbed by New Netherland. How a colony which never exceeded more than 400 people survived for so long, unsupported, and surrounded by much more powerful colonies, is something of a mystery, but let's just get into it.

New Sweden

Peter Minuit was the first leader of the colony, and he managed to secure from the Indians a 50-mile stretch of land along the western bank of the Delaware. He drew up a map and the supervised the construction of the fort before making the voyage back to Europe to attract more settlers. Minuit had a plan for how to grow the population of the settlement. He was from a Wesel, a town on the German-Dutch border. Things on the continent had been rather unstable with the 30 Years' War, and the population was rather unsettled. There was a possibility that these people would be interested in heading over and forming a strong population base, but it wasn't to be. On his voyage back in 1638 Minuit died in a storm in the Caribbean. It was a huge blow.

Back in Sweden, Fleming and Spiring were making their preparations for the second expedition, despite hearing that their Dutch backers were pulling out because the venture had not made immediate profits. They had the supplies, they just needed people to go. Orders were sent out to governors to attract artisans and their wives, but this was unproductive. The artisan class was happy, and didn't want to be moved, so instead one of the governors proposed that they instead collect soldiers who had deserted the army or who had committed crimes. Also collected were a mixture of thieves, poachers, embezzlers, adulterers, debtors and tax defaulters. You know, a good group. Exactly who you want to be the foundation of your empire. I joke, but they really didn't have much of a choice. Nobody wanted to go, so they would take who they could get.

The majority of the population of the settlement was from Sweden and Finland, which had long been under Swedish control. By the 1655 Finns made up 40% of the colony's population. In addition to these were two major groups of foreigners. One was the Dutch. The Dutch were highly involved in setting up the company, and a group of Dutch families from Utrecht arrived and set up a separate base 18 miles to the North of Fort Christina, while to the south a group of approximately 20 English families settled at Varkens Kill, which would become Salem, New Jersey. This group was mostly made up of people from Yorkshire and Cornwall, in addition to an expedition by New Haven.

I haven't actually mentioned New Haven yet, so I'll give a brief background to it here. New Haven was a Puritan settlement and short lived colony founded in 1638 on the Long Island Sound. It was a typical Puritan settlement. Representative government, citizenship was church based etc. Although, an interesting quirk is that rather than basing its legal system upon England, as was typical, it instead based it upon the bible. This gave it a rather unique character. It did not have trial by jury because it was not a feature of Mosaic law. It would form its own little empire, spreading settlements across the sound to Long Island itself, and it had a group of merchants which formed the English Delaware Company who helped found Varkens Kill. It only survived as an independent colony for around twenty years before being absorbed by Connecticut. Tangent over, back to New Sweden.

New Sweden is surprisingly well documented. There were around 300 inhabitants, and we can identify over 200 of them, including 21 women, by name and where they came from. In addition to the Swedes and Finns were Dutch, Norse, Danes, and even an Irishman. It was this diverse, mostly criminal, population that Minuit's replacement as governor, Peter Ridder, had to work with when he arrived in 1640.

His actions all served the purpose of creating a stable foundation for the colony. Fort Christina had been damaged, so he repaired it. Clearings were made in the forests to grow vegetables and tobacco, and he secured friendship with the Lenapes, the local Indians. Ridder was well-intentioned, but not strong enough to force his will upon the colony. Ridder's take on the population was, and I quote, "It would be impossible to find more stupid people in all Sweden." The population was unproductive, unskilled, liable to infighting, the Dutch and Swedes didn't get on, and both Dutch and English traders were constantly trying to extort them by charging outrageous prices for goods. It seemed like the colony was about to collapse, then Ridder was replaced by John Bjornsson Printz. He had served in the Swedish army very successfully, rising to the rank of lieutenant colonel during a series of wars fought in the Holy Roman Empire. In 1640 he was forced to surrender the city of Chemnitz, and then left Germany without reporting the loss or obtaining permission to leave. He was arrested, court marshalled, and exiled to Finland. He had a point to prove, and would hold the governorship of New Sweden for ten years.

These ten years were highly frustrating for Printz. He constantly appealed for reinforcements, determined to salvage his reputation, but he was ignored. Two ships arrived after 1644, and none after 1647. Printz was able to force his will upon the colony. He was a large man. And I mean that literally. He weighed over 400 pounds. He drank heavily, had a fierce temper, and took a highly authoritarian approach. There could be no opposition.

He arrived in January 1643, and found that the population only had 105 adult males. It was small. All his supplies had rotted, and everybody wanted to leave. Relationships with the Lenapes were friendly enough, but were more complicated with the Susquehannocks, who acted as middlemen between the colony and the Iroquois. Printz felt that he couldn't trust either people, not thinking them as any different to the Powhatans who would massacre the Virginians in 1644. They were also not particularly interested in converting to Christianity, leading the Swedes to believe that they should be forced to convert, and killed if they resisted.

Printz never got the reinforcements he wanted. In addition to campaigning in Germany, Sweden was preoccupied with a war with Denmark. This was followed by agricultural depression, commercial recession, and political struggle. The population was down to 183 by 1644, with only 83 adult males.

The Swedes considered the English to be their primary foes in the region. They forced Varkens Kill to change its allegiance to New Sweden, and formed an amicable relationship with the Dutch so that they could mutually protect themselves against the English. They would have a rivalry with each other for the fur trade, but they would otherwise act as partners, for now.

So, let's sum up. The settlement was weak, and only Printz, through sheer force of will, was able to keep it from falling apart. But, he couldn't perform the impossible. Supplies stopped coming from 1646. There was another expedition which would have helped in the late 1640s, but it was shipwrecked off the coast of Puerto Rico. Printz wrote in 1650 that there were less than 30 men in the colony that he actually trusted. If you'll allow me to quote The Barbarous Years by Bernard Bailyn.

> "By 1653 the colony's small population of independent farmers was scattered in isolated woodland encampments that were only gradually becoming cultivated. But while the freemen were more or less content to continue clearing and planting, and proceeded to construct, besides a mill of

traditional Swedish design, a makeshift brewery and a small shipyard, the officials, servants, and soldiers were restless and fearful. The officials and higher-status adventurers were prevented from fully exploiting the fur trade by Printz's restrictive rule; the servants, debilitated and sickly, worked under desperate conditions with little to look forward to; and the soldiers, guarding swampy wilderness forts, were bored, beset by lurking dangers, poorly equipped, and weakly armed. All three groups were eager to escape from the colony, and some began to think enviously of what they had heard of conditions in New Netherland and Maryland."

Dutch Involvement

The director-general of New Netherland at this point was Peter Stuyvesant. It was a position he achieved in 1647, and he would hold it until 1664. He was an equally large personality as Printz, and his arrival in New Amsterdam changed the nature of the Dutch-Swedish relationship as it developed into something more hostile. Stuyvesant started making noises that the Delaware was Dutch rather than Swedish. Printz objected this strongly, which really annoyed Stuyvesant. This is when events took a military turn.

Stuyvesant sent an armed ship up the Delaware to a site a few miles away from Fort Christina, this was followed by a flotilla of smaller ships. He made a deal with the Indians to secure some land, and then constructed a fort in the centre of Swedish territory, less than 15 miles away from Fort Christina, this was named Casimir. Printz objected, and Stuyvesant ignored him. By April 1653, 23 Dutch families had moved to Fort Casimir, and there was nothing that Printz could do about this.

1653 was also the year that domestic problems erupted. 22 colonists, a mixture of Swedes and Finns, delivered to Printz (and by proxy queen Christina) a list of 11 grievances. These included: brutality, restrictions on trading, and restrictions on access to resources. Printz saw this as treachery, and decided that the ring leader was a common soldier, Anders Jonsson. He was arrested, tried by a military court and then executed by firing squad. Printz considered the matter put to rest. But, what really happened was that he lost the trust of the settlers. He felt that he had served his country well, and perhaps for a combination of these reasons he decided to return to Sweden with his wife, 4 daughters, and 25 colonists. He left behind his daughter Armegot and her husband Johan Papegoja in control. His regime did not get off to an auspicious start with 15 colonists immediately defecting to Maryland. But, his time in charge was only short, until a replacement could be sent over. And for that, we need to go back to Europe.

Things were beginning to calm down in Sweden. Their wars were over, and so military recruitment dropped. This created potential migrants. Those most interested were the Finns, seeing New Sweden as a land of opportunity greater than they were ever likely to receive in Sweden itself. They managed to attract hundreds of settlers, and the man selected to lead them was Johan Risingh. Risingh was a protégé of Oxenstierna. He had been a public servant, and had most recently served as secretary of the Commercial College of Sweden. He was very optimistic, and had been promised supplies to turn New Sweden into a great commercial power. Despite his high hopes, the colony was doomed from the moment he arrived at the Delaware in May 1654. This was because as he sailed up river, on his way to Fort Christina, he spotted the Dutch Fort Casimir. It was weakly guarded. The garrison was made up of 9 men who lacked effective weapons and who were no match for Swedish musketeers. The garrison surrendered, and defected to Sweden. Casimir was renamed Trefaldighet, which translates into English as Trinity. Stuyvesant had set up Casimir after Printz had refuted his claim that the Delaware should be considered Dutch territory. The Dutch could build a fort there if they wanted, no matter what sovereignty the Swedes claimed. There was nothing they could do about it. The Dutch were the more powerful state, and there was nothing the Swedes could do about it. They were the junior side in this partnership, and they had better remember that. So, I hope you realise how bad an idea capturing this fort was. And how that helps explain why the colony did not last 16 months.

Governorship of Risingh

Risingh had a lot of work to do. The colonists had no trust in the government, relationships with the Indian tribes could be better, and there was a need for economic development. He first settled the new arrivals, and tried securing food supplies for them from New England. He expanded Swedish land, hoping to prevent the English in the Chesapeake from encroaching. Importantly, the land that Risingh distributed was given away permanently, it wasn't a temporary grant. He tried to make the government more open and accessible, and he tried to bring the Dutch into the fold, hoping to keep the settlers from returning to Manhattan. There were conflicts with the Indians, this was unavoidable, but without the combative Printz relations improved. Trade became more common, and he managed to secure a block of land from the Susquehannocks which was rather sizable, 250 square miles, which gave the Swedes access to the Chesapeake. Things were suddenly looking coherent, as those it was coming together to form a real colony, not a smattering of settlers who wanted to be anywhere in the world other than there. Things perhaps could have gone well, had he not offended the Dutch.

Taking Casimir was a huge mistake. When the next supply ship came, it accidentally wound up at New Amsterdam rather than at Fort Christina. Rather than returning the ship, Stuyvesant took it and refused to listen to the protests of Risingh. But this was only the start. In 1655 Stuyvesant left Manhattan, and arrived in late August. The Swedes had 75 soldiers and armed farmers. The Dutch had 317 soldiers and 7 armed ships. Trinity/Casimir instantly defected to Stuyvesant's forces. Risingh prepared to make a last stand at Fort Christina while Stuyvesant surrounded them.

Risingh made a plea to Stuyvesant that they make peace through negotiation in Europe. Sweden and the United Provinces were allies, and they didn't want to cause huge complications for their countries back in Europe through a drastic act in the colonies. Stuyvesant replied that he had orders to destroy New Sweden and claim the territory. They ravaged the surrounding lands for three weeks while conditions inside the fort worsened. Risingh realised that all was lost, and he came to terms. They were favourable to the Swedes as the Dutch were preoccupied with a war with the Indians around Manhattan, but New Sweden from this point ceased to be an independent colony, and it (along with its 600 or so inhabitants) became a part of New Netherland. Something which we really should get back to.

You'll recall that the Dutch became interested in sailing to the Americas, particularly with respect of the fur trade, once they were no longer able to trade with the Spanish. They wound up in the area around the Hudson following the expedition of Englishman Henry Hudson. Eventually the Dutch West India Company was created, and it set up several settlements in the colony of New Netherland, the most important of which were Fort Orange, the future Albany, and New Amsterdam, the future New York City.

There was growth, but it was too slow for Dutch merchants. Between 1624 and 1628 New Netherland exported 31,024 beaver skins and 3,097 otter skins for a combined value of 225,495 florins. This sounds quite good, at first. But the value of goods imported to the colony was 110,895 florins. That was half of all profits. The other half was pretty much whipped out by overheads. It seems that the investors were left with either very little profit, or none at all. Meanwhile, those in the colony itself didn't have enough supplies. We've seen how long it took all of the colonies to become truly self-sufficient, but the Dutch West India Company thought that New Netherland would be able to manage it just two years. When it didn't, and more supplies were not sent, they were forced to trade their meagre possessions. It was in this context that the company turned to creating patroonships.

Patroonships

Patroonships were the small feudal settlements which someone could receive if they brought over

50 people. They would be able to conduct trade, as long as it was on the North American continent between Newfoundland and Florida, and as long as they paid a 5% commission to the company. The big issue with the Patroonships was the restriction on fur trade. They could only trade for furs where the company had no agent, which is a rather ambiguous phrase. This was an attempt to increase the size of the colony, and investment into it, since by 1628 New Netherland still had a population which was smaller than 200.

This did nothing to encourage individual migration to the region. The trade restrictions were problematic, and the history of the colony suggested that it was high risk, low profit. Basically, nobody took them up on the offer. The only patroonship to have any sort of success was one set up near Fort Orange by Kiliaen van Rensselaer which became known as Rensselaerswyck. Van Resselaer had a long history with the company and in the region, and was prepared to make a long term investment in the patroonship, but it would make most of its profits until after van Rensselaer died.

While at the time the patroonships were the most visible aspect of reform, of ultimately far more importance was a minor regulation which said that a settler could travel at their own expense and would be granted as much land as they could work. The terms for this were particularly ungenerous, meaning that nothing really advanced during the 1630s.

The initial population of New Netherland in 1628 was about 270, this had risen to 300 by 1630, but by

1640 it was still only at 500. It was troublingly small. During this decade the colony suffered with economic stagnation. There was an official audit in 1644 which discovered that while New Netherland produced around 50 to 70 thousand guilders each year, it had cost the company 550,000 guilders. In order to operate the company needed a million guilders, and it was not going to find that wealth on the Hudson. The States General pushed the company to reform its methods of attracting settlers. In 1638 the States General pushed the company to make more land available. This was done again in 1639, with added emphasis on citizens from friendly states. The result of all this pushing was the Charter of Freedoms and Exemptions which was produced in 1640.

Charter of Freedoms and Exemptions

What this charter laid out were the terms for a new system of land division, with a greater emphasis on smaller groups rather than the large patroonships. If anyone brought with them 5 adult settlers, then they would receive a grant of 200 acres. There was also a guarantee of self-government on the local level. The people could nominate local magistrates from themselves, and the best qualified which would be selected by the director and council. There was, however, an issue. This land could only be granted after it had been secured from the Indians, and what this led to was a flood of private negotiations with Indians for plots of land which were often highly deceptive to the Indians, and then forced through the New Netherland administration. This process got so out of hand that in 1652 the practice was outlawed.

There was another problem. The Dutch themselves weren't particularly keen on making the voyage to New Netherland. Life in the Netherlands wasn't exactly easy, but saying that, life in the seventeenth century wasn't easy anywhere. At least the Netherlands were familiar, it was comparatively safe, there wasn't massive unemployment, and if you worked hard it was generally possible to get by. There wasn't a persecuted religious group like the Puritans of England. There weren't a large number of second sons in the Dutch aristocracy looking for an alternative life. Indeed, opportunity in the New World was quite difficult for the individual because of the overbearing nature of the company. This meant that if potential colonists could not be found domestically, they would need to look beyond their borders. Settlers were found from across Northern and Western Europe. Almost 40% of the colonists to arrive at Rensselaerwyck in the 1630s were either from England, Norway, or the German principalities. This was, to some extent, only a part of the process of the English gaining dominance in the region. The mass immigration to Massachusetts Bay was leading the English population to begin its push west. The English were moving into the Connecticut Valley, and were beginning to create settlements on Long Island.

This too was an important feature over the next two decades as the relationship between the Dutch and English grew mor,e and more tense. It was one thing for the two groups of colonists to be dimly aware of each other, one group on Massachusetts Bay and the Chesapeake, another on the Hudson, but this was altogether different. With the English on Long Island and the Connecticut Valley, they could get a good view of the Dutch at New

Amsterdam, and just as importantly, the Dutch could see the English. The Dutch looked at the English, and didn't understand their need to travel in groups. Whenever they moved to a new area, they always travelled in groups and set up a town. The Dutch were content to travel as families, and didn't feel as though a town was necessary. It was left to the company to create social units, but such things are very difficult to engineer. It took until 1646 for the first Dutch town to reach chartered status, something that only 9 towns would do during the history of the colony. There was another element to this, which went hand in hand with the English village. Democracy. The Dutch were very envious of the townships of New England with their yearly elections. They had no say in the running of their colony.

But, we are beginning to get a bit off track. The 1640 Charter of Freedoms and Exemptions is what we were talking about. Did it work? Yes. Well, sort of. A bit. Kinda. Not really. Actually, no. Not at all. That answer may you leave you a bit confused, so let me explain what I'm talking about.

The population was still around 500 by 1640, but by 1643 it had more than doubled, and was approaching two thousand. On the face of it, it looks like the charter was really successful, but here is a lesson for you from the mouth of Homer Simpson. Facts are meaningless. You can use facts to prove anything that's even remotely true. Yes, that is a Simpsons line, and it's a joke, but like a lot of Simpsons lines it has a lot of truth in it. In this particularly instance you can use the facts that the population more than doubled in around 5 years to prove that the policy was successful, because it is remotely true, but facts can be problematic. Those facts, for example, are highly misleading.

This population boom was not made up of long term settlers, but those eager to make some quick money. As soon as they turned a profit they left. But this wasn't the real reason for the failure of the policy. That had far more to do with Willem Kieft, director of New Netherland between 1638 and 1648. Kieft led New Netherland into a war with all its Indian neighbours which completely exhausted it.

I previously discussed the problems caused by individuals negotiating with the Indians in good faith, and then reneging on their promises. As time went on, the amount of land purchased grew, including Queens in 1639 and the purchase of Brooklyn was completed in 1640. Relations deteriorated, and as they deteriorated it became harder and harder for the Dutch and the Indians to live together peacefully. Then there was the final nail in the coffin when, in order to support fortifications and the maintenance of their military force, Kieft attempted to tax the Indians. It was a foolish decision that provoked a few Indian raids in the summer of 1641, which Kieft responded to with war which lasted intermittently until 1645. It was a war characterised by brutal attacks from both sides. While the Dutch could be reinforced from Europe, and New Netherland would recover under the governorship of Peter Stuyvesant, the Indians couldn't. A thousand Indians were killed, which was a devastating blow. While peace had been brought for the moment, it shouldn't be a surprise that they would remain hostile to the Dutch and would cause them future problems.

The policy was a terrible one. Intimidating the Indians in order to scare them into submission wouldn't work, and the Dutch all seem to realise this apart from Kieft. When this was combined with their observations of the English townships, the Dutch began to develop a political conscience. A council was created which fluctuated in size, but caused a great deal of trouble for Kieft. They wrote back to Amsterdam, and managed to force him out in 1645, although it would take two years for the new director to arrive in the colony, which at this point had a population of a thousand people in New Amsterdam, in addition to several smaller settlements around what would become New York, and those up the Hudson.

I want to at this point include a quote from Colonial New York: A History, by Michael Kammen.

"This was New Netherland after two decades of settlement: several months' sail from Amsterdam, with fully four months not uncommon. The voyage home was easier – one to two months – because of the favourable westerlies. The company had pursued a series of seemingly contradictory policies, vacillating between colonisation as a priority and the simple preservation of its fur monopoly. Between 1624 and 1628 the company made almost no concessions to its colonists. From 1628 until 1631 it opened the possibility of patroonships and just as quickly fell under the influence of directors who stressed the need for short-term profits. But little economic growth occurred anyway, so that the 1630s were years of regression. In 1639-40 the company committed itself to a policy of colonisation through agricultural development; and once Kieft's insane policy of intimidating the Indians had ended in 1645, the planting of institutional roots and social growth became possible. That was the story of the Stuyvesant years, 1647-64.

Some fifteen men tried to govern New Netherland and New York during the course of the seventeenth century. They were not, on the whole, an impressive lot. A considerable number, including Minuit, Van Twiller, Kieft, Lovelace in 1673, and Andros in 1680, were recalled in disgrace and required to defend themselves against charges of maladministration. Several of them, certainly, did serve as scapegoats for the sins of others or for circumstances beyond anyone's control. But by and large, the early governors were not especially able. The exceptions were Stuyvesant, Nicolls, and Dongan. Stuyvesant ruled for seventeen years – the longest tenure of any governor in the history of colonial New York –

and he most certainly left his stamp upon the province."

Peter Stuyvesant

Peter Stuyvesant was born in the Netherlands around 1612. He received an education, and joined the Dutch West India Company in 1635 during his early 30s. He rose quickly through the ranks, and in 1642, aged 30, he became governor of Curacao, an island in the southern Caribbean, about 40 miles off the coast of Venezuela, which is still Dutch territory. He would spend two years in command there before his time in charge was cut short. In 1644 he led an unsuccessful assault upon the Spanish fort of St. Martin which resulted in him receiving a cannonball to the right leg. It had to be amputated, and he spent the rest of his life with a peg leg. It would have made life difficult in the seventeenth century, but was infinitely preferable to the aternative. He returned to the Netherland, and he must have impressed sufficiently for him to be made director of New Netherland.

We've already sort of introduced Peter Stuyvesant, but that was in our side story of New Sweden. I introduced him as a strong character, and that is certainly true. He was stubborn, and had a big personality. He was determined, courageous, and a dedicated Calvinist. He was also able, and a capable diplomat. He is a very interesting figure in wider history beyond New Netherland because he belongs to a very select group of people. He spent his life trying not to be careless. He is remembered positively, even though he was for the most part a loser. Usually when you have historical figures who lose, they get either forgotten, reduced to a footnote in the histories of the winners, or portrayed negatively, but not Stuyvesant.

When Stuyvesant arrived in New Netherland in 1647, he found the place in what has been called its usual state of organised disorder. He took issue with seemingly everyone and everything in the colony. He disagreed with the colonists about everything from taxes to morality, from political participation to administration of justice. He had a disagreement with the company over religious toleration and judicial administration. He had an issue with Rensselaerswyck over the fur trade around Fort Orange, and indeed with all the colonists over trading regulations. It appeared that jurisdictional matters were the source of these conflicts, but that was only how they appeared. The fundamental issue creating tension within the company was twofold: excessive pluralism within political society, and lack of legitimacy within the government. All colonies had experienced this, but they were both particularly strong in New Netherland, and they aggravated each other. This was understood at the time. We have the following viewpoint from a contemporary magistrate.

> "the frequent changing a government, or the power of electing a governor among ourselves, which some among us, as we understand, aim at, would be our ruin and destruction by reason of our factions and various opinions, inasmuch as many among us being unwilling to subject themselves to any sort of government, mild or strong, it

must, on that account, be compulsory or by force, until the Governor's authority be well confirmed; for such persons will not only despise, scorn or disobey authority, and by their evil example drag other persons along, whereby laws would be powerless, but every one would desire to do what would please and gratify himself."

It was a tough situation. The people wanted popular government, but were so diverse that it would be impossible to form one that everybody agreed to, and it would just produce trouble. That, at least, was how the magistrates of New Netherland justified their position. Compounding the domestic divisions were exterior ones as tensions rose between the Dutch and the English on Long Island. This gains a new dimension when you realise that a significant portion of the Dutch population was actually English, and the Dutch elements in the English colony of Plymouth. The complications caused by English self-government would be the dominant political undercurrent for the period of Stuyvesant's directorship.

Whenever reform seemed likely to take place, it was generally done with a twist to keep power in the hands of the elite. For example, when the States General instructed Stuyvesant to have a Court of Justice in New Amsterdam, this should have been done with elected officials. However, when Stuyvesant implemented the reform he made sure that he appointed the officials. He also created a legal distinction between the citizens. These were greater and lesser burgher rights. The greater rights were necessary for holding public office, and were reserved for people who held, or their ancestors had already held, office. This right could be purchased for 50 guilders.

His administrative and political reforms were only one facet of his greater programme of measures, all of which he did in order to improve the public good. Stuyvesant assured the people that developments were being made which would answer all of their questions and solve all of their problems. These involved domestic matters to try and keep people and their property safe. Fencing laws were revised, and the fire code was made stricter.[65] Improvements were made to the state infrastructure, such as repairs to their defences and the construction of the first pier on Manhattan. He also sought to improve relationships with the Indians by making sure that they were paid properly for services that they might perform. However, this wouldn't quite work. The Indians would not forget the wrongs that had been done to them, and they would wait. Revenge is a dish best served cold. He also ventured into the realm of public morals, reflecting Stuyvesant's strong Calvinist position, by requiring all to attend Sunday services.

Stuyvesant was determined to strengthen the position of company. He clashed with the patroonship of Rensselaerswyck, fearing that it would gain a monopoly of the fur trade in the north. In response he seized a village just to the north of Fort Orange which he named Beverwyck.[66]

---

[65] You cannot underestimate the threat of fire in settlements mostly constructed out of wood.
[66] This is of significance because Beverwyck would

He also clashed with private merchants in New Amsterdam, and Stuyvesant tried to regulate all aspects of economic life. This upset the States General, who did not like the idea of internal regulations, thinking that such regulations would disrupt growth. They would also make New Netherland even less attractive to potential settlers. The actions of the company were very much at odds with Stuyvesant. While he was eager to force the state into all aspects of life, the Company was taking a different opinion. They felt that economic freedom was of primary importance to the economic growth of the settlement, and that the state's monopoly on the fur trade was only causing problems rather than being a benefit. The monopoly was rescinded in 1647.

But, for all this rhetoric, it's important to look for more detailed explanations and hard evidence. If you'll allow me to borrow a phrase from the 1976 classic All the President's Men, follow the money. Or, in this case, follow the lack of it.

The Dutch West India Company was in dire financial straits. This had an awful lot to do the Dutch stepping back on their monopoly. Simply put, they couldn't afford to upkeep it.

The company stopped having its own traders in New Netherland from 1644, and from 1650 it ceased to sell goods directly to the colonists. The company's strategy wasn't working. It needed a new approach if it was going to survive. Commercial activity was put firmly in the back seat, particularly

---

become Albany.

in New Netherland. They were not making enough money in the fur trade for it to be worth the investment. Dutch priorities were their New Holland colony in Brazil, and their Caribbean islands. New Netherland could serve a purpose of supplying food to those colonies, but beyond that they had very little interest. In order to increase agricultural production, they needed to increase the population of the colony. How would they increase migration? The monopoly on trade was one factor which was discouraging people, so it makes complete sense that such a policy be dropped. But, of course, the matter was far more complicated than that.

Trade restrictions have very little to do with agriculture. The policy might encourage immigration, but it would encourage those seeking commercial opportunities, not farmers. What they needed was a way to import people to the colony, and to keep them as farmers. They needed a way of preventing people from turning to trade instead of agriculture. There was an obvious solution to the problem, and I suspect you can see where this is going. They turned to slavery.

Slavery had been a part of the Dutch colony ever since its foundation, but it was only in the late 1640s and 1650s that their import became regular. The New Netherland slave owners found that slaves taken directly from Africa, so they developed a system known as seasoning. A slave would be brought over to the Dutch West Indies and stay there for a while. They would teach the slaves 'European values', and wear down their resistance. Slavery in New Netherland was less intense than on the plantations, which may explain why they seemed happier than those brought to New Netherland directly. African slaves became an important element of the New Netherland population. When the English took over the colony in 1664 the population stood at around 8,000, and of those 700 were of African descent.

Slavery in New Netherland

Now, this is a very uncomfortable topic, but it is an important one. Slavery and racism are two evils, often associated, but they are not the same, and it is very important to remember that. While slavery was present in New Netherland, it was done for its economic benefits. It was cheaper to buy slaves than bring over and pay free workers, and there wasn't a risk they'd turn into traders. But this was how the world was in the 1640s, and there wasn't a great deal of prejudice there. This led to certain key differences between the sort of slavery which emerged in New Netherland, compared to what emerged in the other colonies, and indeed in other societies.

Slaves had the same rights in court as did a free white man. This is not insignificant. I know I talk about Rome a lot, but it's interesting to note that in the Roman Empire, a state considered the foundation of western law, a slave could not freely give testimony in court. Testimony was only valid if obtained by torture. There was nothing like that in the legal code of New Netherland.

Also, the company was flat broke, and it couldn't afford a monopoly on slavery. This led to a bizarre legal situation where slaves could be temporarily hired in a half-free function. It wasn't full citizenship, but they had more rights than normal slaves. It was also possible for blacks to become free, and if they became reformed protestants then they could even intermarry and have their own indentured servants. Racial prejudice certainly existed in the colony, but it was not the overt racial prejudice which we will deal with later in the narrative.

In these years, the early 1650s, the major element of foreign policy for New Netherland was something we've already covered, the growing tension with New Sweden. This led to Stuyvesant launching an invasion to eliminate the competition. I'm not going to repeat this, but I instead want to expand slightly upon the story. I mentioned when we were covering the endgame of New Sweden that Stuyvesant was forced into accepting peace terms which were favourable to New Sweden because of an Indian War in Manhattan. This deserves a bit more of an explanation.

Dutch and Indians

Relations had been tense between the Indians and the Dutch, and once they realised that the governor was out of the province they decided to take advantage of the situation. In mid-September 1655 a group of tribes comprising the Esopus, Hackensacks, Mahicans, and Pachamis, launched a raid to devastate the Dutch settlement. 60 Indians died compared to only 50 of the Dutch, but they were more interested in property destruction. They destroyed 28 farms, 500 cattle, and thousands of bushels of corn. It was this raid that prompted Stuyvesant's hasty withdrawal.

Stuyvesant had several methods of dealing with the aftermath. He increased the defences of the settlement, which were grossly understrength. He stopped the practice of settlement in isolated areas as this made the farmsteads particularly vulnerable to Indian attack. He also stopped the practice of allowing Indians to stay overnight in New Amsterdam, or of brining arms into the town. This worked to great effect. 1655 was the last time Manhattan was invaded by Indians. There were issues with invasions further up the Hudson, but Manhattan itself would not be invaded again.

As time passed, and foreign elements grew stronger within the colony, New Netherland took on a distinctly English character. For example, in 1652 the New Amsterdam Consistory sent a request for a pastor who could speak both Dutch and English, and Stuyvesant regularly employed English officials. New Netherland was attractive for those seeking freedom of religion, the type which had been difficult to achieve in several of the New England colonies. This was another complication in what was already a strained relationship. We've discussed elements of this before, such as the fact that English democracy in Long Island was an issue in New Netherland, and that there was a great deal of overlap in territorial claims, but to really understand what was going on here, we need to turn towards Europe.

Anglo-Dutch Relations

Now, for much of our story so far, we've always dealt with the English and Dutch as allies. This was the case at the beginning of the seventeenth century. However, things got complicated during the 1640s. The Dutch were on good terms with English, but what this really means is that the Dutch were on good terms with the English monarchy. Relations strained during the civil war, and the execution of Charles I horrified the Dutch. Oliver Cromwell considered the Dutch enemies. This might seem odd. You would expect that as they were both protestant Northern European republics the English Commonwealth and the United Provinces of the Netherlands would be allies, but international politics are far more complicated than that. As we enter the 1650s, the Dutch and English detested each other. All that was needed for war was a specific cause of dispute; a cassus belli. This was found in the colonies.

At this point in history, England and the Dutch Republic represented two opposing systems of economic thought. The English were firm believes in Mercantilism, while the Dutch believed in free trade. The distinction between the two is actually very important.

Let's begin with the basics. What is mercantilism, and what is the difference between it and free trade? Well, they are both theories on how to best help a country's economy. Mercantilism is the believe that an economy should be designed to reduce the loss of wealth to foreign countries. In order words, an economy should be geared towards avoiding a trade deficit. This is done by placing tariffs on foreign goods. This will raise their cost, and make domestic goods more appealing. This stops money leaving the country, reducing the trade deficit. In contrast, free trade is the believe that such tariffs cause more problems than they solve. While they help foster domestic industry, they also reduce that countries ability to export. A country cannot supply all its own goods, so higher import duties complicate things more many industries. These complications slow down economic growth, and ultimately harm the economy more than a trade deficit. Those are the theories. Mercantilism is, at least in the Anglo-centric world, the older tradition. It was the basis of the British Empire that was forming around the Atlantic, in contrast to the more famous nineteenth century Victorian British Empire centred on India. That empire was dedicated to free trade and to spreading it around the world. As the British Empire declined, the position of principle backer of free trade was taken up by the United States, this led to the globalisation of the twentieth century. Free trade has indeed been something of an American orthodoxy, which is why it is academically interesting that it became an issue in the 2016 election. Bernie Sanders of the Democratic Party and Donald Trump of the Republican Party were two surprise candidates, and they both took mercantile position, taking issue with the trade deficit. But, what does this have to do with the Dutch and the English in the 1650s?

Well, the English fully subscribed to the mercantile approach. The economic approach that was all about reducing the trade deficit. This was done through the Navigation Acts, which began in 1651, and you'll recall that we covered them when we looked at Virginia and the economic depression this caused in the 1660s. The Dutch, as we've seen, were in the process of expanding their merchant fleet and moving into free trade. They were busy removing trade restrictions to support this. Mercantilism was making English goods more expensive than Dutch goods in the New World, and as Dutch goods spread into English colonies, the Commonwealth could not stand by and watch. The Dutch were abhorred by the English Commonwealth, and the English were infuriated by Dutch violations of the Navigation Acts. We have an insight into English grievances through a petition which was given to Oliver Cromwell in 1658.

> "The Dutch eat us out of our trade at home and abroad; they refuse to sell us a hogshead of water to refresh us at sea, and call us 'English Dogs,' which doth much grieve our English spirits. They will not sail with us, but shoot at us, and by indirect courses bring their goods into our ports, which wrongs not only us but you in your customs."

Conflict was inevitable, and a skirmish off the coast of Dover led England to formally declare war, beginning the First Anglo-Dutch War in 1652.

The First Anglo-Dutch War

The Dutch were the premier maritime power of the day, and so it is understandable that they began the war on the front foot. They were led by the capable Admiral Maarten Tromp who managed to defeat the English in December 1652, but the tides were changing, and the English man-of-war ships were superior to the Dutch. They were victorious in 1653, and again in a large battle in 1654 in which Tromp was killed. Peace was brought about, but it was more temporary than anything else. It didn't fix the underlying issue of tension. The English were bothered enough by having New Netherland between New England and their Chesapeake colonies to pass another Navigation Act in 1660, and their trade rivalry off the African coast was very intense. Even the restoration of the English monarchy could not restore relations. One spark was required to set off this powder keg, and it took place in March 1664.

King Charles II of England issued a grant to his brother James, the Lord High Admiral of England. The grant contained Maine, the islands of the New England coast, Long Island, the Hudson River, the land west of the Connecticut River and east of the Delaware. In short, it gave him New Netherland. James organised a fleet to be commanded by Colonel Richard Nicolls, which set sail to enforce these claims, at it arrived around Coney Island on August 26. Stuyvesant sent a messenger to Nicolls to see what exactly he intended to do. Nicolls claimed the island of Manhatoes, along with all its forts and its town, by which he meant New Amsterdam. Stuyvesant responded by detailing Dutch claims. Stuyvesant, rather than answering Stuyvesant's complaints, simply told him that he had 48 hours to surrender.

Stuyvesant was horrified, and determined to resist, but the officials of New Amsterdam, not so much. They knew that they had week defences, not much food, and the English were stronger and better equipped. The matter was lost, and the terms for surrender were not horrific. They, and the rest of the population, forced Stuyvesant to surrender. The English entered, and Stuyvesant signed a letter of surrender. As Nicolls wrote to Massachusetts to inform the New Englanders of his victory, he signed the letter, from New York, truly beginning its history. However, the Dutch would not just let this go.

A Brief History of Indonesia

If you are reading this, I'll assume you've read the 295 pages before it. You've probably got a pretty good idea of how my mind works, and how I'm continually going off on tangents which add bits to the story. At least that's what I claim they do. Now, we are going to begin with a bigger tangent than normal. In history, context is everything. You see, if we are going to understand what is happening in New York, then I really need to get into the history of Indonesia. Everything is connected. How I'm going to introduce this tangent is with a passage from A History of the World by Andrew Marr.

> "The coming British world domination was not yet obvious... The rise of the British as a naval and trading power is now so firmly part of world history that it may come as a shock to find that in the most lucrative contest of all, they were soundly beaten by... the Dutch.
>
> Very broadly, the story of European mercantile expansion can be divided into three phases. First, from the late 1400s, came the Portuguese, whose ships explored the African coast. Then, discovering that the Cape could be reached by veering off far west into the

Atlantic, allowing the winds to carry them round, they got to India and the Far East. The Portuguese operated as violently monopolistic traders rather than as empire-builders, setting up fortifications to protect their sea routes and repelling all rivals. The Spanish were next to get in on the act, but did not really try to oust the Portuguese from 'their' routes, focusing instead... on the Americas....

The second phase saw two more northerly nations, the English and the Dutch, join the adventure. To begin with they were no more consciously imperialist than the Portuguese, also being driven by merchants hopes of profit. Europe had long had a near-desperate desire for the spices that grew only in the East. The most delicious and (it was thought) healthful of these were to be found in the Spice Islands, wedged in the dangerous seas between Borneo and New Guinea. Nutmeg, cloves, mace, pepper and cinnamon had been bought from the islanders there by Muslim seafarers; then taken to India, thence through the Islamic world to Constantinople, and finally through Venice to Europe. A profit as made at leach stage, so that the aromatic nuts and seeds were hugely expensive luxuries by the time they reached Paris or London. Yet before the advent of refrigeration, in an age of rank meat and dull eating, the appetite for them was as insatiable as it was for fur. Most spices were also thought to offer protection against illness: nutmeg was supposed to cur syphilis, and even plague.

Meanwhile, Portuguese seamanship had found a shorter way.... Ships from Europe could now get direct access to the spices. The losers were the Arabs and Indian traders, suddenly and brutally cut out of the chain.... The next losers would be the Portuguese themselves, confronted by better-built ships and bolder adventurers, this time from the lowlands of northern Europe. In particular, the Dutch....

Rival Europeans tried to batter their way through the Arctic ice or penetrate the Canadian wilderness, still looking for a shorter way to the aromatic islands. In London, they tried to mimic the Dutch by founding their own East India Company, but the British discovered, not for the last time, that it is hard to be second into a new market. The Dutch were dug in, determined and utterly ruthless... The Dutch businessmen

319

realised that to repel rivals, they
would need forts, protected
warehouses, secure anchorages and
a permanent arrangement with the
local rulers whose produce they
were after. This meant that the
Dutch – even though they were
God-fearing republicans – were
turning themselves into
imperialists. The third phase had
arrived. Indonesia became their far
Eastern base, with a new, Dutch,
capital, 'Batavia'."

Okay, so we have a bit of context. The Dutch were
the dominant force in the Spice Islands, and the
English were late to the party. They did, however,
manage to become friendly with the inhabitants of
the island of Run. Run is an island about 2,000km
(1,200 miles) east of Java in Indonesia. It is 3 km in
length by 1km in width, and now only appears on
specialised maps. It's importance four hundred
years ago was due to nutmeg, and the large supply
of nutmeg on the island. These spices were highly
desired in Europe, and it was possible to make
ridiculous profits. And when I say ridiculous, I mean
ridiculous. The quantity of nutmeg which could be
purchased for one penny on Run could be sold in
London for 50 shillings. That is something in the
region of a 60,000% mark up. That's why the Dutch
and English were so desperate to have a piece of
the Spice trade, and why they were both so eager
to force the other ones out.

The English, as I've said, were late when arriving in
the East Indies, around 1602, almost a decade
behind the Dutch. The Dutch were not happy about

the English presence there, but they could not abide by the English having Run. Run was one of a group of ten islands known as the Banda islands, and they were where almost all the nutmeg in the world grew. This is why the Dutch decided in 1616 to launch an attack to take it. The English did not give up, and launched a defence. The siege of Run lasted four years until 1620, when the English commander was killed and the island finally fell to the Dutch. It was an incident the English would not forgive the Dutch for. They were on friendly terms back in Europe, and so it wasn't too much of an issue, but following the execution of Charles I and the rise of the English Commonwealth, it was a grievance the English had not forgotten. The return of Run was one of the terms of the treaty of Westminster in 1654 which brought to a close the First Anglo-Dutch War.

On the face of it, this looks like the matter was closed. But, as I'm sure you've already guessed, it wasn't. The Treaty of Westminster didn't really do anything to solve the issues between the English and the Dutch. Just as tensions continued in Europe, resulting in the 1660 Navigation Act, and as they continued in North America, leading to the English invasion of New Netherland, they also did not go away in the East Indies. The Dutch wouldn't give up Run. They were supposed to, and the English tried on several occasions to take back Run as per the terms in the treaty, but the Dutch wouldn't give in. Run was considered highly important, and they wouldn't let the English traders back on the island. These issues in all three theatres led to a declaration of war in 1665, beginning the Second Anglo-Dutch War.

The Dutch had learnt their lessons from the first war. Their ships were outmatched by the English, and they set upon rectifying that position. They began construction of a new navy almost as soon as the first war ended, and it was more than a match for the English fleet. The English suffered defeat after defeat in the waters of the English Channel and the North Sea. The English war effort was then made more difficult by domestic issues. England suffered an outbreak of bubonic plague, and the Great Fire of London. It seems like the Dutch would win, and that would be the end of it. But it wasn't. You have to adapt to the political realities of the situation, and international political realities are never simple.

Okay, step back for just a moment, and look at Europe in your mind. You have England and the Dutch fighting each other as neighbours, but look at the bigger picture. The United Provinces of the Netherlands had three other big neighbours, and their actions always had to be taken into account. There were the French, the German principalities, and the Spanish.

The war at sea wasn't going well for the English, so they sought to launch a land war. They enlisted Munster as an ally to invade the United Provinces. At the same time, the English approached Spain. It must be remembered that the Spanish were still in the Spanish Netherlands, present day Belgium. On the face of it, this looks like a good idea. Getting allies together to fight the Dutch seems sensible. However, this provoked a reaction from France. France was at the time ruled by a man with great ambition, Louis XIV, the Sun King. He was in his late 20s, and really wanted to conquer the Spanish

Netherlands. He was alarmed at the prospect of a Spanish land invasion, and so joined the war on the side of the Dutch. Now, this seems like a good thing for the Dutch. Who doesn't want a strong ally? Well, the Dutch.

The Dutch were very proud of their independence; they had just spent the better part of a century fighting the Spanish for it. The last thing they wanted was to win a war only because of the French. If the French became the dominant power in the region, the Dutch would be relegated to the position of a French vassal. The English didn't want that either. And so the war continued for a few years, but with the intention of returning to a position which didn't really change anything.

It's not really necessary for me go into the details of the various naval battles fought of the Dutch coast, so we'll skip to the conclusion. The Dutch won the war, but they won it in order to mostly revert to the status quo with England. I say mostly, because the Dutch did win the war, and so they were in control for how exactly events played out. For instance, the Navigation Acts were altered to give special trade rights to the Dutch, they would be able to sail English goods up the Rhine for example. However, what mostly concerns us is what the situation was with the colonies.

Here was how the situation looked to the Dutch in 1667. The East Indies were the centre of the Spice Trade, and they were highly profitable. Again, remember the 60,000% mark up on Nutmeg. It was the heart and soul of their maritime empire. In contrast, New Netherland had been a bit of a disaster. The profits made off the fur trade had not justified the costs of setting up the settlement. It was losing money. They had tried to transform it into an agricultural base, but the Dutch had a very small rural population. There was no land hungry populace, and no persecuted religious minority. It wasn't working. Therefore, it was decided that in the peace treaty they would simply keep the status quo. The English would be granted New Netherland, henceforth known as New York, which they in practice already controlled. And, in exchange, the Dutch would be granted the valuable spice island of Run, which they in practice already controlled. At the time it was seen as a good deal. How times change. If, at the next social gathering of your friends, you drop the knowledge that the Dutch traded New York to the English in exchange for an island nobody has heard of in the middle of Indonesia, well... they probably won't care if we're being honest. But, if they are also history lovers, they will be really shocked and surprised. It's one of those bits of historical trivia that on the surface doesn't make a lick of sense, even though it does, given the historical context. Which is why we spent so long talking about Indonesia when all I really needed to say was that after the English invaded New Netherland, the Dutch were so dissatisfied that with the project that they were happy to trade New Netherland for a Spice Island, but where would the fun have been in that?

Part 4

The New England Confederation

Chapter 14 – The Plymouth Republic

We last left Plymouth in 1628 at a rather interesting moment in its history. The colony, you'll recall, had a great deal of trouble with funding itself. The first wave of colonisation is a very exciting moment for investors. It gives them a chance to get in on the ground floor, as they say. It is very difficult to be second into a new market. This is fine, but it also meant that there was a desire for quick profits. Gold mines, or something similar. New England was not suited to quick profits.

It did have many opportunities for wealth creation. It would have a thriving whaling industry, it could produce ships, and the regions fast flowing streams could be used to harness energy. There was also plenty of iron in the bogs of the area. It was low quality, but it was useful for household objects as it was far cheaper than importing it from England. New England wasn't a great agricultural centre, but it could produce food. All these were valuable, but they would take time for these industries to develop. And people are impatient. While the Pilgrims set up their colony, they struggled to get people to keep funding it for the early years, with their investors constantly funding new projects and new colonies instead of sticking with Plymouth. These never worked, of course. The following Simpsons' quote seems appropriate: "This is finally really happening. After years of disappointments with get rich quick schemes, I know I'm going to get rich with this scheme! And quick!"

So, after continual rebuffs from London merchants, the Pilgrims bought themselves, legally in the name of 8 senior figures in the colony, William Bradford,

Miles Standish, Isaac Allerton, Edward Winslow, William Brewster, John Howland, John Alden, and Thomas Prence. Plymouth was rather unique as a self-owning colony, although this didn't end their difficulties with London. Allerton sailed over to London as the representative of Plymouth, and then abused his position before being fired and expelled from the colony after a couple of years for gross incompetence. In 1630 a patent was given to Bradford, the governor, securing possession of the land, but he transferred this patent to the colony itself in 1640. The only thing Plymouth lacked was a Royal Charter and in 1630 it spent £500 trying to acquire one, but thanks to Allerton it was never approved.

I cannot overestimate the importance of Allerton's untrustworthiness as it made the process of paying off the loans used by the colonists to free themselves from London merchants infinitely more complicated. We have Bradford's complaints preserved. It would take until March 1646 for the debt to finally be paid off.

Over the course of the 1630s, more and more settlers arrived in New England. We've dealt previously with how this began the westward push that would so define America, and how it began with the setting up of several other colonies such as Connecticut and Rhode Island. It also altered Plymouth, and the way the colony was structured. Plymouth had, for the first ten years or so of its existence, essentially been a city state. There was only settlement in the colony, Plymouth. That was where everybody lived, and where everything took place. But, as more people arrived, it was only natural that several other smaller satellite settlements spring up around Plymouth. This began around 1630, but over time the process was formalised and these small clusters of housing developed into townships. These were formally organised, Scituate in 1636, Duxbury in 1637, Taunton, Sandwich, Barnstable and Yarmouth in 1639, and then Marshfield in 1640. Within a few years the political layout of Plymouth had altered. The direct democracy that had worked for the past two decades was no longer possible, and so in 1639 a change was made. The colony became the Plymouth Republic, a representative democracy. Plymouth was the capital, and was the seat of the assembly. It would have four seats, and each other township would have two. There were two houses, the lower made up of deputies and the upper of the governor and his 7 assistants.

Relations with the New Colonies

The 1630s had seen a great deal of domestic upheaval within the Republic, but ever greater changes were happening externally. The most obvious factor is Massachusetts Bay, the larger and more powerful colony which had appeared directly to the North. Connecticut too was emerging to the West. Relations were not exactly hostile. Religious differences between the colonies faded over time, and they had a similar perspective economically. The greater resources of Massachusetts livened up the area, and helped stimulate the Plymouth economy. There was, however, some underlying tension. It could not be forgotten that the development of the new colonies altered the regional balance of power.

Plymouth had long been the most organised force in the region. It had been Standish and the Pilgrims that dealt with Thomas Morton at Mount Merry only a couple of years previously. But this changed. In 1634 there was a legal issue to do with Pilgrim trade, but Massachusetts took legal action despite the affair being out of their jurisdiction. The message was loud and clear. Plymouth had become a junior colony. It was no longer the only English settlement between Canada and Virginia. It was one of many, and a not particularly important one at that. This problem was exacerbated the next year when the Plymouth settlement of Windsor was taken by Connecticut. There was very little Plymouth could do about the situation.

Economically, the town should be considered a success. It had a slow beginning. In 1621 its population was 86, this had increased to 180 by 1624 and then about 300 by 1630. This reflected the slow economic beginning as the Pilgrims set up the basis of their agriculture and industries, and of securing their independence. It was only during the migration period of the 1630s that the population seriously began to increase at a steady rate, reaching about 3000 by 1644.

No great wealth was created in Plymouth, but there were a lot of small industries. The fisheries were productive, and there was work in agriculture and lumber production. The Pilgrims were comfortable. That it of itself is notable. We'll see for much of history in the American story that it would take a very long time for a majority of the population to reach some level of economic comfort. Life in the seventeenth century was hard. It was no small achievement for a group of individuals to set up a representative democracy, govern themselves, and secure some degree of prosperity.

Plymouth showed the way. It was the foundation of New England, but it was destined to be absorbed into the Commonwealth of Massachusetts. You see, while New England was deeply Puritan, Puritan was a bit of a catch-all term. There were many different variants of Puritanism which gave each of the New England colonies a distinctive character. Plymouth was founded by separatists, which gave it the deeply democratic organisation that we discussed at length in the previous episode. In stark contrast to this, Massachusetts was more oligarchical. It viewed government as sacred and a God-given institution rather than something that had anything to do with the people. It took until the mid-1640s for political pressure to build up to the degree that popular reform was made, and finally the General Court became a bicameral legislature, a lower house of deputies and an upper house of assistants to the governor. I can indeed summarise this by quoting the historian John Dickinson, whose essay "The Massachusetts Charter and the Bay Colony 1628-1660" appears in the book, Commonwealth History of Massachusetts: Colony, Province and State in 5 Volumes.

> "The essential feature of Massachusetts government during the first generation of its history can be summed up in one word, centralisation — a concentration of influence, power, offices, functions of every kind, in a small and compact group of leaders. Yet under the surface of this

centralization a development was going on which was ultimately to undermine it. This was the growth of towns and town-government. Massachusetts was settled at the outset by groups rather than individuals, - not by isolated pioneers, but by parishes and congregations which transplanted themselves from England and sought to reconstruct their communal life in the new environment...

The leaders at first looked with dislike on this process of dispersion and sought to keep a firm hand upon it. They passed an order that no new plantations were to be set up without leave of the Governor and Assistants and they assumed the right to appoint local officers, constables and the like, for those which had already been established. But the process of town-formation outran the control of the magistrates, - new communities came into existence as squatter settlements, and named officers and levied rates without authority form the government of the Company. The leaders soon bowed to the inevitable... Each town was given the right to manage its own affairs, to make ordinances and enforce them by penalties, and to choose its own local officers; and an even more important function was conferred on the towns in connection with the distribution of land....

As town after town was set off, the greater part of the land in the colony ultimately came into their possession for subsequent distribution to individuals... Each town thus became a close economic community with a direct interest in admitting or excluding new members."

Now that we are fully refreshed, we can begin to press on into new material.

Chapter 15 – The United Colonies of New England

The defining feature of the American colonies during the seventeenth century is their mutual independence. Each colony was effectively in control of itself, almost an independent state. We saw this take itself to its logical conclusion in Virginia in Bacon's Rebellion. The English reaction to Bacon's Rebellion, which we'll get to eventually, forced the eighteenth-century empire to be very different to the seventeenth, focused instead upon subjection of each state by the motherland. But that is all to the future. For the moment I want to talk about mutual independence.

There were, at this point, two groups of English colonies. In the north was New England, and in the south where were the Chesapeake colonies, although they were developing into what will form the heartland of the South. Of these southern/Chesapeake colonies we've only dealt with Virginia so far, but there was also Carolina and Maryland. While there might have been occasional border disputes, for the most part these each had clear boundaries and were all set up by royal charter. In contrast, the position of the northern/New England colonies was more precarious.

Their land holdings were not based on royal charters. Connecticut and Rhode Island didn't gain royal charters until the 1660s, New Haven did not have a charter either. Plymouth had tried to get a charter but, because of Allerton, had been unable to do so. New Hampshire and Maine were both sort of provinces due to the complicated system of land grants, but were both dominated by Massachusetts.

The Colony of Massachusetts Bay was the only colony to actually have a royal charter, but it was technically in open rebellion against the crown. The point I'm trying to make here is that in contrast to the relatively simple legal organisation of the South, the North was a mess.

Despite this, and all the contradicting land grants, there was a lot to be said for the unity of the New England colonies. They had a similar religious and legal system, and collectively enjoyed popular government. They were also surrounded by many potential threats. The French were to the far north on the St. Lawrence, but there were closer concerns. There were many potentially hostile Indian tribes in the area, and then there were the Dutch. We've already covered the rising tension between the English and Dutch in the 1640s and 1650s extensively, so I won't needlessly repeat myself here. They were also worried about events back in England. King Charles and Archbishop William Laud might make a move to repress them. This gave the various colonies an idea. Wouldn't they be safer if they formed a union?

Now, I don't want to stretch this too far, but it's impossible to ignore what this is. What was being suggested here was the first union to ever occur between the American colonies. The United Colonies of New England is the first in a series of experiments which will lead to the Philadelphia Convention in 1787 and the United States of America. It was only small, and no one at the time had any idea that this was where the idea would eventually take them 150 years later, but a union was first mentioned by Puritan leaders in 1637.

Plans became more concrete in 1638. Massachusetts made a proposal to form a union with Connecticut, Plymouth and New Haven, but the other three colonies rejected the idea, worrying that the proposal would give too much power to the newly created federal government. Had he been there, I'm sure Thomas Jefferson would have approved.

The two most influential men in Connecticut, Hanes and Hooker, tried to revive the idea in 1639, fearing possible encroachment into Connecticut from New Netherland, but they were unable to get Massachusetts on board. The idea came up again in 1640. Connecticut, New Haven and Rhode Island sent a joint letter to Massachusetts again proposing some sort of defensive pact. Massachusetts was in favour in principle, but had to reject this proposal because she would not be involved with Rhode Island. There was a great degree of hostility involved in the foundation of Providence.

Nothing happened for two years, but the matter came to a head in 1642. There was an increase in Indian activity and the New England states were greatly concerned. Connecticut drafted a proposal for Massachusetts, this one including both Plymouth, and Maine, although I'm cautious about mentioning this. Maine shouldn't be considered a full colony, more an area of Massachusetts with a complicated legal background. Massachusetts considered this idea, and it was decided to move the matter forward to something which will become very familiar to us as we advance in the story, what I might hesitantly describe as a constitutional convention.

The First Constitutional Convention

In the spring of 1643, Massachusetts, Plymouth, Connecticut, and New Haven sent delegates to Boston in order to draft Articles of Confederation. The delegates were Winthrop, Dudley, Bradstreet, Gibbons, Tyng and Hathorne from Massachusetts; Winslow and Collier from Plymouth; Haynes and Hopkins from Connecticut; and Eaton and Grigson from New Haven.[67] What they created was a Puritan league, which is why Rhode Island with its religious toleration could not be admitted. It also wasn't particularly important since it was surrounded by the English colonies and had a very small population. It wasn't mandatory that it needed to be in the union.

At the time it wasn't clear in what direction this would go. England was entering into its Civil War, and for the moment the colonies would have to look after themselves. The delegates were treated like ambassadors from independent states, reflecting the character of seventeenth century colonialism. It's impossible to not view this as a precursor to Philadelphia. Although, history decided that this wasn't the moment the colonies would launch their bids for independence just yet. So, let's discuss what they decided.

They created the United Colonies of New England, also known as the New England Confederation. Each of the four colonies would elect two

---

[67] It's also worth noting that the short lived Saybrook colony sent a single representative, Fenwick, but Saybrook was absorbed into Connecticut the Next Year so it's not really worth paying much mind to this.

Commissioners, who both needed to be members of the congregational church. They would meet yearly, every September. They would manage peace, war, and foreign relations for the colonies. They would also determine how each foreign expedition would be financed in terms of manpower and currency between the colonies (the determining rate being the number of men aged between 16 and 60 in each colony). If the confederation was invaded, Massachusetts would immediately raise 100 men, and the three other colonies 45 men each, although this would then have to be ratified by 6 of the 8 commissioners.

The Confederate government also had some civil power, but it was made certain that it would not infringe upon the power of each colony. Any action needed 6 commissioners to vote for it, and if a motion received less support than this it would need to be voted on unanimously by all four general courts. The body would meet in all of the capitals of the colonies, but in Boston twice as much.

It is interesting to note that this confederation would only have a legislature. There was no executive branch. I don't mean this in the sense that there wasn't a president, there was, but it was more of a presiding officer. What I mean is that it is the function of the legislature to legislate, and then of the executive branch to execute the order. But there was no executive, and therefore in order to implement any decisions taken by the legislature it relied upon the four general courts.

There was a provision in the body that a dissenting opinion must be noted and a reason given. It's interesting to note that this feature has survived, and exists in the Supreme Court of the United States. Though dissenting opinions were rare. Discussion was open, and it seems like the representatives acted as statesman.

First Tests

The first task the confederation would have to deal with was an Indian war between two of the powerful tribes of the region, the Narragansetts and the Mohegans. These two had recently signed an agreement to discuss any potential differences between the two with the English before war broke out. It seems that this was ignored, and the Narragansetts attacked a collection of other tribes. The Narragansetts were defeated, and their chief captured. It was decided that the best thing to do with their prisoner was to bring him to the English, directly involving the colonies.

The English feared the captured chief, and trouble that he could potentially cause for them, therefore it was decided that the safest option would be to have him killed. This would come back to haunt the United Colonies as it earned them to antagonism of the Narragansetts. They would continue to be a danger to the English. After it became clear that they wouldn't directly attack the other Indian tribes because of the involvement of the English, they just decided to attack the English. A surprise assault was planned in 1645, although the efforts of Roger Williams and the swift action of the commissioners prevented war from breaking out. A peace treaty was signed.

However, this was only a piece of paper, not a paper of piece. The Narragansetts did everything they could over the next five years to try and undermine it. They set to work building an alliance which would have been enough to destroy the English, and it is quite possible that had the confederation not existed the colonies would have been destroyed. It took some rather nifty diplomacy and a great deal of luck that the attack never happened. The Narragansetts had managed to bring over to their side both the Mohawks and the Pocumtucks. But when the attack was scheduled, the Mohawks never arrived. Two of their braves were killed by the French and so they turned their attentions northwards towards New France, and the Pocumtucks were persuaded to abandon the efforts without the Mohawks. This left the Narragansetts alone, and they decided against launching the attack by themselves.

The following years of quiet allowed the English to deal with the other reason for the confederation, the Dutch. This was of primary concern to New Haven, the most westerly of the colonies, which was itself trying to launch another colony to the south in what would become Delaware. Their fortunes were thus rather interconnected with both the Dutch and Swedes. Indeed, the trading post set up on the Delaware had bad been taken over by the Swedes, and so the commissioners protested to the Swedes. This was unsuccessful. The Dutch, who would be about to take over New Sweden, sent a letter to the English documenting the wrongs that they had done. Eventually New Haven was forced to abandon the whole enterprise, but it was a sign of the rising antagonism that was growing between the Dutch and the English.

I don't want to get too much into this, since we really have covered an awful lot of this during our overview of New Netherland. But, basically, New Netherland was threatened by the union. New Netherland had enough troubles to deal with, but it could at least try to manage the competition between the various colonies. It would be very difficult, but it was something that could be attempted. However, the union of the troublesome Connecticut and New Haven colonies which were pressing on the borders of New Netherland, with the powerful colony by the bay, spelled trouble. It could no longer compete on equal terms. This soon became obvious as the Dutch could only send angry letters to New England whenever another New England town was set up in Dutch territory. Finally, a treaty was drawn up in 1650 which was a victory for the New Englanders. It drew the boundary line between New England and New Netherland as north of Greenwich Bay, and on Long Island as south from Oyster Bay.

We must also mention another group who will be given a full introduction in time, the French. There were complicated relations between New England and New France after Massachusetts managed to get meddled in French affairs in 1644. This was placed into the wider political context of events back in Europe. It wasn't clear exactly how the English Civil War would play out at this point, and the New England colonies were sympathetic to Parliament. This isn't particularly surprising given their Puritan character. Despite this inclination, they couldn't afford to offend Charles. He still might win. France was on good terms with Charles, and so it was important that while they might have issues with New France, they had to remain friendly in case they needed to defend their actions. Relations managed to calm down to the point that New France proposed a free trade agreement with New England in 1647, and in 1650 proposed joint military action against the Iroquois, who were enemies of the French. Both of these proposals failed to gain traction. Massachusetts learnt its lesson after the 1644 debacle, and had no more wish to be involved in French matters.

Foreign policy was the main concern of the Confederate government, but it was by no means the only one. While the immigrants to New England had a wide variety of backgrounds, Puritanism was the most significant. Puritanism had very intellectual connotations. Puritanism grew particularly strongly around Cambridge. This meant that the New Englanders were naturally inclined to foster this atmosphere in their new home. In 1636 Harvard College was founded, and as an ode to their centre of learning in England, they renamed the town around it Cambridge. The Confederation took effort to secure funding for the college with help from the various colonies.

They also set about economic activities, such as standardising measurements, and the quality of the toll roads. They made recommendations about the best ways to fish, and stopped the sail of grain between the colonies since Connecticut was flooding the market. They also made the ambitious move of setting up a joint stock company to trade with the Indians, proposing to raise £10,000 for use in the fur trade. It was in an intriguing idea which was met with excitement at Massachusetts, but Plymouth refused to be involved and so the idea quickly died. It also had another beneficial function, it could serve as an arbiter between quarrels of the various colonies, and fairly settle issues over such matters as jurisdiction.

Impost Controversy

The most famous of these disputes is known as the Impost Controversy. Until the creation of the railroad, it was of prime importance for settlements to have access to a body of water for trade. This was why the various New England settlements such as Boston and Plymouth clung to the coast. Most of the New England rivers were very quick and unsuitable for transport. The best way of shipping goods out of the New England interior was down the Connecticut river. This produced an issue. Massachusetts was the more powerful colony, and so many of the interior settlements had joined Massachusetts, despite being upstream of the Connecticut. One such example was Springfield.

In 1646, Springfield refused to pay the duty to Connecticut for sending goods through the mouth of the river. Connecticut was offended, and Massachusetts defended her town. Eventually the issue was brought to the confederation level. The Massachusetts commissioners made the case that since Springfield was part of Massachusetts and not Connecticut, Connecticut had no right to force a duty upon those on which she had no legal jurisdiction. Connecticut made the point that the impost was demanded from all settlements along the river, regardless of which colony the settlement was in. This was used for mutual defence by funding the Seybrook fort at the mouth of the river, which offered protection to all settlements on it. Springfield benefited from the protection of the fort, therefore she should have to pay the import. Both Plymouth and New Haven sided with the commissioners from Connecticut. The rate was two pence per bushel of corn and twenty shillings per hogshead of beaver. This was perfectly reasonable.

Massachusetts was not happy with the decision, and appealed in 1648. The commissioners again sided with Connecticut. The next year, 1649, Massachusetts appealed again, but this time tried a rather underhand tactic. Tariffs were imposed on goods from Plymouth, New Haven and Connecticut if they were imported or exported in Massachusetts. This was an action which changed the nature of the relationship. It became clear to all that this wasn't exactly an equal partnership. Sure, Massachusetts, Connecticut, New Haven and Plymouth all sent the same number of delegates to the confederate government, but this hid the fact that Massachusetts was far more powerful than the other three. On issues important to Massachusetts it could throw its weight around, and it became clear throughout the course of events that Massachusetts wasn't exactly afraid of this. In many cases, political organisations, particularly those on the multi-state level, will not work if one element is determined to win. Arguably the most famous example of this in American history will be a long way down the line when we look at the Impeachment trial of President Andrew Johnson. There was no evidence that Johnson committed the crimes he was charged with, Congress just wanted him out of office. He was never actually impeached though. Had he been impeached for fabricated reasons, the legitimacy of constitutional government would have been severely damaged, and we have no idea what the implications of that would be. However, we can perhaps give some insight into this blow to the United Colonies of New England.

New Haven and Plymouth both sided with Massachusetts and Connecticut dropped the issue. Connecticut had been acting in terms of standard international protocol, which is why New Haven and Plymouth sided with them in the first place. Massachusetts wasn't exactly wrong in its defence of Springfield, but it had won by circumventing the system. Plymouth and New Haven were both scared of challenging Massachusetts, and no longer would wish to arbitrate decisions against it. Connecticut was spooked too. It was a very damaging blow. It is worth noting that when the federal government was formed, most of the battles took place between the big states and the small. The small states had fears that they would be bullied by the larger states, and with historical examples such as Massachusetts and the United Colonies of New England, it seems as though they had every right to be. But, as with Andrew Johnson, all that is for much later in the story.

I am, as a rule, opposed to calling things 'inevitable'. Some things certainly are. But, as a rule, if anyone describes something as 'inevitable' I take it as a red flag. Therefore, I'm not going to call the issues which the United Colonies of New England faced inevitable, but they certainly have an unsurprising feel about them. International treaties are difficult.[68]

---

[68] Yes, I know that all these colonies were technically English, but they should be treated as different nations in the seventeenth century (I'm using the term 'nation' to avoid 'state').

International organisations particularly so. Many that which exist today took many different forms to get where they are. Therefore, it is unsurprising that it would take the Americans a few attempts to form what eventually became the federal government, and it would have been truly remarkable had they got it right on the first go. It isn't that surprising that the confederation faced major problems.

Problems for the Confederation

The key issue was Massachusetts. Massachusetts had roughly 60% of the population of New England, with the other 40% spread between Plymouth, Rhode Island, Connecticut, and New Haven. It was not inevitable that things would fall apart, but it was not surprising that if there was something Massachusetts really wanted, such as a favourable outcome in the Impost Controversy, she would be easily able to circumvent the system. It seems that Massachusetts had been uneasy about the Articles of Confederation from very soon after the signing. For example, they made propositions such as having a third Commissioner in exchange for the extra expenditures she had to make. This was rejected.

The Impost Controversy may be partly explained with Massachusetts' growing dissatisfaction with the arrangement, and increasing lack of regard for the confederation itself. When the Impost Controversy made it clear that the Confederacy was toothless when it tried to oppose Massachusetts, from that point it didn't really need to be taken seriously any more. This could be seen in the fate of the other two semi-colonies of New England, New Hampshire and Maine.

New Hampshire and Maine were the remnants of the very early patents made in the region, but they had limited resources to work with. They were quickly overwhelmed by Massachusetts Bay once that colony arrived, and by this point in history it was understood that Massachusetts had some sort of influence over them, but this was very ill-defined. This changed in 1651, when Massachusetts began the process of extending her influence. They were both annexed in 1658. There was nothing the other New England colonies could do about this.

These tensions would push the alliance to the edge in 1653 when rumours began to spread that the Indians, funded by the Dutch, were once again planning to cause trouble. These rumours weren't exactly strange, but they were enough for a special session of the commissioners to be galled in April. They spent two weeks trying to come up with an understanding of events, but things were not cleared up. The Narragansets, the other tribes, and the Dutch Governor Stuyvesant, all denied the charges. However, more evidence indicating trouble was brought to light.

This was not surprising. The First Anglo-Dutch War was raging in Europe, so it made sense that the Dutch would try to create trouble. Matters were very tense, particularly in Connecticut and New Haven. It seemed likely that war would break out. But then Massachusetts, which wasn't particularly interested in picking a fight with New Netherland, did something rather remarkable. The General Court of the Bay Colony set up a committee and interfered with the commissioners, in effect taking it over, and voting against a war.

The defence made was that the Confederation was a defence pact, and no authority to launch an offensive war against the Dutch. It wasn't fair that 6 individuals be given that degree of power. The matter could go no further, and so the commissioners returned to their own colonies to decide what would happen next.

New Haven and Connecticut wrote to Massachusetts, complaining about the action. They then asked permission to raise a military force to attack the Dutch if Massachusetts would block the efforts of the commissioners. It was rather pathetic, and highly embarrassing for Connecticut and New Haven. They were independent colonies, but they were acting like satellites of the colony on the Bay. Massachusetts replied that she would never dream of doing anything against the confederation... but at the same time gave no hint that she would allow a war with the Dutch. New Haven responded by announcing that commissioners wouldn't be sent to the September meeting unless Massachusetts gave in. Massachusetts called New Haven's bluff, which, with even more embarrassment the three lesser colonies, sent delegates to Boston to continue the discussion.

Massachusetts proposed that the Articles of Confederation be rewritten to give the power of declaring war to the General Courts of each colony, and the other three opposed this. Massachusetts finally gave in, but there wasn't to be war against the Dutch. Things seemed like they were back to normal, but only for a moment. Almost immediately thoughts turned to the Indians rather than the Dutch. A group had been attacking Indian allies of the English on Long Island. It was felt that inaction would show the English to be weak, therefore they had no option other than to stop the attacks.

The commissioners from Plymouth, New Haven, and Connecticut all voted to declare war, but one of the commissioners from Massachusetts dissented. He said that while the Indians on Long Island were friendly with the English, they were not allies of the United Colonies. It was an inter-Indian affair, and the English had no right to be getting involved. It must also be remembered that the English were still in quite a weak position. Massachusetts was being very sensible by stopping war from breaking out with either the Indians or Dutch, either could have been potentially disastrous for the colonies. That was why they did what they did next.

The commissioners could declare war on the Indian tribes, but Massachusetts had a nuclear option. It decided to openly defy the Confederate government. It refused to raise troops. New Haven, Plymouth, and Connecticut were all outraged, but there wasn't really anything they could do about it. And without the assistance of Massachusetts, there was nothing that could be done. The damage done to the confederation was great.

There were attempts to resolve the situation. Massachusetts defended her actions, even going as far as to send messengers back to England to explain what happened, but didn't want to break up the confederation. It behaved during the 1654 meeting. The other colonies were hurt, but that didn't get in the way of business. The confederation survived, but its importance had waned and its prestige was damaged.

New Haven was determined to go to war with the Dutch and sent a petition to Oliver Cromwell for supplies which were sent. But, by the time they arrived in the New Haven peace had been made back in Europe. Relations improved slightly, and much trade took place between New England and Monhatoes (as Manhattan was referred to at the time). Once the restoration took place, rumours began to circulate of renewed hostility between England and the Dutch, and so the New Englanders stopped having anything to do with Stuyvesant. This was confirmed when James the Duke of York conquered New Netherland. New York was born, and the animosity between New England and Manhattan was brought to a close.[69] At any rate, the New England colonies no longer had to worry about the Dutch.

Indian relations were less clear cut. The United Colonies did not go to war, but they set up a ship to patrol the Long Island Sound to protect their friendly tribes. There were many other elements to Indian policy, as you can imagine. The Indians were not one single political entity, but many that had to be dealt with. The Ninigrets had to be watched as a threat, the Pequods were allowed to have a settlement which was half-English. Missionary activity took place, and in 1649 Parliament set up a corporation to help spread the Gospel with the money handled by the New England Confederation.

As we enter the 1660s we have to deal with one of the unpleasant episodes of US history. The

---

[69] According to some. Try saying that at a Red Sox-Yankees game.

simplified version of the American story is that the Pilgrim Fathers travelled over from England to the US because they wanted freedom of persecution. That, as I hope you've already worked out, is a myth. The Puritans who travelled to the New World were just as intolerant as the English they were escaping. They didn't want to be attacked by Archbishop Laud, but this meant that they wanted to set up an exclusively Puritan settlement, rather than set up a place to avoid persecution. A resistance to new migrants is a theme which reoccurs continually throughout American history, which is extraordinarily ironic.

So, what we have in New England in 1660 are a skittish group of Puritans, who, as the name implies, wanted to be pure, and not allow impurity into their settlement. This was why Rhode Island was not allowed to join the Puritan League, as you might as well call the United Colonies of New England. So, what was this great danger that arrived in New England that threatened to destroy their way of life? The Quakers.

The Quakers

I'm not going to properly explain the Quakers just yet, other than mentioning that they were a fringe religious group which believed that it was wrong to swear loyalty to earthly magistrates. They are very important in the history of Pennsylvania, that will be a more appropriate place to cover them. Anyway, the puritans were worried by the Quakers, and felt that they were dangerous radicals. The Quakers were expelled from the United Colonies. Any Quaker that returned would be imprisoned and then banished. If they returned a second time, they would be killed. This was done by all the colonies, but Massachusetts was more vigorous than the others. I repeat, don't let anybody tell you that the Pilgrims wanted religious toleration.

The exception was that one little colony, Rhode Island. Rhode Island was a bastion of toleration, and refused to give up the Quakers that fled there. The other colonies threatened Rhode Island with an economic blockade which would have been ruinous. However, Rhode Island didn't give in, and the other colonies never followed through on the threat. Speaking of which, it is about time we return to Rhode Island.

In 1636, Roger Williams fled from the other colonies of New England to Narraganset Bay where he founded Providence Plantation. Williams had several major objections to the other colonies which he intended to fix. He objected to the way Puritanism had invested the governments of New England. Religion was a private matter, and had nothing to do with the state. He also disapproved of the oligarchical nature of the New England governments, particularly Massachusetts. The pastors had too much power. In Providence Plantation there would be religious freedom, and it would be democratic. There was very little actual governance in the area of Rhode Island, but when it was time for government it would be done by the shareholders in the colony. In other words, the landed men. This doesn't seem that radical to us, but it was at the time. Over the years many others seeking religious freedom would flee to Narraganset Bay, and by 1643 four settlements had been established. These were Providence, Newport, Portsmouth, and Warwick. We can call this Rhode Island, although it would take quite a while for this collection of villages to understand itself as the colony of Rhode Island, or even to view the founding of Rhode Island as happening in 1636.

The first history of Rhode Island was written in 1738, a date considered the colony's one hundredth anniversary. Rhode Island is essentially a bay around an island which was known as Aquidneck, but for reasons which are a complete mystery to us was renamed Rhode Island. The other townships were based on the island, and were economically more important than Providence which was located on the mainland. The first of these townships, Plymouth, was founded in 1638, so for some time this was regarded as a more appropriate foundation date. This attitude is found in other places. When the colony finally received a royal charter in 1663 it had the name 'The Colony of Rhode Island and Providence Plantation'. Rhode Island gets top billing over Providence.[70]

Williams has received more recognition for founding the first settlement in the region, and he also did much to organise its infrastructure by securing a patent for Providence in 1644. I hope what this is making clear is that Rhode Island had a very turbulent history. We mentioned this previously in our brief introduction, but there are some things I'd like to revisit. For example, I never really talked about the process by which the land was actually acquired. Not the process by which the Europeans granted lands that they had no right to, but the process by which the land was secured from the Native Americans. To explain that we need to get a bit into Native American history.

Native Americans of Narraganset Bay

It's a shame that there are only a few pre-Columbian civilisations whose history we have a reasonable understanding of. We simply don't know

---

[70] There are also a few who would date the foundation of the colony to William Blackstone who arrived in the region before Williams, but no serious historian actually thinks this. Blackstone may well have been the first European to live on Narraganset Bay, but he travelled there from Boston to escape the crowds, not found a community. He might have lived there, and he is worth an interesting footnote, but no more than this.

most of the history of Narraganset Bay, but we do begin to understand the situation from the early sixteenth century.

There were two tribal groups in the region, both of whom we've already dealt with at various points. These were the Wampanoags and the Narragansets. The Wampanoags lived on the eastern side of the bay, and the Narragansets lived on the western side. It wasn't what you would call a peaceful relationship, and warfare took place between the two tribes for control of the islands in the bay and the coastline. We know that the Wampanoags were the more powerful of the two tribes in the 1520s, but after this initial investigation there was not much interest in the region for the following hundred years.

The next insight to the region we have is the arrival of the Pilgrims, and it seems as the though the balance of power had greatly changed in the intervening century. This was mostly due to the great plague which had devastated the Wampanoags. You'll recall that Plymouth was set up on what was a deserted settlement. In his book Colonial Rhode Island: A History, Sydney James estimates that there were about 25,000 Native Americans living in New England at this time. The largest tribe in the region was the Narraganset tribe which had a population of about 5,000 condensed in an area 20 miles west of the bay, and 60 miles inland. It was one of the highest population concentrations on the North American continent. In comparison the Wampanoag population was something just under 1,500.

This explains the geo-political context, but there is a greater point to all this. Rhode Island wasn't empty. This was a crowded area. Much American mythology centres on taking untouched land. But, this wasn't remotely true here. In fact, this was the least true it would ever be during the European conquest of the continent. It wasn't a case of Williams, Coddington, and the other founders of Rhode Island just going to an empty area and setting up shop, the native tribes had to actively make room for them. Why?

The explanation is both very simple and very complicated at the same time. The Wampanoags reason for going along with it is obvious. They were far weaker than their traditional enemy, the Narragansets. They wanted a buffer, and so were more than happy to give land which they claimed to Williams to get someone between them and the enemy, but which in practice they could not possibly hope to control themselves. Understanding why the Narragansets is a bit more complicated, and it requires both knowledge of Indian diplomacy, and a great deal of what was covered in the previous chapter.

The Narragansets immediately understood that these new arrivals to the region were a threat, and that some were more threatening than others. One colony bothered them in particular, Massachusetts.

Massachusetts was the largest, it was growing the quickest, and it was the most hostile. In our last chapter Massachusetts didn't actively declare war against the Narragansets, well aware that they could be destroyed, but they did kill a Narraganset leader. They were sure that there was some sort of conspiracy to destroy them. The puritans were very frightful. As more and more puritans poured into New England, they pushed west, and tensions with the Narragansets increased. They tried to deal with the Europeans so that they could define their relationship, but the Europeans couldn't understand the diplomatic system. So this, a tense relationship with Massachusetts, was the first issue.

The second lay to the west. There was another powerful Indian tribe to the west of the Narragansets, these were the Pequots. The Narragansets were far more concerned with the Pequots than with the Wampanoags, and even Massachusetts was of secondary importance compared to this new threat. They had a clear ordering of priorities.

The third factor was that while they disliked the Puritans, they got on very well with Williams. He had traded with them, and helped them to ease relations with Massachusetts. They would even briefly unite against the Pequots. So, when Williams was forced out of New England and he asked for land, it made perfect sense for them to grant Williams a strip of land on their eastern territory. He was a friend, it would place someone between them and Massachusetts who could act as an intermediary between them, and it secured the eastern border so that they could give their undivided attention to the West.

The Narragansets would treat Williams very well over the years, and when he asked for more land on the islands in the bay they complied. In return, Williams gave gifts. He had a greater understanding of Indian diplomacy than most. They could use this settlement to get access to English trade, and it would have the benefit of being a buffer between themselves and the Wampanoags. It would be realistic to view Rhode Island as a creation of Narraganset Indian policy. Now, that is a version of the founding of America you will rarely hear.

The land was also rather useful. All the townships were established near sources of fresh water, and there was access to the sea for all of them, as well as land for crops and livestock.

Rhode Island Theology

Socrates is famous as one of the fathers of western philosophy, but his writings almost all come from someone else. Usually his students, Plato and Xenophon. Socrates himself didn't write anything down because he believed that the written word corrupted philosophy by putting into a fixed form. Philosophy was far too complicated to be written down. It needed to be explained and discussed. That was the best way to fully understand ideas. If it was written down, someone could misunderstand, and errors could creep into the creed. That was why Socrates never wrote down his ideas. It is an idea that has merit, but is profoundly frustrating to historians.

Rhode Island was very active in the theological field; it was very energetic. Many sermons were given. But it was felt that sermons were unique things. They were special to the place and time that they were given, and could not be fully understood by anyone who wasn't there. So, it follows, there was no point in writing any of it down. Nobody else would be able to gain the insight from it, so it didn't need to be saved. This is incredibly frustrating to the historian of the period, and it colours everything I'm about to tell you. So, just what can we work out?

Well, the Rhode Islanders were ultra-puritans. This led to interesting results. When you take an idea to its extreme conclusions, it often ends up being against what most people who like the idea believe. This is, in fact, where Rhode Island toleration came from. The puritans wanted a pure church. To enforce this, the church was fused the state. People who didn't believe in church beliefs were expelled from the colony. Roger Williams took this a step further in Providence. There could be nothing in the church which was impure, therefore the church was more selective in who could join. For example, the state was a very human affair, and it couldn't be allowed to meddle with the church. Therefore, they would have nothing to do with each other. The ultra-puritans could have their church, and they didn't really care about who else was in the state. The church was pure, that was what counted. Everybody else was left to their own devices. Forcing people to join, or be pure when they weren't, would only corrupt the church. So, by following through on extreme ideas of exclusivity they created a state of religious toleration. That was where things began.

The Baptists

Then, very early on, the puritans found another error to be purged from the church. An idea that had slowly been gaining influence in Europe for 30 years or so. The idea was child-baptism did no good because children couldn't understand what was happening. It was useless. Therefore, baptism should be reserved for adults, and only those baptised as adults could be allowed into the church. So, what Williams did was establish the first Baptist congregation in the New World. Although perhaps a better way of putting it was that Williams was led into establishing the first Baptist congregation in the New World. It wasn't quite the idea for him. The Baptists would try and organise themselves, and try and understand their own ceremonies. The most important of these was the laying on of hands. The practice has its origins in the bible, most notably Acts 8:14-19. If you'll allow me to quote the King James,

> "Now when the apostles which were at Jerusalem heard that Samaria had received the word of God, they sent unto them Peter and John: who, when they were come down, prayed for them, that they might receive the Holy Ghost: (For as yet he was fallen upon none of them: only they were baptised in the name of the Lord Jesus.) Then laid they their hands on them, and they received the Holy Ghost. And when Simon saw that through laying on of the apostles hands the Holy Ghost was given, he offered them money, Saying, Give me also this power, that on whomsoever I lay hands, he may receive the Holy Ghost."

That the laying on of hands was highly important became a part of Baptist thought.

While the Baptists sorted this out, Williams went out in his own direction. He began to question what right did a church have to control its members, unless that church had received that authority directly from either Christ or the apostles. There was no church like that. The old churches had such authority, but the papacy had broken that connection by introducing many elements into Christianity which had no basis in the bible. This led him to the conclusion that until God set up a new church, there could be no church. He dropped out of the fellowship. He didn't believe in other religions, such as the Narragansett religion, but he didn't see it as anything worse that an incorrect form of Christianity, and since all churches had no authority, almost everyone worshiped some incorrect form of Christianity. This led him to complete toleration. He wouldn't try and convert the natives, or anyone else for that matter. He would preach to, and pray with, anybody who wanted to listen, but didn't force his views on anyone. While Williams went in this direction, the Baptists were going in quite a different one. Without Williams, uneducated minsters were left in control. They wanted to uncover the single absolutely correct interpretation of the bible. So much for Providence. Let's turn to Portsmouth.

Theology of Portsmouth and Newport

Portsmouth was founded by Anne Hutchinson, who was forced out of Massachusetts for Antinomianism. Antinomianism is the belief that salvation is earned through faith alone, and therefore that it was unnecessary for believers to follow biblical law. This was in direct contrast to the view that good works were also necessary for salvation. Antinomianism was very controversial. It was a threat to the purification of the church, and therefore was forced out of Massachusetts. Once Anne Hutchinson had founded the settlement, Antinomianism ran into difficulties.

Hutchinson might have been able to found a settlement, but forming a ministry is something rather different. She was unable to do it, and soon lost religious control of the colony. There was no order, and various people prophesised their beliefs. The most notable was Gorton who went on to found Warwick, but once he was forced out of Portsmouth in 1641 the colony lost its earlier zeal. Hutchinson left in 1643, a sign of her disintegrating religious movement. This isn't necessarily her fault. She might have spread the idea that direct communication with god was possible, as many wanted to hear, but they didn't want to be told this by a woman. A tragic element of the times. Portsmouth would continue with this sort of informal Antinomianism for about twenty years.

Gortonianism

Newport was the most traditional of the four townships that would form the colony. It started out with a Puritan minster who had a traditional place in the community, but he soon returned to Weymouth, and gradually the town drifted to a prophesising version of Baptism.

Warwick had probably the strangest religious origin of the lot. Warwick was founded by Samuel Gorton, a man who had been kicked out of pretty much everywhere else in New England. He was a very controversial man with a strong personality. He preached, but we do not know what he preached. As I explained earlier, nobody thought that history might appreciate it if somebody wrote this down. So then, what can we work out?

To borrow a phrase from James' 'Colonial Rhode Island: A History', Warwick was an elaborate irony. Much like the obsession of Providence with keeping a pure church ironically led to religious toleration, Warwick took this to new levels. We can't be sure what exactly Gorton preached, but it was incredibly controversial. He had been forced out of everywhere he went. It seems that he completely rejected organised religion. He viewed that the state and religion should not remotely be connected. This was a radical view. The people who followed Gorton had been kicked out of everywhere else, therefore they were extremely loyal to him. I think you can see where this is going.

Gortonianism was characterised by controversy, but everybody in Warwick believed the same thing, so they couldn't argue with each other. Everybody rejected the premise of a town church and organised religion, but they all believed the same thing. So, they met socially, as people do. They got together to talk about how they all believed the same thing. By completely rejecting the principal of a church, they formed a church. Elaborate irony.

Gortonianism, much like Antinomianism, wasn't well suited to long term survival. It was, as the name suggests, largely based upon the personality of Gorton. It didn't long survive his death. He hoped that others would find the Holy Spirit within themselves as he had done, but the people were only following him. Upon his death most turned towards either Baptism or Quakerism. The fact that none of his sermons were written down leads to a fascinating series of events, where some Gortonians continued to follow the creed for another century, but because nothing had been written down they had no idea what the creed was. They knew that whatever he had preached was so insightful that it went beyond human comprehension, therefore they couldn't possibly understand what they believed. I don't think irony is quite the right word for this, but it's certainly something.

Rhode Island was utterly incomprehensible to the other puritans of the region. They saw it as a mixture of extreme zealots who embraced madnesses, thought war unchristian, and had uneducated ministers. The state was viewed with suspicion. It seemed like the colony was rejecting religion, and was going down a dark road towards ignorance. It was this Rhode Island that Massachusetts wouldn't allow in the United Colonies of New England.

To those so inclined, it is very easy to be consumed by politics, and to forget that most people don't think about it 24/7. It's a trap a lot of historians fall into. The story of history is often viewed as the story of politics, but that simply isn't true for most people. In Rhode Island, the predominant factor at play here is religion. Most people were far more interested in that than they were in politics, therefore religion is a far better lens with which to view the history of the colony. It is far more revealing about the past.

Rhode Island, in this state, could only exist while the English civil war was raging, and then once Charles I was dead, only by the leniency of the liberal Puritans. Cromwell began the process of taking down some of more extreme Puritan creeds, and the restoration of Charles II saw Rhode Island flung into isolation. England wanted nothing to do with the black sheep of her North American children. Significantly, just before this happened, a new force entered the colony. Quakerism.

Quakerism and Biblical Literalism

Quakerism had some similarities with Antinomianism, such as the focus on inner light, that made many of the Rhode Islanders ready converts. This was a better organised alternative to their existing religion. The church reached high levels of sophistication with remarkable rapidity. Their insistence on refusing to use oaths was troublesome everywhere else, but in Rhode Island this was nothing out of the ordinary. By 1670 most leading figures of the colony were Quakers, but it would be unwise to refer to anything even approaching a Quaker Party which captured the colony, as some historians have been inclined to do.

This rapid shift to Quakerism was a reflection of one of the two underling and counteracting trends in the colony, the drift towards mysticism and the drift towards biblical literalism. Antinomianism opened the way by suggesting that biblical rules didn't apply to believers, the key factor of Christianity was the personal relationship with God. The next step was to gradually abandon the written texts, and to instead focus upon what one person experienced. We've seen this focus on the individual with

Gorton. Quakerism saw the main focus of Christianity become the guiding force of the Holy Spirit. This move away from traditional theology, and indeed from education, was troubling to many.

The other force at work was biblical literalism. The Biblicists believed that the divine revelations would not be achieved by some process of inner search and abandoning the bible, but instead by trying to use the bible, particularly Acts and the Epistles, to try and recreate the practices of the early Christians as best as they could. There were some other similarities to the Quakers. They did not listen to the beliefs of the educated as gospel, and instead preferred a personal relationship with the bible. It was an unsophisticated eye that looked upon the text, but it was certainly direct. Just as the mystical elements of Rhode Island were naturally drawn towards Quakerism, the Biblicists were drawn towards the Baptists. The main feature of Baptist theology was the focus on adult baptism. Infant baptism was not mentioned in the New Testament, so the Biblicists rejected it, and became Baptists.

Christianity has had, over the past two thousand years, a history of arguing with itself. That was what happened in Rhode Island. While the Baptists could agree about Baptism itself, there was a wide verity of other issues which caused schisms very quickly. The first of these schisms was over the practise of the laying on of hands with reference to Hebrews 6:2, which caused a breakaway church led by Thomas Olney. There was a break between Predestinarian Baptists (Five Principle Baptists) and General Baptists (Six Principle Baptists). There were also conflicts about how lawful oaths were, about how lawful war was, about foot washing, and about whether there was a need to sing psalms when worshiping.

There was an argument in the 1660s about whether or not the Sabbath was the first, or last, day of the week.[71]

---

[71] I could give you the very short version of the story, but I like stories, so I'm going to give the long explanation of this debate. While Monday is often treated as the first day of the week, it isn't. Technically, the first day of the week is Sunday. This is why in Judaism the Sabbath is on a Saturday. God created the world in six days, and on the seventh he rested. The Sabbath is on Saturday, the seventh day. During the early Christian period, for what are very confusing reasons, the Sabbath changed. There are many theories, but one is that it goes back to the Emperor Constantine, the first Christian Emperor. Before he converted to Christianity, he was a worshiper of an eastern sun cult which worshiped Sol Invictus, the Unconquered Sun. This was very popular around the turn of the fourth century. When working out which day was special to worshipers of the Sun god, we have to look at names of the days of the week, and therefore to the Babylonians.

Why does a week have seven days? Because Babylonian astronomers could see seven objects moving in the sky. The had a day for the Sun and Moon, and then 5 more for each of the planets they could see. Mars, Mercury, Jupiter, Venus, and Saturn. The planets are named after Roman gods, so are the days of the week. The first day of the week is Sunday, obviously, and Monday is Moon day, or in Italian Lunedi, after the Latin for moon, Luna. Tuesday is Mars, Martedi in Italian. Wednesday is Mercury, Mercoledi in Italian, Thursday is Jupiter, or Jove, Giovedi in Italian, Friday is Venus, Venerdi in Italian, and Saturday is obviously Saturn. So, since the Babylonians, the first day of the week had been associated with the Sun. It made sense that sun

The point for the Biblicists was to exactly recreate the conditions of the early church. Not to get as close as possible, but to literally get it exactly right. This made every small disagreement as significant as the more fundamental points of doctrine, and

---

worshipers have the first day of the week for their holy day. When Constantine converted, he was used to having Sunday as a holy day rather than Saturday, the traditional Sabbath. A Sunday Holy Day was more familiar than the Saturday, so it seems that Constantine changed the date of the Sabbath to make the day more palatable. This is one of a large number of crossovers between the two religions. Even the date of Christmas, December 25th, was selected because that was the festival day for Sol Invictus. That is at the very least one of the theories about why the Sabbath became the first day of the week rather than the last day of the week.

Cut to the 1660s and Rhode Island. A Sunday Sabbath had well over a millennium of tradition, but one of the major elements of the protestant reformation was refuting all the additions to the faith that had been made by Catholicism, and returning to an earlier version of Christianity. Some factors of this tradition were quite easy to throw off. A great many political leaders, such as Henry VIII, enjoyed no longer being responsible to the Pope. Some were more difficult, and not all could stomach the thought that they had been holding the Sabbath on the wrong day. There was a fierce rejection of the notion. It was lunacy to celebrate the Sabbath on a Saturday. If they were going to destroy such a fundamental facet of Christianity, why not just convert to Judaism. The Sabbatarians, as they were called, were accused of deserting Christ in favour of Moses. This was the birth of the Seventh Day Baptist Church. You will not be surprised that this splinter group would splinter even further, but at some point there are diminishing returns on me covering this.

made it so that no church could exist for very long before it completely broke apart.

It is important though to remember that even though they loved arguing amongst themselves, they did not go as far in that degree as Roger Williams. The founder of Providence was so disenchanted with churches that he viewed them all as corrupt, and no different from heathen religions. This led him to have a great degree of toleration. The Baptists argued amongst themselves, but at the same time they were all aware that they had many common ideas. They might fight, but they were all Baptists.

I'd like to conclude this discussion with a quote from Colonial Rhode Island – A History by Sydney James, which I feel captures everything quite nicely.

> "If the idea is not pushed too far, it is helpful to see the two broad types of religion that developed in seventeenth-century Rhode Island, Biblicist and mystical, as stemming respectively from Roger Williams and Anne Hutchinson. From Williams came the determination to purify the church, bringing it into conformity with the divine intent as learned from the revealed Word of God, forever completed in the Bible. From Hutchinson came the exciting hope that the Holy Spirit continued to inspire mortals and would supply direction to the devout in their daily life as well as in their churches. Both these leaders

departed from the fellowships they launched, leaving their followers to settle their own affairs. Loss of leadership surely resulted in accentuation of certain traits – a drift towards the humdrum and the narrow-minded among those who reputed divine inspiration, a drift towards spiritual anarchy among the Antinomians until curbed by the person force of Gorton and the ecclesiastical heavy machinery of the Quakers.

Most of the time no one said or wrote much about the tension between the two sides...

Even if it is reasonable to think of two primary forms of religion in early Rhode Island, it would be a mistake to overestimate the clarity of the distinctions between them. There were many Baptists who agreed with Quakers on ministry guided by the Holy Spirit and on the moral evil of war. Church discipline was practiced in similar fashion by the various communions. If most Baptists were slower to admit and quicker to expel members and the Quakers by contrast prone to embrace people without drawing sharp lines between an inner circle and the rest, the Sabbatarian Baptists stood somewhere in between. The mystical element read the Bible in much the same way as the Biblicist and expected to draw from it the pattern for the church as well as an index to the validity of latter-day inspiration. In a larger sense, moreover, the religious groups of the colony were alike in their differences from traditional Christianity. They rejected the heritage of ceremony, learning, and hierarchy. They went well beyond the ordinary Puritan horror of using beauty or magnificence to piety. Following what they believed was scriptural precedent, the Rhode Island Christians did not even sing Psalms and they met in fields or private dwellings. Before the end of the seventeenth century, they erected only a few meagre buildings: a few small Quaker meetinghouses, a Baptist meetinghouse, and dressing rooms for baptismal ceremonies. They all allowed women to participate in church affairs to an unprecedented extent – the Baptists letting both sexes vote in church meetings, the Gortonians insisting that they and God recognised no distinction between the sexes, and the Quakers welcoming some women as ministers and all as full members for ecclesiastical business until they set up meetings for women alone. The churches around Narragansett

Bay were thus much of one mind on many points in their departures from tradition.

The departures were not purely radical, however. After the early years, the burdens of the Christian heritage of learning and elaborate organisation of ecclesiastical authority no longer had to be thrown off because the Rhode Islands had left them behind. Solemnity and magnificence in the church were no longer appealing either to mirror and sustain the majesty of the state or to counterbalance it. Secular authority struggled along on a modest scale and so did religious. Neither could afford more grandeur. The Rhode Island Christians adjusted their churches to their lives. Hey ended up with simplicity, plainness, home-grown preachers, detachment from power and the trappings of power – altogether a modest do-it-yourself style of religion suitable for straightforward people in a society where all worked hard and even the wealthiest were people of modest means by Old World standards."

Economic World of Rhode Island

Seventeenth century Americans had a fear of the untamed nature of their new home. They worried that the precious gift of civilisation that Europe, and

Europe alone, had developed, could be lost. They had manners, morality, and culture. The Indians had none. Everything must be done to protect their refinement.

The colonists did have some practical priorities. Their first priority was to secure clean water and a food supply. With their various crops and access to the sea, they were able to have a society which was primarily agricultural, but there were a few specialised professions. Each town needed a sawmill. This was a degree of simple self-sufficiency, but this wasn't the ultimate level of civility that the Rhode Islands had mind. For example, they were a very religious people, bibles were necessary. Other books too. Glass windows, iron tools, spices, gin, ammunition. All these were needed, but couldn't be acquired locally. They would need to be imported.

A reoccurring feature of the story of the United States until the twentieth century was the lack of liquid capital on the frontier. While they had things that they could produce themselves quite easily, such as crops, whenever anything more was needed it caused trouble. As the border moved west, financial trouble will be a theme we come back to again and again, but it had its origins here. How were the Rhode Islanders going to acquire the features of western civilisation? Furs were an early solution, but the area was generally quite swampy, and the forests didn't have that many animals to make the trade profitable for any length of time. Particularly with the more powerful colonies surrounding them. What was the Rhode Island fur trade compared to New Netherland, or Massachusetts?

They settled on livestock and other agricultural products, such as some garden produce, cheese, tobacco, in addition to timber. This could be exported. The problem for Rhode Island was, again, the other colonies. Other traders from other colonies had more capital, and so were able to edge out the Rhode Islanders. There were many open markets, such as the Newfoundland fishing fleet, the Caribbean, and the New Englanders themselves, but they would generally get goods from the old world via Boston. Competition was fierce, but eventually a Rhode Island trade network managed to establish itself, mostly centred on the Long Island Sound and the newly established Carolina.

This was the economic world of Rhode Island. Primarily agricultural, with some specialist artisans. This was in addition to a group of traders who created the wealth to bring in the much desired imports. Trading activities usually organised itself, but the agricultural aspects of Rhode Island needed more order, which was the key factor in the development of Rhode Island politics.

Political World of Rhode Island

I want to assume that most of you are familiar with the William Goulding Book, Lord of the Flies.[72]

---

[72] Or, at the very least, the Simpsons version of it. Season 9 Episode 14, Das Bus. The plot is that a group of children are stranded on a desert island. They try to establish order and democracy, but they quickly turn to their baser instincts. Without the rule of law, the children turn on each other and before long there is murder most foul. It makes the point that civilisation, so prised by the seventeenth century colonists, is just an illusion of tradition. Once you are placed into a different land, the

Rhode Island, partly due to its very unusual origin of being the people driven away from all the other colonies, went through a similar crisis in its early years. It wasn't sure where exactly authority came from. They were all immigrants, and so understanding how the system worked where they came from is very important. They lived in an old country. England had a great many traditions going back centuries, some, millennia. There existed an unquestioned public authority which either came from the crown, from the local dignitary, or from local custom. These things went back into time immemorial. You would accept the local town rulings because that was the way it had always been. All of a sudden, they were thrust into a new world. People could set up agreements and agricultural regulations. That was fine. But what happened when someone broke them? A town could give a ruling, but why did anybody have to listen? Their old village would have had centuries to build up prestige and authority so that people would listen, but this village had been founded last year? Everyone had been there just as long. Why did they have to listen to anyone else? There were some social conventions which survived the transition. A town itself couldn't be ignored, but the judicial apparatus of the town could be. Judges could be denounced as having no real authority.

Portsmouth attempted to set out a social compact in the manner of the Pilgrims, being a town run on biblical laws with Coddington as a judge, but they also used town meetings which quickly gained the

---

illusion vanishes, and law and order are notoriously difficult to establish. That at least it the basic version of it.

aura of old England. This couldn't last long. While the idea of biblical judges was attractive in theory, in practice the settlers didn't like such a concentration of power. Elders were chosen to assist the judge, and then they were to report their activities to the town. Gorton stirred up enough trouble that eventually Coddington quit the town and travelled to the other end of Aquidneck to found Newport.

Anne Hutchinson's husband, William, was chosen to be the new judge. This didn't last very long. Many of the citizens of Portsmouth wanted fairer land distribution. They came to terms with Coddington and his new town. He abandoned the practice of Mosaic law, instead adopting English customs and proclaiming his direct subordination to King Charles. He set up a government to govern both the towns on Aquidneck. This system was far more orderly, particularly once Gorton was expelled and William Hutchinson died.

This new government lasted for several years. It loudly proclaimed both its democratic element and its subordination to King Charles. It would have a governor, and two assistants who were elected from each town. In practice it wasn't a democracy, but more of an oligarchy dominated by Coddington.

Meanwhile, in Providence, Roger Williams tried basing their government upon the laws that governed human society, rather than a theoretical concept. He saw society as based upon families, and so Providence was based upon family units. Each head of the family would have one vote, and arbitrators or judges could be appointed case by case to settle specific disputes. This was very idyllic, but there were several practical issues. How could someone who violated the agreement be punished, aside from being attacked by the rest of the citizens? There was also no way for individuals to be brought into a social system based upon family blocks. How were new settlers to be introduced to the mix? How were they to deal with the Indians? A more sophisticated government was necessary.

Land was set aside for original settlers; this was an attempt to prevent later reluctance to allow new immigrants who were also fleeing persecution. Newcomers needed to swear to obey the town rules before joining, something which in 1640 became the Combination (a sort of social compact). Gorton was again part of the process of disruption that led to these developments.[73] There were still issues about the authority of these actions, with many viewing that the only source of authority could come from the King. Indeed, this same conclusion was reached by people all over Rhode Island. All other theories simply weren't enough. This is why it was so important for the Rhode Island to get a royal charter. The towns might base their laws upon English precedent, but that simply wasn't enough. The process of this finally taking place and forming a cohesive colony would take most of the seventeenth century.

The process began in 1644 by a patent given to Providence Planation. It implied that the towns of the region should gather together under some sort

---

[73] It's quite ironic that Gorton's own Warwick never had to deal with these issues because by the time it became a settled community the governmental structure had settled into place.

of central government. This was what was needed, a judiciary with authority from the king in order to solve their disputes. But, in practice, they were too independent for this to work. The towns kept setting up their own courts which would contest decisions of the central judiciary. They wanted the authority from above, but not the regulations that came with it.

The patent caused other problems. Massachusetts did not like Rhode Island. The very last thing it wanted was for these upstarts to get legitimacy from parliament. Aquidneck also resented the primacy that was given to Providence. It seems that Coddington didn't want to be in the same colony as Gorton, and also feared losing power. He attempted to keep Aquidneck as an independent colony, seeking out protection from Massachusetts and Plymouth, but both wanted nothing to do with Aquidneck, aside from perhaps annexing it.

Williams spent the immediate years trying to gather recruits to his tentative new regime, while gradually the government of Aquidneck fell apart. The legislative element of the government had already collapsed by 1646, and as things got worse Aquidneck was forced to agree basic terms with Williams for the new government, and a constitutional convention of sorts was held at Plymouth in 1647.

It was to be a democratic government with a general court which would act as a legislature, but already existing rights and political bodies would exist. A pledge was taken, oaths after all being a controversial subject. A body of 8 officials was to be elected to act in a judicial function. These would include one assistant from each of the four towns, a general secretary, a general sergeant, a general treasurer, and President who would act as a chief officer. The president and the assistants had powers as magistrates and were the bench of the judges. The secretary, known as the recorder, would be the clerk at trials. The general treasurer was the only official with something resembling administrative duties, and these were not many. The colonial government didn't have much in the way of finances for quite some time. The judicial focus of the body was further made clear when two more elected officials were added to the roster, a general attorney and a general solicitor.

The code of laws which was drawn up was mostly based upon English statute, with elements from scripture and English common law. Essentially, a mixture of scripture and authority from parliament was used to give authority to the new system, and the details were worked out by law. The Rhode Islanders were very optimistic with their brand new system. I'm sure that you'll be surprised to learn that this system was a complete failure.

Chaos in Rhode Island

First of all, it was very quickly realised that their citizens were unsuited to work as legislators. The spent a year at it, and got nowhere. It was a failure. Since direct democracy had failed, they tried a shift towards representative democracy. The General Assembly voted to transfer its powers to a body of representatives, 6 from each town, who tried to include popular democracy into their actions. They experimented with versions of referendums, but none of these proved successful either.

What followed was a reaction against the central government. It wasn't getting anything done, so why not just return power back to where it belonged: with the towns themselves? Rights were given back to the towns, they were allowed to design their own constitutions and their own legal structures, they were then allowed to elect town councillors to administer government, and not even this worked because some towns chose simply to not have certain bits of the government, or elected people who didn't wish to serve. Coddington refused to serve as president. Public authority crumbled. The new government had been established in 1647. By 1648 Rhode Island was falling into chaos. Fighting started between the various towns, one man was actually killed. Warwick feared that Massachusetts would take advantage of this infighting, and then out of nowhere Coddington appeared with a document that he claimed had been sent over from the Council of State in England, which re-established the government of Aquidneck and named him President for life. Meanwhile he sent friends to London to try and get the 1644 patent rescinded. This horrified the mainland towns, who sent Williams to London in order to reaffirm to patent and selected Gorton to be their president, replacing Nicholas Easton who had no intention of resigning. There were now three separate governments in operation. This was how things continued until into the 1650s.

In September 1652 Coddington's agents returned from London. they reported that the 1644 patent was still in effect. The men on Aquidneck took this to believe that Easton's government was the legitimate government, and mostly sided with him. Some on the mainland did too, but many there viewed Gorton as the remnant of the original government. Nobody supported Coddington, though he was determined to revive his government. He met with agents from both Boston and New Netherland in an effort to secure their support, but nobody wanted to back him. This state of affairs lasted for two years until Williams' own return to the colony in 1654.

By this stage the Aquidneck government of Easton was prevailing due to its vastly greater resources, and Williams persuaded those still resisting on the mainland that they would be better served by uniting with Easton rather than fighting under Gorton. Having reunited the colony, Williams was elected president and he spent three years bringing harmony to the region. With some help from Oliver Cromwell, he was even able to get Coddington to cease trying to set up a counter-government, and finally join the administration.

By 1658, 14 years after the patent had first been given, it could be said that Rhode Island had something resembling a government. They had support from the Protectorate of Cromwell in England, Massachusetts' persecution of Quakers had reminded them of the value of religious liberty, and the conflict between the Indians and the United Colonies of New England reminded them of how fragile their little slice of the world was. They finally established a judicial system, and were able to enforce laws. The government had authority. Things were looking good. And then it all went wrong. Again.

In September 1658, Oliver Cromwell died. With him fell the Protectorate. Charles II restored the monarchy in 1660, and the position of Rhode Island suddenly became rather uncomfortable. The patent of 1644, which the colony was based on, had been issued during the English Civil War by Parliament. The monarchy had nothing to do with it. The colony had been backed by Oliver Cromwell, and it is not hard to understand why Rhode Island may not be Charles II's favourite of all the New World colonies.

Charles II was proclaimed king by Rhode Island about three months after news reached them of events in England. Three months wasn't the quickest reaction time in the world, but it was a quicker response than the other puritan New England colonies manage. This was a good start, but Rhode Island very quickly ran into problems caused by inactivity. Rhode Island wasn't the only colony that ran into issues by not having royal approval, Connecticut had the same issues. Connecticut had a bit more going for it though, such as the support of the other New England colonies, while Rhode Island was something of a pariah.

Rhode Island had an agent in London named John Clarke, but the Rhode Islanders gave him no instructions, or resources, with which to act, until very late in 1661. By this stage, it was to some extent already too late. Connecticut had acted first, and their agent in London, John Winthrop the Younger, was already very advanced in the process of securing a royal charter for that colony. Winthrop the Younger had pressed to secure the eastern border of Connecticut as Narragansett Bay, effectively taking control of mainland Rhode Island. Clarke protested, but all he was able to achieve was a promise that when the Rhode Island proposal was made that it would be treated fairly. A very frustrated Clarke spent half a year fighting to get the Rhode Island case going. His case was turned down for hearing by the Privy Council, and who knows what might have happened had Connecticut not had other matters to deal with.

Problems for Connecticut

Connecticut did not like Rhode Island, and if the royal charter could grant her Providence then all the better for Connecticut and the other New England colonies. But while dealing with Connecticut was the only real issue that Clarke had to deal with, Winthrop had many problems in determining the exact jurisdiction of Connecticut. For instance, there were issues on Long Island. Long Island had been torn between the Dutch and the English for some time, and as the Dutch left the New World it wasn't exactly clear how Long Island would enter the English system. The Long Islanders wanted to be a part of Connecticut, Plymouth had some claim to the land. While all this was going on the English were dealing with the Dutch, and were about to invade and bring about the creation of the Province of New York which claimed all islands along the Long Island Sound, including Long Island itself. It would be decided in 1664 that Long Island belonged to New York, but for the moment it was something Connecticut was fighting for. It was also fighting for New Haven.

New Haven was sandwiched between New York and Connecticut. It was small, it was isolated, its land wasn't brilliant, and it had a political structure which didn't encourage new arrivals. It was desired by Connecticut, although it had no wish to be a mere piece of its more powerful neighbour. In the grand scheme of things for Connecticut, Long Island and New Haven were more important battles to fight for than Rhode Island, and so it was agreed that Rhode Island could keep her territory on the mainland. The initial charter for Connecticut was granted in 1662, but it would take until 1664 for it to be determined that Long Island belonged to New York, but that Connecticut was allowed to absorb New Haven. Without the interfering power of Winthrop the Younger, Clarke was finally able to advance with his charter and it received official confirmation in July 1663. Interestingly, the charter gave the newly created Governor and Company of the English Colony of Rhode-Island and Providence Plantations land to the east. The charter vaguely defined the eastern border as three miles east of Narragansett Bay, which included land which had traditionally belonged to Plymouth. And, with that, the colony of Rhode Island was formally created.

The battle for the borders was by no means over, even though it had effectively been decided. Connecticut was upset with the actions of Winthrop the Younger. They said they had granted him no permission to make concessions, and would spent the greater part of the next forty years trying to annex the land he had given up, although the matter would not be decided for good until a meeting of the Privy Council in 1727. The disagreement with Plymouth, and latter Massachusetts, over the eastern border of Rhode Island would take even longer, and that matter would not be resolved until 1747, a whole 84 years after the charter had been granted.

Charter of Rhode Island

The mode of government in Rhode Island was altered by the charter. Powers of the magistrates were increased. It was determined that each May the freemen would elect a governor and a deputy, in addition to ten assistants. They would meet at least twice a year with the representatives from the towns in a General Assembly. All the original towns would have four representatives, aside from Newport which would have 6. Newly created towns would have two. There were other benefits to this official recognition diplomatically.

Rhode Island was still the black sheep of the New England family, but it could no longer be bullied to quite the same extent. Its citizens were protected, and had the right to travel in other colonies. Massachusetts would have to finally stop persecuting its citizens. It had many standard colonial government features, such as its laws needing to go along with English law as far as possible. It was also granted land regulation relatively free of old medieval relics, and it had complete freedom of judgement and conscience, reflecting its culture of religious toleration.

A few alterations were made by the Rhode Islanders, such as the distribution of magistrates. It was concerned about how many were given to Aquidneck, so it was changed to give 5 representatives from Newport, three form Providence, and two from all other towns. There was debate about whether the legislature should be bicameral or not. It was decided to go with a single chamber, although that would change in 1696.

The magistrates served both as a war council and a judicial council, in addition to advising the governor. The Assembly was a legislature, but it also appointed some officers and served as a court of appeals. The old offices were kept, but now appointed by the Assembly rather than directly by the freemen.

All in all, it was a more powerful central government than had existed previously, but despite the conditions of the charter a great deal of power still lay in the hands of the towns. What was created was, in essence, a federal structure. It is a theme that keeps coming back, which is certainly of interest when you consider the role that federalism will play in the wider history of the United States. Although, it must be noted, that there were still roles to be played by England. The central government had little power commercially, instead being a part of the English commercial web. But, despite these weakness, it is undeniable that a colony genuinely existed in Rhode Island.

Now that we have brought Rhode Island, and indeed most of New England into the 1660s, it is time to look towards the creation of New York and Delaware.

1664 was one of the most important dates in the history of New York. In that year, the colony was taken from the Dutch, who no longer really wanted it. New Netherland had not produced the promised profits, and Dutch merchants had other, greater interests. For example, the Spice Islands. The English, however, were in the process of setting up their dominion over the Atlantic Seaboard, and the Dutch controlled land between their Northern and Southern colonies was an unpleasant mark on the map. The ownership of the land transferred from the Dutch West India Company to become the property of James the Duke of York, the future James II. This is why rather than becoming the Colony of New York in the model of the Colony of Virginia, New Netherland instead became the Province of New York.

Transition to New York

In some ways, the transition was immediately felt. Many Dutch farmers recognised the change and were happy to go along with it. They took surnames, and they anglicised their names. For example, Carel van Brugge became Charles Bridge. Yet, in deeper ways it would take the colony at least a generation to make the transition from Dutch to English, and there would be many ramifications because of this. Indeed, for some time New York was something of a backwater.

To brand new students of the subject of American history, there are some things that you know from general knowledge. One of those is that New York is important.[74]. New York is a larger than life name, and you have the assumption that it was a very important place in American history. New York was, but this was a reputation it acquired in later centuries. For much of early American History, Boston and Massachusetts were far more important than New York. It might be obvious to a lot of you, but there are others, such as me when I first became interested in the subject, who didn't understand the colonial balance of power. We've already discussed the problems New Netherland had in attracting settlers from the Netherlands. There wasn't an excess of Dutch population willing to move to shacks on the Hudson. It was a huge gamble; the benefits did not look as good as life in the Netherlands.

---

[74] I have a very clear memory of being 7 years old, and a family friend gave me a placemat which was a map of the United States. It had all the state names on it, and the state capitals. Thinking about it, it's more than likely that my interest in America has a lot to do with this placemat. Every morning I'd get up and my parents would make me breakfast before school. I'd sit at the dining table, and I'd look at my placemat. Gradually I'd learn the states, I'd learn state capitals, but there were some things in particular that really confused me. I couldn't understand why New York wasn't the capital of America. New York I'd heard of. California, I knew about. But what on earth was Washington DC? My friends at school would use our newly gained ability to read to go through the first Harry Potter book, but me, I was on a quest to understand what on earth the District of Columbia was. My quest would take me several years. Back then we didn't have the internet, and while my small primary school in Manchester had a library, we didn't have many books on the American political system. It was all very frustrating to seven-year-old Jamie.

This process was made even worse by the English capture of the region. The Dutch weren't particularly inclined to travel to New Netherland, and immigrating to the English New York was an even less appetising proposition. The English weren't that interested either. Why would they travel to a weaker, mostly Dutch colony, when they could travel to either the strong Agricultural bases to the south such as Virginia and Carolina, or the more secure puritan merchant settlements of Massachusetts, Connecticut, and the soon to be founded Pennsylvania? New York was rather unique, but it would take time for this to become a positive feature rather than a negative.

The first thing to be understood about New York was its size. It was huge. HUGE. It contained under its jurisdiction the land of the Hudson and Delaware Rivers. It also, due to the shortage of willing immigrants, was sparsely populated, particularly in contrast to its more active neighbours. This meant that the very first thing to happen to New York after the conquest was that it was broken up into several different areas. I want to deal with these in order of complexity, starting with the simplest division and then advancing to ones more complicated as I feel this is easier to follow than going strictly chronologically.

Long Island

We have been dealing with the arguments between New Netherland and Connecticut for some time. Dutch-English tension had a great deal to do with what has been going on for the last twenty years, and all the events that led up to the conquest of New York. Many of the New England colonies had various stakes in this game, but the two which caused the greatest issues were Connecticut and New Haven. Under its royal charter, Connecticut took over control of New Haven, but this was just one of the many battles it was fighting for its frontiers. It was locked in a bitter struggle with Rhode Island for control of the mainland around Narragansett Bay, and it was furious that its London representative, John Winthrop the Younger, had abandoned that particular struggle. Its other concern was Long Island. Connecticut was just across the Long Island Sound from Long Island itself, and it had supported the English townships on the island against the Dutch settlements on the tip of the island, in what will eventually become Brooklyn and Queens. It made more sense that they belong to Connecticut than New York, but they were given to New York in 1664. Connecticut was not pleased, and it represented one of the many such reasons that its neighbours didn't like New York. Western Connecticut, which had become part of New York, was granted back to Connecticut in 1667 in a move which I suspect was motivated at least partly in annoyance at the Long Island decision, but that is just a hunch on my part.

New Jersey

The next most complicated issue was the land to the west of the province. In addition to the land stretching north of the Hudson, there was also a degree of land to the east which belonged under the jurisdiction of New York. This was the land between the Hudson and the Delaware. It was rather ill-defined, like many of the details of seventeenth-century colonialism. Therefore, in 1665, the Duke of York decided to break off this piece of territory into its own colony to be controlled by Lord Berkeley and Lord Carteret. It was to be based around the Dutch settlement of Bergen and was given the name New Caesarea. The name didn't really stick though, and so this new colony became known by its other name, New Jersey. That is also relatively simple, but now we have to deal with the real trouble causing areas. It's worth taking just a moment for me to recite a passage from Kammen's Colonial New York: A History.

> "By giving away all the land lying between the Hudson and Delaware rivers, the Duke left his subjects feeling 'cooped up' (Governor Thomas Dongan's phrase) between New England and New Jersey and competitive with them for immigrants and economic growth. The remote settlements beyond the Delaware were a military liability, as they had been for the Swedes and Peter Stuyvesant. As for upper Maine and the New England islands, they were about as useful as dead limbs on a dress and knots on its trunk: quite visible, but uncongenial to active growth. They added administrative costs, produced almost no revenue, and brought New York into conflict with Massachusetts as well as France."

After New Jersey and Western Connecticut had been taken out of the equation, there were what we can call three classifications of New York Land.

The first was the heartland. It was the city of New Amsterdam, now renamed New York City, on Manhattan, and the settlements up the Hudson as far as Albany. This was the populated area, indisputably part of the colony. Next came the more loosely populated areas of the colony. They were under New York jurisdiction, but didn't have the same connection with the colony that the settlements along the Hudson did. This included the areas which had been given to New Jersey, Connecticut, and the area of what had been New Sweden on the far side of the Delaware. The third area were those that New York claimed, but were not populated, at least not heavily populated, and only really caused disputes. This included an area of Northern Maine, the upstream areas of the Connecticut River, and even a stretch of land going into the interior about as far as what would become the state of Missouri. Now, this claim of the interior is something we don't need to talk about, but the Delaware, the Upstream Connecticut, and Northern Maine, all require a bit of discussion.

Further Land Issues

Northern Maine wasn't particularly an issue for New York. It was very far away from the Hudson, and it wasn't very profitable. It was ceded to Massachusetts in 1691. Upstream Connecticut was more of a battleground between the two colonies. The land to the east of the upstream Connecticut had a bit of an odd history, alternating between independence and as a province of Massachusetts, while at the same time being claimed by New York. Eventually, in 1689, this area became the independent Province of New Hampshire, and then New Hampshire resumed the conflict with New

York about who owned the land to the west of the river.

The matter was settled during the revolution, when this area declared its independence from both states to become the Vermont Republic in 1777. This enterprise would be short lived, lasting until 1791, when it joined the Union, becoming the fourteenth state in the process.

And then, after all of this, we have Delaware. New Jersey was an odd colony to create. The lands between the Hudson and the Delaware Rivers may sound nice, but what it did was leave a small slice of land on the far side of the Delaware River belonging to New York. It would have made sense to grant the land to New Jersey, or even to give it to Lord Baltimore who wanted it for his Maryland enterprise. But no. It belonged to New York. The area became what we call Delaware Colony in 1664, although that implies that it was an independent colony. It certainly wasn't. This is revealed by the fact that at the time it was known simply as the Three Counties. It was administered by New York until 1682 when it was granted to William Penn, who had founded his colony, Pennsylvania, in the previous year. Penn tried to merge the Three Counties with Pennsylvania, but this pleased nobody. In the end the two colonies would share a governor, but the Three Counties would have their own legislative assembly from 1704 onwards. This was the state of play until the Revolution when the Three Counties broke free of Pennsylvania, taking the name Delaware after the Baron De La Warr, a former governor of Virginia. His name had been used to describe the bay and river, and eventually the adjoining land.

The idea of joint governors may sound odd, but was something that did happen. New Jersey had the same governor as New York until 1738, but then New Jersey has the added complication of spending 26 years between 1676 and 1702 split into East and West. So much for the issues regarding land claims, but there were other problems. The colony had to deal with the major issue of merging its English and Dutch characters together. This was not something any other English colony had to deal with before. They were all distinctly homogenous. The other major factor at play was the inverse of Rhode Island.

Reversed Rhode Island

New York struggled to understand its legitimacy, but in reverse when compared to Rhode Island. Rhode Islanders attempted to understand how their townships worked through various theories based upon the consent of the governed and democratic ideals, but at the same time needed some connection with the old world. This is why they fought so fiercely for a royal charter. New York had exactly the opposite problem. It was a province controlled by the Duke of York, the bother of the king. He had absolute power in the region, and its inhabitants swore oaths to the king. The process was made even simpler in 1685, when James became King and the intermediate step could be skipped. New York was a royal colony. This sounds very straightforward, but in practice it made for a complicated set up.

Had James taken an active role in the province, things might have been different. However, he was an absentee landlord. He never visited New York. He had tremendous power, but he never allowed for institutions to be seriously developed. Representative democracy was not encouraged, in stark contrast to the New England colonies. This produced a void. There was a higher power at work, sure, but that power didn't enter people's lives. They found it very difficult to understand the system. It would arguably take until the 1760s for this process to be sufficiently resolved that New York had an infrastructure resembling other colonies. But, this century of confusion is an oddity, one which would surprise the new student of American history, but when you realise that New York should be considered a backwater, begins to make sense.

That isn't to say that nothing was done about the situation. The first governor of New York was Colonel Richard Nicolls. He executed the decision to conquer New Netherland, and then took over as governor and began the process of making sense of the situation. It was a position he would hold for three years until 1667. He began to set up something of a colonial governing apparatus, but he is most famous for creating something known as the Duke's Laws.

The Duke's Laws were designed to rule over a number of Dutch and English settlements on Long Island, and later spread out for use over the whole colony. They were a mixture of English and Dutch law, and as a result they were a mixture that nobody was familiar with and that nobody particularly liked. He removed English ideas such as freemanship, public education, and an elected assembly, and introduced Dutch elements of religious toleration and double nomination of officials. He also ordered that all land owners surrender their land grants and then issued renewals. This made sense as a way to break legal authority to the Dutch, but was viewed as unnecessarily complicated by most people. The code was rather vague, and New York experienced a great deal local variation, something perhaps beneficial because of its mixed population.

Many Dutch changed their names to sound more English, but it is equally important to talk about the things that didn't change in the transition. While the names of the offices became English, the offices still existed, and in many cases their holders continued to be Dutch. The names of some places did change, Beverwyck famously changing to Albany, but many others did not change. The Dutch Lange Eylandt stuck as Long Island, despite efforts by the English to rename the island Yorkshire. Similar efforts were made to rename the village of Harlem, now an area of New York City in Upper Manhattan, to be Lancaster. Needless to say, both of these attempts were spectacularly unsuccessful. Frustrating it may have been for the new English governors, but it was a very interesting time for the English language as many Dutch words entered the language during this period. Just a few are coleslaw, boss, cookie, and waffle.

An additional problem for the governorship was what to do about Rensselaerwyck. You'll recall that to encourage immigration to New Netherland, the Dutch West India Company offered Patroonships to those who brought over enough people with them. This was a slice of land on the Hudson that they could rule in a feudal manner. The patroonship experiment, like many of those tried by the Dutch West India Company, did not go well, but it had one notable exception. On the upper Hudson the Van Rensselaer family set up a patroonship known as Rensselaerwyck. The collapse of the Dutch government undermined Rensselaerwck greatly. The nearby Beverwyck was problematic to Rensselaerwick, but once it received support from the English under the name of Albany, then there were plenty of issues.

The Van Rensselaers made contact with the Duke of York directly in order to try and resolve the situation, but it would ultimately take 20 years for the matter to be settled. The feudal era of Rensselaerwyck was over. They would have an economic privilege that was allowed to remain, but it lost its political independence. The patroon was allowed a seat on the Albany court, and he could nominate other members, but it was a great weakening of his old powers of maintaining a court.

It was difficult for Nicolls to manage the English takeover of the Colony. It took a great deal out of him, and he asked to be replaced. The man selected was Colonel Francis Lovelace, a staunch royalist who had spent time in the colonies. He was selected in April 1667 and arrived in March 1668, and he continued his government in much of the same manner.

One of Lovelace's priorities was improving the infrastructure of the colony by improving roads, expanding the colony's shipbuilding industry, and promoting more commercial activity. While there was Indian activity, and we will get onto King Philip's War shortly, defence was neglected. This would come back to haunt the region. To explain what was happening, we need to go back to Europe.

Third Anglo-Dutch War

England was rather humiliated after losing the Second Anglo-Dutch War. She had gained New York, but the spice island of Run was lost, and her prestige was dented. King Charles took great issue with this, and so he plotted to get revenge. The reason that the Second Anglo-Dutch War didn't go very far was the French. King Louis XIV of France wanted control of the Spanish Netherlands, and the English didn't want a French client state there. The Dutch didn't want to be a French client state, but they were forced to accept French help against the English. Charles decided that this was his weakness, and so he sought to break apart the alliance.

He made warm movements towards the Dutch in the open, meaning that they naturally drifted away from France, while at the same time Charles made the secret Treaty of Dover in 1670, planning to effectively divide the Netherlands between French and English control. It did not take long for action to take place, and the Third Anglo-Dutch War began in 1672.

The Dutch were unhappy about how their Atlantic Empire had been weakened, and so the States General ordered raids against the English in the Caribbean and the Chesapeake. As the Dutch fleet sailed north, it soon found itself off the coast of New York and found that the colony was defenceless, just as it had been when they lost it to the English. In addition, Lovelace was out of the colony, having a meeting in Connecticut. The Dutch sailed in, New York City surrendered, and on July 30th, 1673, New Netherland was born again.

New York City was named New Orange, a new government was set up, and it began the long overdue process of setting up a real defence for the colony. Lovelace was captured upon his return and expelled. He returned to England, and was seized for debt by the Duke of York. He was placed in the Tower of London in 1674, and died a year later. The New Englanders were very unhappy about this, but they couldn't organise a response. There was really nothing that could be done. It was lucky for the English that the Dutch didn't really want New Netherland.

In 1674 a peace treaty was agreed in which New Netherland was returned to the English, and New York was back. This time for good. They also paid an indemnity to the English, and Suriname was confirmed as a Dutch colony. This would mark the end of Dutch and English conflict for over a hundred years. In 1677 Charles II forced his niece Mary to marry the Prince of Orange, William, something of huge importance to history.

There were two key military events in the 1670s that mark the end of the early colonial era. The first of these that we dealt with was Bacon's Rebellion, but this cannot be taken in isolation. Just as the Southern Colonies dealt with a potential independence movement, the north was dealing with a crisis of its own. King Philip's War.

Origins

Pressure between the Indian tribes and the English began as the English began their westward push. The first townships were set up along the coast of Massachusetts Bay in the 1620s, and as more and more people arrived they worked their way across the region. This initially caused no problems. In the years before the arrival of the Pilgrim Fathers, a devastating plague had struck the region. There were empty sites for the Pilgrims to settle at, but more and more arrived problems began to emerge. Before long, the English dominated Eastern Massachusetts, going about 25 miles inland, and were pushing into the Connecticut valley. This was going to cause problems.

Due to the haphazard nature of expansion, with each town acting quite independently, there was no grand plan. There was no systematic defence. The Connecticut villages in particular were isolated from those on Massachusetts Bay. Communities were not interested in defence, in constructing stockades, or refuges. The frontiersmen neglected military matters completely. This was going to cause problems.

Aside from the odd incident, there was little trouble between the English and the Native Americans for some time after the English arrival. The Pilgrims had quite friendly relations. Matters began to change in the 1630s when a war was fought with the Pequods. It did not reflect well on the English. They massacred an Indian village, killing 600. There were also incidents of taking Indians out to sea in boats and then killing them, and taking women and children as slaves. The English seem to have been quite panicky, regarding the Indians as threats. It is ironic that the only reason they could possibly be a threat would be because the English sold them their firearms in the first place.

The other defining feature of Anglo-Indian relations was attempted conversion. Some Indians were very interested in what the English had to say when they weren't fighting. There was even an effort to educate the Indians, to teach them about laws and democracy. It comes across as quite condescending to modern ears. The Native Americans had their own political organisations, even though they might not be as complex as those of Western Europe. They were admittedly not on the same level of civilisation, but they were not wild savages.

Native Americans did not fit with the Western understanding of creation. The people of the time understood all civilisation in terms of the bible. There were three continents, Europe, Asia, and Africa, one for each of the sons of Noah. Just how did the Native Americans fit into this? Well, they didn't. It was thought that they were of a different creation, from something before the fall. They were not quite human. They might do nice things, they might create art, but so could spiders and bees. It didn't make them human.

There was thus some confusion over what a Christian Indian was. If they weren't human, they couldn't be considered the same as white Christians, but they were a step above heathens. The term 'Praying Indians' was invented to describe them, although it was doubted that they understood or believed in the faith. It was this that would destroy any potential cooperation. While a few good folks had managed to accidently nurture friendly relations, it was all about to be destroyed.

In 1661, Massasoit, the old friend of the Pilgrims died, and he was succeeded by his son Wamsutta, known to the English as Alexander. This was at a time when the pressure for land was making it harder and harder for the two civilisations to live side by side. Wrongs were committed by both sides, and mistrust became the status quo. Wamsutta began to prepare for war against the English, and attempted to bring the Narragansets to his side. The English tried to fix the situation, but during this process Wamsutta fell ill and died. The Indians suspected that he had been poisoned. Relations soured further. In 1662 Wamsutta was replaced as king by his younger brother Metacomet, sometimes known as Pometacom or Metacom, who adopted the English name Philip. This of course brings us to King Philip's War. I will, for the purposes of this narrative, refer to him as Metacomet.[75]

Metacomet could see what was happening to his people. The English would not stop coming. They

---

[75] I dislike anglicisation of names.

would take more and more land, and eventually his people would be overrun. The English needed to be forced out. He wasn't going to just launch a war he knew that he would lose, but it seems that he realised that war was inevitable, and so he waited for it to happen. And it did.

Breakout of King Philip's War

In an early deal, the English greatly manipulated the Indians. They came to terms in talks, and then a document was signed. The Indians assumed that what was written down was what had been agreed, and so made their mark, not realising that the English, who's law valued written contracts, had changed the terms of the agreement. This took advantage of the Indians. It must be said that the English believed that all diplomatic and political deals were done in this way, and they were ignorant in assuming that the Indians would know this. It doesn't excuse their behaviour, but it does explain it. The English honestly thought that they had done nothing wrong.[76]

Metacomet had other grievances. He was frustrated that the English would not sell weapons to friendly tribes. He took offence that the English would treat the actions of individuals as the actions of tribes, and he was affronted that the English insisted in forcing themselves into legal matters that concerned only natives. They had no jurisdiction. Their strengthened position over the last 50 years had made them arrogant. This made the English very paranoid. They assumed that every action

---

[76] It's not the historian's role to moralise and judge. It's the historian's role to understand.

taken by Metacomet was in some way a preparation for war.

There was a confrontation in 1671. Metacomet admitted to the English that he had less than noble designs, and promised to be friendly. As a show of faith, he turned over his firearms to the English, but it was just that: a show. He promised to send over the rest of the weaponry his tribe held, but, of course, he never did. Relations grew more tense. In 1671 Plymouth and Rhode Island were getting worried, and by 1674 the concern had spread north to Massachusetts.

The English sent representatives to Metacomet to investigate just what he was doing, and to try and negotiate a treaty with him. He ominously responded that he was not going to negotiate with underlings. If they wanted to talk he would talk with King Charles, and that was it. The English were terrified, but equally were unwilling to make the first strike. If there was a way they could peacefully dominate the Indians they would try that, but Metacomet had no intention of being peacefully dominated. It is suspected that Metacomet intended to launch his attack in 1676, but in 1675 his hand was forced.

An educated Indian, who seemed to have had knowledge of Metacomet's plans, travelled to Plymouth where he was suddenly murdered. Three Indians on Metacomet's council were arrested and found guilty. The evidence was circumstantial at best. The Wampanoags were furious with the English for once again trampling upon their sovereignty. It was the final straw. Vengeance was demanded.

On June 20th 1675 a raid was made against the English town of Swansea in Massachusetts, and one Indian was wounded in the attempt. On June 24th, an Indian raiding party attacked and killed ten Englishmen. The shroud of darkness had fallen, begun King Philip's War had. Massachsuetts fell into chaos and numerous Indian tribes joined in with the raiding, including the largest tribe of the region, the Narragansets. The conflict is sometimes known as the Great Narraganset War for this reason.

King Philip's War

Throughout the next 6 months, Indian attacks ravaged the region. No area of New England was safe. It was for this reason, you'll recall, that the United Colonies of New England had been created, to mutually protect the region in case of an Indian attack. Had this infrastructure not been in place, it is very likely that New England would have been completely wiped out, such was the unprecedented scale of the attack. But the organisation did exist.

At first it was all the English could do to defend each town on a case by case basis. It's hard to make long term plans when you don't know if you might live to see tomorrow. Boston raised 120 troops, and other settlements had raised forces, but there was nothing that could be done. On October 19th, Metacomet made an assault on Hatfield with 800 men, but this was rebuffed. He then tried to encourage an attack from the tribes on the Hudson, before he set up winter camp in a swamp in Narragansett land around Rhode Island.

This gave the English the opportunity to put together a fighting force which had been called for in September. In November a force was finally gathered. New Haven had by this point been absorbed into Connecticut, but the other three colonies contributed to a force a thousand strong. Massachusetts provided 527 soldiers, Connecticut gave 315, and from Plymouth came 158 and the commander-in-chief, Josiah Winslow, the son of our old friend Edward Winslow. This was in addition to a force of about 150 allied Indians. They made their way to Rhode Island with the plan to attack the Indian winter camp, at which about 3,000 were stationed. The attack, known as the Great Swamp Fight, began on December 19th. The result of the conflict was mixed. The camp was destroyed, but this wasn't particularly important. It was just a camp in a swamp, of no strategic importance. It also brought the Narragansets more firmly into the war. About 70 militia were killed and 150 wounded, while it seems that hundreds of Indians died. Determining exact numbers is difficult.

In 1676 the raids continued. Metacomet launched an attack on Lancaster in February, the first of a series of devastating attacks that destroyed many English towns. Providence was burned in March. The war dragged on, but the Indians struggled to develop a strategy. They won many battles, but they were unable to do anything with these victories. Meanwhile, the English, with their superior marksmanship, inflicted heavy casualties. The Mohawks, who were on good terms with the English, helped to stop the rebellion to spread. Indian tribes were brought into the English army, and helped annex the territory of enemy Indians.

A huge blow was dealt to the Indian war effort when Metacomet was killed in August 1676. From that point, it was only really a matter of time before the war was brought to an end. By this date, the Wampanoags, the Narragansetts and the Pequods were completely wiped out, and the English were now in complete control of Southern New England. The war dragged for two more years in the north and east in what would become New Hampshire and Maine, but by that point the remaining Indian tribes and the English were both exhausted. Neither of them was in a position to achieve a decisive victory, and so a peace was signed on February 12th 1678.

Consequences of King Philip's War

The war had been very costly. There were between 30 and 40 thousand English in New England by the time of the war, about 6 to 8 thousand of these were men of fighting age. By the end of the war, one in ten were dead. About half of the 90 or so towns were attacked, and a dozen were destroyed. The war cost was £100,000, a tremendous amount for the colonies.

The Indian losses were devastating. Several thousand died in the war, thousands more died of starvation, and thousands more left the region either fleeing or in chains. Three tribes were destroyed. It is estimated that the Indian population of Southern New England dropped by anywhere between 40 and 80%.

The war was important because it demonstrated the benefits of the colonies working together, something we shall see when we when we advance the narrative into the late seventeenth century, and something which will reach its conclusion in the eighteenth. It also changed the nature of New England. No longer was it a border region in the same sense. It had established its dominance over the Indian tribes. Sure, the Iroquois were lurking beyond the Hudson, but that was a matter to be dealt with by New York and New Jersey. The history of New England would become more domestic and political as it advances towards the revolution.

This is defining moment in our narrative. It was a lot harder to bring New England up to the end of the 1670s than it was Virginia. This section of the narrative has allowed us to get a much wider understanding of the early American story than the episodes solely on Virginia did, of a distinctive northern character. We now have one final topic for this book. We need to return to the south, and recap the events of Maryland and Carolina.

Chapter 19 – A Southern Detour

Following the invasion of the New World by Columbus in 1492, the Europeans began to probe numerous areas. Despite the odd venture by the Portuguese into Brazil, the Americas were immediately dominated by the Spanish. This was confirmed by the 1494 Treaty of Tordesillas which gave the Spanish authority over all of the Americas aside from a bit of Brazil, which belonged to the Portuguese. As I'm sure you can imagine, a lot of people were not particularly fond of this treaty. The most important were the European powers: France and England.

Both these powers were curious about the New World, but neither was in a position to do anything about it. The English made probes around the North American continent with the expedition of John Cabot in 1497, and inspired by the voyage of Magellan, Francois I of France decided to fund an expedition. Giovanni da Verrazzano travelled to the North American landmass, and on March 21st 1524 he sighted land around Cape Fear. Verrazzano found the land in good quality in what is the first description of what would become North Carolina. Interestingly, Verrazzano made a mistake while in North America which would go on to confuse cartographers and explorers for the next 150 years.

It's been a frequent element in our narrative that Europeans have been certain that the Pacific was just beyond the Atlantic. That this wasn't a huge continent. It would take them a long time to understand just how big a mistake this was. But there is the question of why they thought this was the case. The answer is that Verrazzano landed at

North Carolina, specifically at the island chain just off the coast. He saw the water on the other side of these islands, but couldn't see the mainland beyond it, so he assumed that this body of water was the Pacific Ocean. In reality, it was the Pamlico and Albemarle Sounds, a body of water not 20 miles wide. He reported his findings, and came to the conclusion that Carolina was an isthmus, and the Pacific was just beyond it. This is why so many people believed that it would not be difficult to find the Pacific from Virginia.

Verrazzano was eager to conduct further exploration of the area, but he was unable to. The Francois was preoccupied with his wars, and Henry VIII was dealing with the reformation. Neither wanted to fund an expedition to the area when they had more pressing matters to deal with. The expedition was, however, not without consequence. It stirred the Spanish.

Spanish Interest in Carolina

They had been primarily focused on their conquest of New Spain and solidifying their position in the Caribbean. Suddenly, they realised that their new colonies could be threatened if another European power had the chance to gain a foothold, so this must be prevented. As the 1520s advanced, they began to send expeditions to the region. There was even an attempt to found a colony on the Cape Fear river, but this colony was beset with problems. One of their ships was lost as they arrived in the region. They settled in an area that was swampy, and thus many fell sick. They pressed on, but over time they realised that they had lost more provisions in the sunken ship than originally thought. They tried

410

finding a better location, but were unable to do so, and soon winter was upon them. They returned back to Santo Domingo. Of the 500 to set sail, only 150 were still alive. It had been a disaster, and the Spanish resolved that it was simply not worth making a settlement that far north.

It must be said that the region was not abandoned completely. The Spanish might have lost interest in founding a civilian settlement, but they were curious in what resources the area might hold. In 1539 an expedition was sent out northwards from Florida commanded by Hernando de Soto. De Soto reached North Carolina by the Spring of 1540. They were unable to find anything, but thought the region seemed promising. They then began to travel westwards, eventually reaching the Mississippi in 1541. It spread knowledge about the South of the North American continent, which was still largely unknown, but De Soto greatly exaggerated the size of the mountains he found, and put off future explorers and settlers from travelling to the region.

The Spanish continued to make occasional voyages northwards, even travelling into the Chesapeake, but this was only visiting. The French became briefly interested in founding a colony in South Carolina, and they tried, but failed to establish a settlement. This again stirred the Spanish to action. They set about exploring the region in more detail, but once again determined that the country was a wilderness of no value. This action is a bit of a microcosm for Spain with regards to North America in the sixteenth century. Spain did not want North America, aside from her colony in Florida, but just because she didn't want didn't mean that any of the other countries could have it either.

Roanoke

But other countries did want it. England was jealous of the riches Spain had acquired, and wanted a piece of the action. This was the age of the great privateers, Drake, Cavendish, and Raleigh. Raleigh was interested in settling up a new colony, and in 1578 Elizabeth gave a patent to Raleigh's half-brother Sir Humphrey Gilbert to found a colony. That year he sailed to the Indies, but was unable to do anything worthwhile. He tried setting up a colony in Newfoundland in 1583, but this failed. He gave up after a month and tried finding another location, but one of his ships sank while he was sailing and he became discouraged, turning home. He was then caught up in a storm, and died.

In 1584 Elizabeth decided to renew the charter, but this time she did in Raleigh's name. He sent an expedition party later that year which found Roanoke. They stayed there for 6 weeks, found that the land was good, and then set sail back home to report their findings. Raleigh was greatly excited, as was the queen. She named the country Virginia after herself. The next year, 1585, was when a colony was to be established along military lines with 600 people, although most travelled back that year, and a force of only 100 or so was left behind. Drake arrived in 1586 with some supplies, but these were not enough to keep the company going. Roanoke was abandoned. Although Raleigh's supplies for the colonies just missed Drake leaving. Perhaps a permanent English presence in the region could have been created 20 years earlier, were it not for 5 days. This new party decided to leave behind only a handful of men at Roanoke. This didn't go particularly well.

Raleigh made another attempt to establish a colony in 1587. There was again the problem of reinforcing the colony, as the English became rather distracted by the Spanish Armada in 1588. By the time they were finally able to check on the colony in 1590 it had been abandoned, giving the mystery of Roanoke colony and what happened to the English settlers. It seems that the Powhatans probably attacked it at some point. A few of the English might have survived for some time, but they were never found. Raleigh's rights to found a colony expired in 1590, so it was vital to him that his colony still exist, because otherwise he would not be able to continue his plans, but it was not found. Nothing happened after this. Raleigh held the rights to the region, but he couldn't found a new settlement. Raleigh's hopes were finally doomed with the death of Queen Elizabeth in 1603.

The new King James was not a fan of Raleigh, believing that he had been working with the Spanish to prevent his ascension to the English throne. Within eight months of Elizabeth's death, Raleigh had been found guilty of treason. This was crucial in the story of the colonisation of America. Nothing had been able to happen due to the odd legal situation of the land belonging to Raleigh and a colony which half-existing, but when Raleigh was found guilty he lost his rights, and control of the area essentially reset and power returned to the crown. It was this that allowed James to create a new colony, Jamestown and Virginia. Indeed, the experience of Raleigh was vital in the survival of this new colony. If you will allow to quote Colonial

North Carolina: A History, by Hugh Lefler and William Powell:

> "Raleigh's attempts to establish an English colony in America were costly in terms of both his own personal fortune and the considerable loss of lives. Surely those who were brave enough to risk their future in the New World hoped that what they did would be of future benefit to England, but they could not have known this with any certainty. The knowledge they gained of the natural resources of the region was of inestimable value to those who followed. Their glowing reports and encouraging promises for the future ultimately bore fruit in the 1606 charter of the Virginia Company. Before issuing this charter, which was to establish the first English colony, King James sought the advice of men who had worked with Raleigh and who had invested their own personal funds in his ventures. Once he had assurance from these individuals that England would undoubtedly benefit from further investments in the area, he granted the new charter, under which Jamestown was planted and eventually survived."

For more details on that story you can restart this book. Indeed, a lot of what I've just said we've already covered, but now I want to focus on the land to the south, the land that was forgotten with the foundation of Virginia. The charter given to the Virginia company covered the land between 34 and 45 degrees latitude north, this was the land between Bangor, Maine, in the north, and Cape Fear in the south.

While Jamestown and Virginia were being created, the land to the south wasn't quite forgotten. John Smith wrote of the area, calling it Old Virginia. In fact, it could be explored in greater detail. Exploring Old Virginia wasn't the first priority of the Jamestown settlers, but it was a lot easier for them to do than expeditions from London. As Jamestown became more settled they looked around the coast, and the Pine forests of Old Virginia were of great interest, as were the stores of tar and pitch. England had long been reliant on such material from Sweden, and the chance to reduce this dependency was certainly of valuable. The natives seemed friendly and eager to trade. It was also possible to get two harvests in a season. There seemed to things of value here that the Spanish had either not noticed or not cared about.

Perhaps something could have been done more speedily, were it not for the horrific management of the Virginia Company. You'll recall from the early episode how much of a mess all of this was, so that in 1624 the company's charter was invalidated and Virginia became the first Royal colony. This brings us to 1625 and the death of James.

The Stuarts were one of the absolutist royal families of the early modern era. They were just one among many. There were the Bourbons, the Mughals, and the Hohenzollerns, to name but a few. The absolutist royal family would be undone by the enlightenment, and the English revolution against the Stuarts is an early example. Charles, as yet unaware he was destined for execution, began his reign trying to extend the reaches of his personal control, and so in 1629 Charles gave a royal charter to his attorney-general, Sir Robert Heath. This created a province located between 31 and 36 degrees latitude north, an area with a southern limit 30 miles north of the Florida state line, and extending as far north as the Albemarle Sound. Heath was the sole proprietor of this territory. He would have large feudal powers. He could raise an army, and collect taxes. He was only subject to the king, a point which was made clear by the stipulation that there always be a twenty-ounce gold crown, just in case the monarch decided to visit. And then, just so that nobody could miss the point that he was a super powerful and fantastic guy, Charles decided to name the province after himself. No longer would it be Old Virginia. This land was now Carolana, or, as it is known today, Carolina.

Sir Robert Heath had a huge tract of land, and his first issue would be finding people to settle it. This was problematic. Carolana would suffer the same problems as New York would later in the century. There was very little reason for people to go there. If people wanted to travel to the south, to be farmers, then they would travel to Virginia, by far the largest and most powerful colony. If they were Puritans escaping persecution, then they would travel to New England. There was little reason for them to go anywhere else. This was why he turned to another group.

Wars of Religion

We haven't really been covering what exactly has been happening on the European continent, but following the reformation Europe was full of revolutionaries. Some countries switched to Protestantism quite easily, such as some of the German states, and others stayed staunchly Catholic, such as Spain. England had its share of issues, but it wound up a protestant country eventually, without too much trouble. France would find things a lot harder. There was a large minority of French Calvinist protestants known as the Huguenots which caused continual trouble throughout the sixteenth century.

The trouble began almost immediately following the reformation. There was persecution until in 1562 something known as the Wars of Religion broke out. The war lasted, in various phases, for almost 40 years. The situation began to get out of control during the reign of Henry III in opposition to his pro-Protestant policies. He was the last in his line, and had problem finding an heir, eventually choosing Henry, the King of Navarre. A protestant. This enflamed the Catholics, and the Holy League grew in power. Henry III tried to mollify them, but was unsuccessful. He was assassinated in 1589. This passed the throne to Henry IV who founded the Bourbon dynasty.

If the French Catholics were unhappy about the heir being Protestant, you can just imagine their reaction to having a protestant monarch. Eventually, the wars were brought to a close by the Edict of Nantes in April 1598. The deal was that the protestants would be allowed the keep their freedom of conscience, they would be permitted to worship openly anywhere other than Paris, and would keep their military positions. In exchange, Henry IV converted to Catholicism.

This was the way the situation lasted until the civil wars returned during the reign of Louis XIII. The Huguenots were defeated, and a peace was established with the Peace of Ales in 1629. The Huguenots would retain most of their rights, such as freedom of conscience, but lost their military advantage, and their political position was greatly weakened. This was not appealing to many a great many of the French, and was understood immediately by Heath as a possible source of settlers. Just as the Puritans had turned New England into a base of English civilisation, with a Dutch element, he felt that the same could be done in Carolana, but with a French twist. This could have been of immense benefit to the colony, but the government of Charles I had a remarkable ability to shoot itself in the foot. The privy council degreed that only those acknowledging the Church of England would be allowed to settle.

Instead, the Huguenots would not travel to Carolana, but remain in France until the Edict of Nantes was retracted in 1685 by Louis XIV. In the next few years, some 400,000 mostly urban Huguenots would leave France, travelling to England, Prussia, the Netherlands, and, of course, America. It is interesting to think the effect of this loss of urban population had on France, and how a more urban France would have handled the oncoming Industrial revolution. The Huguenots would be persecuted throughout the eighteenth century, until during the latter part of the century public opinion turned against it. Religious freedom would finally be assured by the French Revolution, but we're getting rather off topic.

Carolana

The process of attracting settlers to Carolana was made immensely more difficult by this. The Huguenots were the best option, and with them no longer a possibility Heath was forced to scour England in an effort to find anybody willing to settle in his territory. But Carolana was simply not an attractive proposition. Religious dissidents would travel to New England, those who wanted land would travel to Virginia. There wasn't much insensitive to travel anywhere else. So, while thousands of people were immigrating to the new world, Heath was able to gather 40 people. Even this went wrong. Heath transported them to Jamestown in Virginia, but then he was unable to secure passage south to Carolana. The potential settlers then split, some deciding to stay in Virginia while others headed home, but nobody went to Carolana. This was as close as Heath got. He became frustrated, and preoccupied with affairs back in England. In 1638 he transferred the rights to Carolana to Lord Maltravers.

As the English Civil War broke out the colonies became less important in general. The number of migrants reduced across the board, and there was no interest at all in Carolana for at least a decade. Once the Commonwealth was founded in 1649, the area suddenly had potential. We've dealt with the Puritan colonies in the North which sided with Parliament, but the more aristocratic south was royalist. In particular, our old friend, Governor Berkley. The area to south was regarded with envious eyes, and slowly, and surely, plans were drawn up about what to with this land to the south, called variously Roanoke, Carolana, or South Virginia.

In the 1650s, the process really began to get underway with grants being made and people moving into the area. It must be noted that this wasn't considered a rebellion against, Virginia. It wasn't anything of the sort. Rather, the area of North Carolina was simply considered the frontier region. A vague term which reappears continually throughout the American story. Land hungry settlers moved there. There wasn't anything particularly novel about it. It seems that by the early 1660s over 500 settlers had colonised North Carolina. It was in fact so large that it was beginning to become an administrative nuisance. But the state of affairs was about to be forever altered in the region due to events back in Europe.

Perhaps, had things been allowed to continue, Carolina would have become just a region of Virginia. However, the monarchy was restored. When Charles II came to the thrown in 1660 he was indebted to a number of influential figures who had secured his return, and who needed to be handsomely rewarded. So, with this in mind, it isn't at all surprising that in 1663 a new charter was given for Carolana, except now it was spelled with an I, making it Carolina, in the name of 8 proprietors.

Carolina

This immediately sets up the main conflict in the politics of Carolina. There would always be a battle made up of those who were themselves settled in the region, and outside pressures, such as the royalty. This is clear from the wording of the royal charter of Carolina. For example, it included something known as the Bishop of Durham clause, which is a bit of a weird way to define power, so I'm just going to quote Colonial North Carolina — A History to explain it.

> "This provision gave the proprietors as much power in Carolina as the Bishop of Durham had in England. As feudal lords of his frontier county, the bishop could collect taxes and raise an army; he was also expected to protect England from invasion by the Scots. Similarly, the proprietors were expected to manage and protect the province in the interests of England."

This makes it appear as though the proprietors had total control over the province, but it was countered by another element in the system: the following clause in the charter, that no law should be enacted without, "the advice, assent, and approbation of the Freemen of the said Province, or of the greater part of them, or of their Delegates or Deputies". This indicates that there was to be an assembly for the proprietors to call. This democratic assembly would represent the people, while the governor was appointed from back in England.

There was another very interesting point included in the charter. It was decided that while the Anglican Church of England was to be the established, exactly as was the case back in England, there was to be religious toleration. Other protestant groups, such as the Quakers, would flourish there, making it a real alternative to Virginia and the puritan colonies of the north. It is also deeply ironic that this clause was included, considering a rejection of religious toleration was exactly what halted the development of the province over thirty years previously.

The powers reserved for the king in the charter were one fourth of gold and silver which were found in the province, as well as the usual royal customs and duties. The proprietors could appoint judges, magistrates, and officials. They could issue titles, but not the same titles as existed in England. They could raise an army and construct forts. The colonists were made naturalised English citizens, and so enjoyed all the benefits that came with it. There was also a provision that if they became involved in a legal dispute, it would be permissible for them to be tried only by a court in either Carolina, England, or Wales. The properties were, to quote the charter:

> "our right trusty and right welbeloved Cozens and Councellors Edward Earle of Charendon, our high Chancellor of England; and George, Duke of Albemarle, Master of our horse and Captaine Generall of all our fforces; Our right trusty and welbeloved William, Lord Craven; John, Lord Berkeley; Our

right trusty and welbeloved Councellor Anthony, Lord Ashey, Chancellor of our Exchequer; Sir George Carterett, Knight and Baronett, Vice Chamberlainie of our household; and our trusty and welbeolved Sir William Berkeley, Knight; and Sir John Collecton, Knight and Baronett."

A very distinguished list, but I hope that you noticed more were distinguished than others. Sir William Berkeley and Sir John Collecton in particular could not be considered key figures in the grand scheme of things at the time, but they nonetheless had merited their inclusion. It was realised that it perhaps wouldn't be the best idea for a bunch of English aristocrats to simply organise a huge tract of land that none of them had ever been to before, so it was better to get people involved with some local knowledge. Collecton knew the area well having spent time in Barbados, but William Berkeley was invaluable. We have after all met him previously in the narrative as he was the long-time governor of Virginia. The knowledge of these two men, combined with the influence of the other six, would make for quite a formidable team. There were some tensions though.

For example, Berkeley was tasked with appointing a governor since he knew the region best, but then the proprietors went back on this deal and gave the position to William Drummond of Virginia. Berkeley did appoint a council of six who themselves appointed civil and military officers. The Proprietors also started the process of giving out land grants. These started small as it seems they didn't realise just how large Carolina was. It took until 1665 for them to have a clearer impression of just what they were doing, and what they wanted Carolina to look like. It was decided that Carolina would be split into three counties. Albemarle was in the north east, then there was Clarendon based upon the Cape Fear River, and then finally there was Craven, occupying what was to become South Carolina.

The government was to be quite small, with a promise that it would be expanded later. To begin with, there would be a governor who would appoint the council. They were responsible to the proprietors and were to follow their instructions. In addition, there were twelve representatives of the freeholders. These 19 were to form a legislature for the moment, and there would be some other more powerful general assembly down the line, although this was all vague and not mentioned in the charter.

After some initial struggles, the colony soon began to pick up colonists. These were particularly from puritans dissatisfied with life in New England, and colonists from Barbados, who all settled around Cape Fear in Clarendon. However, these were done independently, and they began to run into problems with the proprietors. At one point, the proprietors chose to just ignore this colony, which had been called Charles Town and at one point had about 800 people living alone a 60-mile stretch of the Cape Fear River. The assembly wasn't interested in helping this group, and neither was London, preoccupied as it was with the more pressing matters of the great plague, the great fire, and war with the Dutch. There was then trouble with the natives. In an open fight the colonists had the advantage. Guns will beat bows and arrows every time. But the Indians had no need to wage an open fight. They instead stole the cattle from the settlers, crippling the colonial economy. People began to leave Charles Town by late 1666, and by Autumn 1667 it had been completely abandoned. The farms and homes were left to be reclaimed by both the advancing tree line and Indians. It was a rather pathetic end to the Cape Fear section of the colony, and when it was eventually settled again there would be confused future colonists, with no idea of the demise of its earlier form.

If Clarendon was a failure, the more northern Albemarle would prove to be a success. It had a governor and a charter describing the government by early 1665, beginning what was to become North Carolina. It had the immediate quality of showing the divide between the settled population and the outside force of London. But this did not mean that they could not work together.

For example, I mentioned earlier that only small grants of land had been made to the various settlers. The maximum land holding was less than half the size of those in Virginia. This was an issue for the Carolina citizens, and the proprietors could be sympathetic. They gave them the same landholding rights as Virginians in 1668. More concessions were made in 1669 to attract citizens, such as making it so that their citizens would be free from prosecution for debt for the first five years they were settled there, and that only they would be permitted to trade with Indians. None-Albemarle citizens were forbade.

This caused some issues with Virginians who were not at all happy about the situation. They were forced to watch as indebted Virginians fled to Carolina in order to escape from prosecution, as well as cutting off their trade to the south. They didn't notice the irony that Albemarle was merely copying laws which had been passed in Virginia nearly 30 years previously.

The government of Albemarle changed in 1669 to reflect the growing number of colonists as the proprietors feared being overwhelmed, and something called the Grand Model was created. Control fundamentally belonged to the proprietors who planned to rule in a feudal manner. They would grant titles which carried tracts of land. Below the nobility were the landowning and slaveholding freeholders, but this class, while free, was to have a minimal role in government. Below them was a group of tenant farmers, the Leet-men, who were effectively serfs. They were bound to the land, and had to serve the lords. The Church of England was the established church, although there was to be toleration for those of differing opinions. The eight proprietors would rule from the Palatine Court, the supreme body of the land. The Grand Council had a mixture of executive, legislative and judicial powers, and there was also a parliament which would represent both the proprietors and the freeholders. This was all designed by the proprietors to foster their ideal social system. It is a very interesting product of the early enlightenment, offering a vision of the future much closer to the past than what would eventually be produced by the period. It placed great personal power in the hands of the proprietors and the council, but you will notice that I haven't yet mentioned the governor, whose power was greatly reduced by the settlement. Likewise, with the main bodies of government being the Council and the Palatine Court, Parliament, the sole body which partly represented the people, was weakened. It lost its ability to initiate legislation, which is quite a problem for a legislature.

This is what the proprietors wanted. It was an issue for them that there is a huge difference between writing a fancy constitution and actually enforcing it. The Grand Model would go through significant revisions multiple times, but would never be fully implemented. It was finally abandoned in 1700. One of the lessons of history that those in power frequently fail to heed is that the people must have an avenue to initiate change. If they do not have a way to do this through peaceful civil channels, or that existing civil channels no longer work or are not listening, they will turn to other means of trying to initiate change. It's really not hard to think of examples of this. Ultimately, it will drive the American revolution, and it would drive the citizens of Carolina. When Parliament lost its ability to initiate legislature, people became frustrated with the lot they were given by the proprietors, and this anger vented itself through the only option left, violence

The Carolina of the late seventeenth century was a very disorderly place, while the region was hit by plague, hurricanes, floods and drought. Goods were expensive to important as they usually came via Virginia (Carolinian ports couldn't support the large ocean going vessels) and so smuggling and the black market thrived. The people were suffering, and the proprietors were not listening. Their attentions having already turned towards new areas which might offer a faster profit. It is not at all surprising that a rebellion broke out in the mid-1670s, at the same time as Bacon's Rebellion was going on in the north. This was known as Culpeper's rebellion, but it was soon suppressed. The proprietors were not harsh once they regained control of the region, and they tried to act wisely, but it is a very difficult task to manage a colony on the other side of the ocean.

Albemarle was even distanced from the centre of power within the colony. In 1670 the Proprietors had begun to look towards the south, and then founded Charles Town, which over time would of course become Charleston, South Carolina. It formally took the name in 1783. But, for convenience, I shall just call it Charleston. Charleston had a much better harbour than the settlements in the north, something immediately recognised. It would take a decade or so to establish itself, but by 1690 it was the fifth largest city in North America. This will all be in the future though. For now, we have only to note that the founding of Charleston indicated that the proprietors were looking southwards.

Maryland

The last colony to be covered in this book is Maryland. Maryland is a remarkable colony in its foundation. While the other colonies had been established either by groups of powerful figures, or by mass movements, Maryland existed due to the efforts of a single person, George Calvert, the First Lord Baltimore. George Calvert was raised in the flurry of activity of the early colonial period, and he was a member of both the Virginia Company and the Council for New England. He was given a grant of land in Newfoundland in 1622, where he established the colony of Avalon. Soon after this he retired from public life, almost certainly because of his conversion to Catholicism. He moved to his Newfoundland colony, but he found the climate too bitter and cold, and so he wrote to Charles I to see if he could move his colony southwards. He travelled to Virginia in 1629 and found the climate much more agreeable, but Virginia was an Anglican colony. George Calvert couldn't stay there, but he liked the area, and he set his sights on the land towards the Northern end of the Chesapeake.

He wrote to Charles I to see if he could have this. Virginians were furious, but Virginia was a royal colony so Charles was free to ignore them. Calvert was his friend, and so Charles happily gave him the land, and indeed to a large extent let him write the charter. Calvert died while the charter was being written, and so it was issued in the name of his son Cercilius, the second Lord Baltimore, in 1632. He was given the land between 40 degrees latitude in the north, all the way to the south bank of the Potomac river. It was some 10 million acres, and he was given the powers of the Bishop of Durham. This was to be named Maryland.

The king had the right to two Indian arrows each year to symbolise the feudal relationship, as well as one fifth of any Gold and Silver which was found in the colony. While the colony was in essence a private estate of Baltimore, it was also intended to be an area of refuge for Roman Catholics. Catholics were experiencing a period of great uncertainty in England. This is not to say that protestants were unwelcome. Indeed, the majority of early settlers were protestants.

The first expedition left Southampton in November 1633, and arrived via Barbados at the Chesapeake in late February 1634. It contained two Jesuits, 17 Roman Catholic gentlemen, and about two hundred others. They settled at St. Mary's on the mouth of the Potomac River. They managed to learn from Virginia and Plymouth by choosing a location with high ground, there were also friendly local Indians who traded for land, meaning that Maryland suffered no starving time. Baltimore's younger brother, Leonard Calvert, was made the first governor, and he distributed the land in a feudal manner. The gentlemen were given manors, about 60 of which would be set up over the course of the seventeenth century. These varied in size from one thousand to three thousand acres, and they would give land to freeholders. There were also other freeholders out of the manorial system. Everyone gave a portion of their earnings to the proprietor, making the only comparable system in North America the patroonships on the Hudson. Many colonies had intentions to replicate the feudal world in the new world, but none managed it to the extent of Maryland.

The colony was immediately prosperous, and was able to begin trading with Boston from its first year. But, it rapidly changed. The system was rigorously hierarchical and was not built for the frontier. The strict social stratification never disappeared, but other elements of the feudal system did.

The early years of the colony were defined by conflicts with the Virginian William Claiborne who kept trying to take Kent Island, and by Baltimore's attempts to enforce religious toleration. The Jesuits kept trying to convert the protestants who found them very annoying, and the protestants were not happy with the dominant social position of the Roman Catholics. This only grew worse in the 1640s.

Puritans were unhappy with the power of the Anglican Church in Virginia and so moved to Maryland with its religious toleration, something they found very appealing. In particular they settled at Providence, a self-governing Puritan town based upon New England precedent, which would become Annapolis. This made the imbalance of power with the Catholics all the more jarring. Then there was the Jesuits, who seemed to be determined to control a great area of land and hold it in the name of the pope rather than Baltimore. This led to an entrenchment of religious freedom, but not exactly as we would conceive it. It was a very seventeenth century sort which only guaranteed freedom of conscience and freedom from religious trouble for Christians. The puritan element in the colony inserted a clause that denying the divinity of Christ was an offence punishable by death. So, not freedom of religion as we could characterise it. That said, it remained a significant step in the American liberal tradition.

Leonard Calvert was the governor for the first 14 years of the colony's existence, and after a few years it was decided that the people should have some say in its government. An assembly was created in 1637, but it had no legislative authority and most of its members were appointed by the governor. It could have been replaced with a rubber stamp. But, by 1642, it had managed to gain the power that resolutions needed to be passed by it to take effect. It was split into two houses in 1650, both of which had protestant majorities. They took inspiration from England, where parliament had dismissed its king and began to make noises that they should remove their proprietor. When news arrived of Charles' execution, Charles II was declared king by the deputy governor, but Baltimore was unaware of this and managed to prevent parliament from punishing Maryland as happened with Virginia. The effect in the change of circumstances was the repeal of the legislation protecting Catholics, and the colony became divided into two factions. A protestant faction favoured direct control by the government in England and a representative democracy in the colony itself, while a more conservative faction rallied around the governor and wanted genuine religious toleration. This would be how Maryland looked for the rest of the seventeenth century.

This led to a Maryland civil war in 1655 when Baltimore's governor, William Stone, was driven from office, and the puritan faction set up an alternative government under William Fuller. Baltimore appealed to Cromwell, who sided with Baltimore against the Puritans, and his position was restored in 1658. He was further strengthened following the restoration of Charles II. In 1661 Charles Calvert, his son and the future Third Lord Baltimore, was made governor with almost absolute power, and he quickly organised the upper house of the assembly to make it of the lords of manors in Maryland. It was essentially a Catholic House of Lords. This was in contrast to the elected lower house which remained staunchly Protestant, and which liked to view itself as a House of Commons. It managed to achieve such recognition in 1670. Government was mostly based upon a continual battle between the two houses of the assembly, and this is all I want to say for the moment about Maryland. Indeed, that is all I want to say in this book.

This is the conclusion of A History of the United States Volume 1. What have we covered? Well, we've covered the European discovery of the continent, and their first colonies. We've seen the origins of many American characteristics. We've seen the commitment to freedom in various tones, we've seen the north take on a mercantile character, we've seen the south remain agricultural. We've looked at the establishment of a developed political class in Virginia, the most dominant of the English colonies. We've also seen the Dutch and Swedes fail where the English succeeded. I hope that you have enjoyed this project, an adaption of the podcast series A History of the United States Episodes 1-60. You can listen along to the story there, or wait for Volume 2 which will include a history of the Native American Peoples, and move the general narrative up to the Seven Years War.

Select Bibliography

Abad del Vecchio, J. *Songs of Motherhood and Marriage: Catullus and Virgil in Statius' Achilleid.* 2015.

Andrews, C. *The Colonial Period in American History.* 1934.

Bailyn, B. *The Barbarous Years. The Peopling of British North America: The Conflict of Civilisations 1600-1675.* 2013.

Bliss, R. *Revolution and Empire: English Politics and American Colonies in the Seventeenth Century.* 1990.

Brogan, H. *The Penguin History of the United States of America.* 2001.

Dabney, V. *Virginia: The New Dominion.* 1989.

Davis, W.T. & Jameson, J.F. *Bradford's History of Plymouth Plantation 1606-1646.* 2013.

Goodwin, J. *The Pilgrim Republic: An Historical Review of the Colony of New Plymouth.* 2017.

Hart, A.B. *Commonwealth History of Massachusetts.* 1927-1930

Horn, J. *A Land as God Made It: Jamestown and the Birth of America.* 2005.

James, S.V. *Colonial Rhode Island: A History.* 1975.

Kammen, M. *Colonial New York: A History.* 1996.

Lefler, H.J. *Colonial North Carolina: A History*. 1973.

Marr, A. *A History of the World*. 2013.

Savelle, M. *A History of Colonial America*. 1964.

Richard, S.C. *The American Colonies: From Settlement to Independence*. 1981.

Webb, S.S. *1676: The End of American Impendence*. 1995.

Weir, R.M. *Colonial South Carolina: A History*. 1997.

Made in the USA
San Bernardino, CA
05 June 2018